Music and Capitalism

Big Issues in Music

A project of the Chicago Studies in Ethnomusicology series
Edited by Philip V. Bohlman and Ronald M. Radano

Music and Capitalism

A History of the Present

TIMOTHY D. TAYLOR

The University of Chicago Press
Chicago and London

Timothy D. Taylor is professor in the Department of Ethnomusicology at the University of California, Los Angeles. He is the author of several books, most recently *The Sounds of Capitalism*, also published by the University of Chicago Press.

The University of Chicago Press, Chicago 60637
The University of Chicago Press, Ltd., London
© 2016 by The University of Chicago
All rights reserved. Published 2016.
Printed in the United States of America

25 24 23 22 21 20 19 18 17 16   1 2 3 4 5

ISBN-13: 978-0-226-31183-8 (cloth)
ISBN-13: 978-0-226-31197-5 (paper)
ISBN-13: 978-0-226-31202-6 (e-book)
DOI: 10.7208/chicago/9780226312026.001.0001

Library of Congress Cataloging-in-Publication Data
Taylor, Timothy Dean, author.
    Music and capitalism : a history of the present / Timothy D. Taylor.
        pages ; cm. — (Chicago studies in ethnomusicology: big issues in music)
    Includes bibliographical references and index.
        ISBN 978-0-226-31183-8 (cloth : alk. paper) — ISBN 978-0-226-31197-5
    (pbk. : alk. paper) — ISBN 978-0-226-31202-6 (ebook) 1. Music
    trade. 2. Music—Economic aspects. 3. Music—Social aspects. 4. Music
    and globalization. 5. Capitalism. I. Title. II. Series: Chicago studies in
    ethnomusicology.
    ML3790.T393 2015
    338.4'778—dc23

                                                          2015014449

♾ This paper meets the requirements of ANSI/NISO Z39.48–1992 (Permanence
of Paper).

For Sherry

One can behold in capitalism a religion, that is to say, capitalism essentially serves to satisfy the same worries, anguish, and disquiet formerly answered by so-called religion.

—WALTER BENJAMIN

What will become of human beings and their capacity for aesthetic perception when they are fully exposed to the conditions of monopoly capitalism?

—THEODOR ADORNO

Contents

Tables

Audio and Video Examples

These can be found on the Music and Capitalism *website:*
www.musicandcapitalism.org.

Acknowledgments

First thanks must go to Ronald Radano and Philip Bohlman for inviting me to participate in this series. I would also like to thank the staff at the University of Chicago Press, starting with the editor extraordinaire, Elizabeth Branch Dyson, who skillfully shepherded the book into production, and Nora Devlin, Susan Karani, and Ryo Yamaguchi. Thanks also go to copy editor India Cooper.

There are plenty of students to acknowledge from various classes and seminars over the years: graduate students in my capitalism seminar at UCLA in 2010, Shelina Brown, Julius Reder Carlson, Jeroen Gevers, Drew Schnurr, and Zachary Wallmark; and graduate students in my neoliberal capitalism and music seminar in 2014, Farzad Amoozegar-Fassie, Monica Chieffo, Wade Dean, Albert Diaz, León F. García-Corona, Deonte Harris, Kevin Levine, Breena Loraine, Alyssa Mathias, Badema Pitic, Eric Schmidt, Darci Sprengel, and Schuyler Whelden. I have benefited from the wisdom and insights of these and other UCLA graduate students in recent years: Catherine Appert, Shelina Brown, Logan Clark, Chloe Coventry, Mike D'Errico, Oded Erez, Jennie Gubner, Joanna Love, Andrea Moore, Alex Rodriguez, Sam Weeks, and Dave Wilson.

I would also like to thank Anthony Seeger for his critique of an early version of chapter 2 and for his sage advice in helping me de-monolithize my portrayal of the music industry, as well as recommendations of, and introductions to, people in the indie label world.

Sincerest thanks are due to all those who consented to be interviewed (all of whom are also listed in the references section). The UCLA Office of the Human Research Protection Program approved most of the interviews in this study as IRB#11–002035-CR-00001. Thanks are due to Shelina Brown for transcribing most of the interviews, and most of all for helping me navigate the Southern California indie rock world.

I would also like to thank Charles B. Ortner of Proskauer LLP, for helping not only to identify but to open doors that might otherwise have remained unknown and closed.

I auditioned chapter 2 at a number of colloquia around the world, and I would like to thank those institutions for their invitations and those audiences for useful feedback: attendees at the Culture, Power, and Social Change colloquium series, Department of Anthropology, UCLA; attendees at the Midwest Graduate Music Consortium Conference, Northwestern University, in 2012; attendees at the Music, Politics, Agency Symposium, University of East London, in 2012; the Department of Music, University of California, San Diego, in 2012; the Department of Music, University of California, Santa Barbara, in 2012; attendees at the Barwick Colloquium Series, Department of Music, Harvard University, in 2013; and the Irish World Academy at the University of Limerick in 2013. I presented chapter 5 at the Nazir Ali Jairazbhoy Colloquium series in the Department of Ethnomusicology at UCLA in 2014 and would like to thank all in attendance for their stimulating comments and questions.

I would also like to think Vicki Mayer of Tulane University, who solicited a chapter for her edited volume *Media Production* in Wiley-Blackwell's *International Companions to Media Studies*, which allowed me to try out some of the ideas in this book, as well as their organization.

Thanks also go to the members of the "Anthropology Salon" at UCLA, who provided many stimulating conversations: Andrew Apter, Jessica Cattelino, Akhil Gupta, Chris Kelty, Gail Kligman, Purnima Mankekar, and Sherry Ortner.

Heartfelt gratitude goes out to a few friends and colleagues over the years who have kindly taken the time to discuss these and other ideas with me: Steven Feld, Robert Fink, Tamara Levitz, Brent Luvaas, Louise Meintjes, Ana María Ochoa, David Novak, Ronald Radano, Anthony Seeger, Martin Stokes, Bob White, and Deborah Wong.

I also benefited from three extraordinarily detailed, smart, and useful anonymous readers' reports, which helped make this a better book.

It has been some time since I thanked my parents, Lee and Jane, in one of my books, but that does not mean that I have forgotten them or outgrown their influence. As we age, the magnitude of the gifts they have given me over the years only becomes clearer. Thanks, folks.

Finally, deepest thanks go, as always, to my partner in life, Sherry B. Ortner, to whom I lovingly dedicate this book.

Capitalism, Music, and Social Theory

Social theorists since the nineteenth century have understood capitalism as one of the most powerful forces on people's everyday lives. Since the publication of Karl Marx's and Max Weber's enduring writings, capitalism has become the most powerful influence in American and Western European life—and, increasingly, beyond—having supplanted even religion. These larger patterns have been the focus of many fields such as history and anthropology, which have long histories of addressing the workings of capitalism, though most of us in music studies have paid little attention until fairly recently.

The only major author with continuing influence after Marx and Weber who made the study of capitalism and its effects on cultural production such as music a central focus of his work was Theodor Adorno (1903–69), whose voluminous writings considered such questions as the commodification of music, the growth and meaning of a market of mass culture and its implications for artistic cultural production, and the changing relationship of people to music with the rise of new sound reproduction technologies such as the phonograph and radio (see Adorno 2002 for a useful selection, as well as Adorno 1987).

But since Adorno's pioneering work in the middle of the twentieth century, there has been little advancement in thinking about music and capitalism. There have been virtually no thoroughgoing studies of the production and consumption of music that engage substantively with major theories of today's capitalism, studies that understand it as a social form that profoundly shapes not only production, distribution, and consumption but also the cultures that musics and listeners inhabit. This is despite the fact that, after a period of some neglect, there has been a fair amount of attention devoted to today's capitalism by a variety of scholars (e.g., Boltanski and Chiapello 2005;

Doogan 2009; Duménil and Lévy 2004 and 2011; Fisher and Downey 2006; Harvey 2005 and 2010; Piketty 2014; Taylor 2012b; Thrift 2005; Wood 2005; see also Schuessler 2013). This study draws on these and other new publications to take up where Adorno's work left off by studying music in today's capitalism.

Yet even those fields that had traditionally devoted some consideration to capitalism neglected it for a time. Part of the reason is the increasing humanities-ization of the softer social sciences that came in with the cultural studies boom beginning in the 1980s, despite its Marxist inclinations. It became more common to theorize the supposed effects of capitalism without attending to causes. It was interesting, for example, to see Fredric Jameson's influence (in Jameson 1984) filtered into subsequent publications with all of the thinking on late capitalism excised, so that postmodernism as the "cultural logic of late capitalism" was reduced to a list of traits or characteristics such as "depthlessness" or "waning of affect" or "pastiche." The predictable effect was a seemingly ever-expanding number of lists of stylistic qualities, which I have written about elsewhere (Taylor 2002). Postmodern culture registered the effects of late capitalism, which was largely ignored or forgotten by many scholars.

Much of my past work has been concerned with attempting to apprehend the present and recent past in the West, a period that has been characterized in many ways in the last couple of decades, as postmodern, late capitalist, a network society, an information age, an era of globalization, and far more. It has long seemed to me, however, that the primary representation, and thus focus of analysis, ought to have something to do with capitalism, not in an economistic sense, but with the understanding that capitalism as a social form profoundly shapes people's relationships to each other, and their relationships to cultural forms such as music.

Without capitalism, after all, most of what we think about music wouldn't be possible. Indeed, most music wouldn't be possible, since most of the music most people hear is industrially produced as a commodity, mass distributed as a commodity, and widely consumed as a commodity. Capitalism has powerfully shaped not only the production, consumption, and distribution of music but also the roles that music plays in people's lives.

Studying such things has been undertaken all too infrequently. There is some of Adorno's work, and the lone book after Adorno's death that systematically tackles the question of music and capitalism, Jacques Attali's *Noise: The Political Economy of Music* (1985), an alternatingly frustrating and exhilarating read. Attali essentially has a functionalist conception of society, which is why he can claim that music can be prophetic (or "premonitory" in his translator's word), foreshadowing the future. He assumes that society is a total, bounded entity where if something shifts, everything else will shift as well. Attali is a Marxist drawing on various aspects of Marxian theory but is also nonetheless a Weberian in his arguments that some parts of the superstructure—in this case, music—precede or even anticipate developments in the base, and in the rest of the culture.

Attali posits four stages of the mode of production of music, the first three of which he calls "Sacrificing," which refers to the premodern era in which music was not notated, or was notated but not printed; "Representing" refers to the era of published music, and "Repeating" to the era of recording. The final stage, "Composing," is a rather optimistic take on recent capitalism, a regime under which people will begin to compose for themselves. To some extent, this has indeed happened, as digital technologies have made the production of music possible for those who don't know how to play a musical instrument, and it has made it possible for people to record their own music in affordable, high-quality home studios and distribute it online. But, overwhelmingly, most people in the West today still consume music much more than they produce it.

Attali's book was written in a period before most commentators were discussing a more virulent strain of capitalism that is now most commonly called neoliberal. Giorgio Agamben has exhorted us to take Walter Benjamin's assertion that appears as an epigraph to this book—that capitalism is akin to a religion—seriously and literally. Capitalism today has become, he says,

> the most fierce, implacable and irrational religion that has ever existed because it recognizes neither truces nor redemption. A permanent worship is celebrated in its name, a worship whose liturgy is labor and its object, money. God did not die; he was transformed into money. (Savà 2012)

In this religion, corporations, especially banks, have replaced churches (see Crouch 2011).

What is new about today's neoliberal capitalism is the achievement of elite social groups, which engineered shifts in state policies in the United States and much of Western Europe in the 1980s (as well as benefiting from other alterations in policies and practices that happened to occur [Stedman Jones 2012]) that emphasize the individual, free markets, deregulation (even as new regulations are put in place that favor corporations and the wealthy), privatization, the withdrawal of the state from many of its former responsibilities to its citizens, and, in general, the imposition of ideologies of the free market on virtually every arena of life. This new form of capitalism from the last few decades has witnessed the increased hegemony of these elite groups. Neoliberal policies, combined with globalization and financialization—aided by the rise of new technologies—have resulted in new sorts of capitalist cultures. Neoliberalism also emphasizes a kind of hyperindividualism by wielding ideologies of consumer choice and fostering what has become known as the "care of the self," including the use of music, whether parents are playing Mozart to improve the cognitive powers of infants or listening to New Age music to calm themselves during yoga class. The use of music, like other commodities, has become a powerful means of fashioning one's self in an era of heightened consumption.

This set of ideologies was a reassertion of familiar liberal ideas from the eighteenth and nineteenth centuries (I use *ideology* in one of the classic Marxian senses here, referring to the ideas of the ruling classes that are hegemonic; see Marx and Engels 1970, 64.) "In a general way," writes Pierre Bourdieu, "neo-liberalism is a very smart and very modern repackaging of the oldest ideas of the oldest capitalists" (1998, 34). This often makes it difficult to sort out what might be new about neoliberal capitalism. While neoliberalism may well be a new phase or form of Western capitalism, it is not wholly different than what has gone before, and has not wholly succeeded what has gone before. In many ways, neoliberal capitalism resembles its predecessor, except that it works faster and is more pervasive and corrosive.

With the term *neoliberal capitalism*, I mean to refer to an ideology, a mode of governance, and a policy package (Steger and Roy 2010, 11). Globalization and the employment of new digital technologies were two means by which neoliberal goals were realized. Gérard Duménil and Dominique Lévy note that the twenty-first-century economy is more than ever a global economy, arguing, "Neoliberalism gave specific features to globalization . . . but neoliberalism is more than a phase of globalization" (2011, 35). These authors also link globalization to financialization, intending that term to refer both to the increased role of financial institutions and to the use of innovative procedures, as well as the imposition by owners of managerial criteria; they give as an example the focus on the creation of value for shareholders (35). There are now countless ways for those in the financial industries to create profits for themselves (Harvey 2005, 161). Globalization and financialization, Duménil and Lévy write, were the means by which high incomes were obtained by the wealthiest (2011, 36)—facilitated, of course, by neoliberal policies.

All of these developments have resulted in new modes of the production, distribution, and consumption of cultural commodities such as music that are the subject of this book. I should make it clear, if it isn't already, that my focus here is on the United States and, to a lesser extent, Europe. For this I make no apology—I am based in the United States, and that is where my ethnographic and historical work has been. But even though neoliberal capitalism is increasingly hegemonic over the globe, it is not uniform. In addition to local variations of forms of neoliberal capitalism, in many places in the world, neoliberal policies have been forced upon countries following military coups or wars or natural disasters (see N. Klein 2008). I have nonetheless been influenced by writings about neoliberal capitalism in other places, especially Jocelyne Guilbault's work in Trinidad (2007), which does address cultural production under neoliberalism (Guilbault 2007), Martin Stokes's work in Turkey (2010, about which more later), Jennie Gubner's work on tango in "post-neoliberal" Argentina (2014), and Alexander Dent's study of Brazil (2009). These and other works help capture the different ways that neoliberal capitalism works on the ground, with different effects and different reactions.

What we now call neoliberalism in the West began following the economic crises of the 1970s, when elite groups conceived ways of using these crises to recover lost income. Economists, politicians, like-minded journalists, and others began to assert ever more strongly the power and beneficence of the free market in what Bourdieu has called "work of inculcation." The press contributes very strongly to this "symbolic drip-feed," which produces profound effects: neoliberalism comes to be seen as inevitable (1998, 30).

In other words, the inculcation of neoliberalism is in part a way of making it seem to be natural, inevitable, and an almost universal explanation for everything, as religion once was. Bourdieu, Michel Foucault, and many others have written of how neoliberalism has become seen as an inevitability, naturalized. That is, through the efforts of politicians, willing journalists, faux "think tanks," some academics, and the media in general, neoliberalism has been almost rendered invisible. Today, in public discourse (at least in the United States), neoliberal capitalism has been largely hidden or replaced by the concept of "globalization," about which more in chapter 4.

Bourdieu, drawing on Goffman, writes that neoliberalism is not just a discourse but a "strong discourse," one that is difficult to counteract "because it has behind it all the powers of a world of power relations which it helps to make as it is, in particular by orienting the economic choices of those who dominate economic relations and so adding its own—specifically symbolic—force to those power relations" (1998, 95). Foucault has similarly argued that neoliberalism in the United States is not just an economic or political choice taken by those in government but is, rather, "a whole way of being and thinking" (2008, 218).

All this is to assert that neoliberalism is not simply an economic system but a cultural system, an ideological system, deeply embedded in whatever culture it finds itself. But it has local variants. Neoliberal or any other capitalism doesn't simply have cultural "effects"; it is, rather (as all capitalisms are), *cultural*: it shapes culture as it is shaped by culture, not some kind of externality that can be easily apprehended, an economic base that "determines" a cultural superstructure.

Music and Capitalism

Music and Capitalism focuses on a number of phenomena and issues that immediately present themselves when one views music by taking the long view of shifts within Western capitalism, attempting to historicize the present: How is our capitalism different than what has gone before, and what does this mean for the production and consumption of music? The main issues that concern me in this book are the new means of the production, distribution, and consumption of music, the branding of musicians and new forms of marketing of them, and changes in social structure in terms of social class and habitus.

Unfortunately, there is little to go on in terms of theoretical predecessors. Despite the prominence that capitalism played in the work of the founding social theorists, it must be acknowledged that writings by Marx and subsequent Marxians have been of little help on the question of the production of cultural forms such as music. Marx wrote in several places that the maker of a musical instrument is engaged in productive labor while the player of it is not, thereby asserting that to make an instrument is to make a commodity, but to make music is not (1973, 305; n.d., 180), a distinction that Raymond Williams once described in terms of its "extraordinary inadequacy" (1977, 93). But Marx didn't spend much time on questions of cultural production, and later Marxians are variable on this question as well, though some of these issues have been usefully addressed by some authors, such as György Lukács (1971) and Mikhail Bakhtin (1981), the Frankfurt School, Williams and the Birmingham School, and others, all of whom have been influential on what follows.

And then there is Adorno. Any work on music and capitalism in the West must grapple with Adorno's voluminous work, which does consider questions of capitalism and the production and consumption of music. Adorno is an important precursor to this study, even though his work can be seen, perhaps most significantly, as a complex working out of the anxieties and fears many European intellectuals of his generation felt as a result of the advent of mass culture and the technologies of the mass dissemination of artworks. For Adorno and other artists and intellectuals of the era, the rise of mass culture constituted a real menace (see Lee and Munro 2001), threatening not only the undisputed superiority of high culture and the individual's relationship to it (a relationship famously and influentially described by Walter Benjamin [1969] as partaking of the "aura" of the artwork) but also the cherished conception of the individual and her unique relationship to artworks created by other individuals. Those holding such beliefs tended to be from solid bourgeois families, or families even more privileged, as was Adorno's, in whose home the making of classical music was normal and common. He once wrote, in a trenchant critique of American-style "music appreciation" on the radio in the 1930s:

> It may suffice to mention that a person who is in a real life relation with music does not like music because as a child he liked to see a flute, then later because music imitated a thunder storm, and finally because he learned to listen to music as music, but that the deciding childhood experiences of music are much more like a shock. More prototypical as stimulus is the experience of a child who lies awake in his bed while a string quartet plays in an adjoining room, and who is suddenly so overwhelmed by the excitement of the music that he forgets to sleep and listens breathlessly. (2009a, 167)

For Adorno and other artists and intellectuals of his class, in his place and time, this was the normal—even "prototypical"—relationship to classical music, threatened not only by new technologies of the recording of music but by what was on many of those recordings.

Despite (and sometimes, I think, because of) this vantage point, the shadow of Adorno continues to loom large over studies of music and culture, both positively and negatively; that is, he has his proponents and detractors. Many of his assumptions and assertions about popular music as a commodity, which were not always supported by empirical study, continue to this day. But it is not often recognized in music studies that Adorno's main project (or one of them) was to attempt to understand what he (and Max Horkheimer in Horkheimer and Adorno 1990) called "late capitalism" (though Adorno also employed terms such as "monopoly capitalism" and "finance capitalism"). Early in his career, Adorno wrote that he was occupied with this question: "What will become of human beings and their capacity for aesthetic perception when they are fully exposed to the conditions of monopoly capitalism?" (Adorno and Benjamin 1999, 305). It is this and related questions that drove the bulk of Adorno's writing on music, the culture industry, and more, and they help explain what looks simply like a snobbish attitude toward popular music and jazz. In music studies, it has been all too easy to dismiss Adorno for this perceived snobbery, or his bias against Igor Stravinsky and toward

Arnold Schoenberg and the Second Viennese School (Adorno 1973), and overlook—or fail to perceive—the broader perspective from which he was operating.

Instead of reading Adorno for what he had to say about composers, music, and listening—which is the norm in music studies—what if we read Adorno for what he had to say about capitalism and cultural production such as music in it? Approaching Adorno this way results in a rich experience of encountering a major intellect grappling with the capitalism of his time and what it meant for cultural producers and cultural production more generally, and helps us move beyond the simple impressions of Adorno being a snob or partisan.

Adorno's positions on art in Western capitalist cultures are well known. While he viewed the artwork in capitalism as possessing a unique ability to allow its author to critique society—its very purposelessness its purpose (see Adorno 1984)—this ability was being threatened by late capitalism. In Adorno's view (and many others' as well, including mine), capitalism was increasingly encroaching on everything, not just commercial or mass culture. Art was no less susceptible to creeping capitalism than mass culture; both high art and low, Adorno wrote,

> bear the stigmata of capitalism, both contain elements of change (but never, of course, simply as a middle term between Schoenberg and the American film). Both are torn halves of an integral freedom, to which, however, they do not add up. (Adorno and Benjamin 1999, 130)

Late capitalism wasn't just creating "stigmata," however; Adorno later argued in "On the Social Situation of Music" (first published in 1932), "Through the total absorption of both musical production and consumption by the capitalistic process, the alienation of music from man has become complete" (2002, 391).

Apart from his famous article "On the Fetish-Character of Music and the Regression of Listening" (first published in 1938, collected in Adorno 2002), Adorno's most sustained focus on the question of music and capitalism can be found in his writings on the culture industries (Horkheimer and Adorno 1990; Adorno 2001), about which he was deeply critical and profoundly pessimistic. Late capitalism in the form of industrial production of commodities for profit was infecting all aspects of the making of music and culture, to the extent that art renounced its own autonomy and took its place among other consumer goods (Horkheimer and Adorno 1990, 157). All products of the culture industry were essentially the same, they believed; individuality was being liquidated (see also Adorno 2001). In a passage that seems to anticipate

Walter Benjamin's famous essay of a few years later (Benjamin 1969), Adorno wrote in 1931 in an essay entitled "Why Is the New Art So Hard to Understand?":

> The reification of art is the result of a socio-economic development that transforms all goods into consumer goods, makes them abstractly exchangeable, and has therefore torn them asunder from the immediacy of use. The autonomy of art, its quality of being a law unto itself, the impossibility of arranging it at will according to the dictates of use, is, in contrast to the religious and ceremonial function of earlier artistic practice, the expression of that reification. It is a reification that we accept more or less lightheartedly where even consumer products retain something of their use value, but that is profoundly disturbing and denounces the entire situation as soon as the possibility of use vanishes entirely, and art, instead, wants to be seen merely as a mysterious sundial from whose face one imagines one can read the state of consciousness, without, oneself, any longer having power over it. (2002, 128–29)

Art was becoming a commodity like any other, a condition accepted largely without question, with an important difference—the absence of use value, leaving artworks to be viewed as reified and ineffable. This was a new form of capitalism in which exchange value had triumphed.

Whether or not one agrees with Adorno's assessment, I would point out that just because something is a commodity doesn't mean it is somehow debased. There are plenty of musicians who want their music to be commodified simply so they can make a living, and it would be difficult for someone with a stable job to criticize them for that. And commodification is now the main means by which music moves about, so that one can hear music from faraway places that one might have been deaf to in the past. Further, commodities are never "simply" commodities. Any sort of good, whether or not it is a commodity, whether or not it is a cultural good, can exist in different regimes of value and is never static in any regime. Many ethnographic and historical studies from the Birmingham School on have shown the complex ways that commodified music (and other goods) are invested with meaning and value by various social groups. What Adorno was really objecting to was the ascendance not just of mass culture, which in itself was a threat to art, he believed, but of new regimes of value that people created for the mass culture commodities that they consumed. Mass culture, Adorno thought, wasn't merely inferior to high culture in and of itself; the ways people related to it were inferior to the relationships people had to high culture. I will have more to say about regimes of value below.

So far as I know, a coherent and reasonably complete statement by Adorno on music and capitalism doesn't exist (it is rather surprising how little capitalism is mentioned in *Introduction to the Sociology of Music* [1976], for example).[1] And Adorno's ties to the social sciences, frequently tenuous in my view, tend to be more oriented toward sociology and its historical concerns (particularly the nature of society), rather than anthropological questions of culture, which is where my interest lies. Adorno's theorizing was often too lofty, too far removed from the messiness of the real world—what real people were actually thinking and doing, how they negotiated the capitalism of their time and place, where they found meaning. For him, there was one capitalism, dominant, uncompromising, and inexorable. Additionally, Adorno's understanding of capitalism, and society more generally, was idiosyncratic—partly derived from Marx (though he blew the commodity fetishism of Marx out of proportion to Marx's treatment of it) and partly descended from Weber and Freud, among others.

But Adorno was also right about many things: capitalism has increasingly encroached on all activities and practices and consciousnesses. All who toil in it lead even more managed and surveilled lives than in the twentieth century when Adorno was writing. The cultural industries, especially after the mergers and acquisitions of the 1980s (about which more in the next chapter), are even more motivated by profit than they were in Adorno's time.

The tools and perspectives offered by Adorno only take us so far; particularly limiting is his conception of use value of cultural goods. As the following pages show, music, like all goods, cultural and otherwise, exists in different regimes of value, sometimes as a commodity, sometimes as a gift, sometimes as something else altogether—never fixed. Thus, much of this book is concerned not just with Western neoliberal capitalism as a hegemonic structure but also with those who labor in it and those who toil at its fringes. What sorts of regimes of value are they operating in? If capitalists become interested in the products of these other regimes of value, what happens? How do cultural producers operating in other regimes of value negotiate their relationship to capitalism? When music is clearly an industrial product as a commodity, Marx's, Adorno's, and others' writings on commodities are helpful, and I will employ them. But other modes of production continue to exist and other ways of understanding labor, production, consumption, value, and cultural goods are necessary.

I have found the anthropological theories of value to be particularly useful, for the question of value of cultural commodities has historically been a difficult one. Marxian exchange value is easy enough to understand with respect to cultural or other sorts of commodities, but use value is usually more complex, requiring ethnographic or historical study to understand use values of particular social groups in particular times and places. Appadu-rai's consideration of goods and his introduction of the concept of regimes of value—that goods are not static but enjoy careers, have social lives (1986) and cultural biographies (Kopytoff 1986), and can be valued by different social groups in different ways, in different times and places—is particularly use-ful, especially as it has been employed by Fred Myers (2001 and 2002). These and other authors help us understand that there are other sorts of value in addition to economic value (value derived from gift exchange, for example, the other main stream of theories of value in the anthropological literature), that the value of goods is never static, and that there can be competition over regimes of value, as Adorno's reaction to mass culture reveals. Value, as I have written elsewhere, can be a way of remembering Geertz's exhortation that we should aim our ethnographic and analytical gazes on individual social actors and what is meaningful for them (Geertz 1973; Taylor n.d.a). Focusing on the question of value is also helpful in understanding moments of transforma-tion, when a noneconomic regime is made to be commensurate with an eco-nomic one.[2] One of the aims of this book is to study how various social actors in and out of the mainstream music industry negotiate—when they are able to—their relationship to today's capitalism as a system of the production of certain forms of value in an economic regime, while at the same time attempt-ing to protect or cultivate conceptions of value in other regimes.

Last in this review of writings influential on my thinking in this book, I am drawing significantly on that body of writings usually known as practice theory. It is important to grasp that capitalism as a dominant force does not simply produce musicians or other subjects who are merely reactive to it. The capitalism of various historical moments shapes cultures, which also shape it in ongoing processes. In conceptualizing capitalism thus, I am deliberately in-voking the language of the problematic of structure and agency, an important part of what has become known as practice theory (see Bourdieu 1990; Gid-dens 1979; Ortner 2006; Sahlins 1981; Sewell 2005). Capitalism can be concep-tualized as a "structure," which is, as Sherry B. Ortner points out, something that makes human action, but at the same time, one must remember that human action "always makes and potentially unmakes" structure (1996, 2).

I also employ Bourdieu and others on the subject of fields of cultural pro-duction (1993 and 1996). By focusing on production in these chapters, I am more aligned with production studies (e.g., Caldwell 2008; Ortner 2013) than with reception studies, which are an entirely different sort of project, though I do occasionally examine the writings of critics as a way of understanding the reception of some musicians' work.

Western Neoliberal Capitalism as a Cultural System

Since I am interested in today's capitalism not simply as a series of abstract policy decisions and business practices but as a shaping force in which those decisions and practices affect everyday life and everyday culture, I want to spend some time theorizing today's capitalism as a cultural system rather than a strictly economic one. There seem to be proliferating studies in the humanities that thematize neoliberal capitalism and/or debt, linking economic observations to interpretations of literature or film or some other form of cultural production, but often doing so in a simplistic base-and-superstructure, cause-and-effect manner that bypasses culture, a problem that is somewhat hidden by these authors' theoretical sophistication in other respects.

Let's look back to Clifford Geertz's classic writings on cultural systems to lay out the underlying assumptions of this study. Culture is an idea that has undergone a fair amount of criticism and critique, and is a contested category even among anthropologists. But culture is real, however one conceptualizes it. The critiques and updates I have found to be the most useful are just that, critiques and updates, which make Geertz's idea about culture more political and also seek to flesh out Geertz on the question of the social actor, which Geertz, like Weber, carves out a space for but doesn't spend much time examining as an agential subject. For such critiques and updates, I am most indebted to Sherry B. Ortner, whose practice-theory-inflected concept of culture is a useful revision; for her, Geertz's conception of culture must be understood as consisting of "(politically inflected) schemas through which people see and act upon the world and the (politically inflected) subjectivities through which people feel—emotionally, viscerally, sometimes violently—about themselves and the world" (2006, 18; see also 1999).

So, capitalism as a cultural system. The historian Joyce Appleby calls capitalism a "cultural system" in *The Relentless Revolution*, though she conceptualizes it in a way that separates capitalism from culture by saying that capitalism "impinges on society constantly" (2010, 20); she is right to claim later that capitalism, as a cultural system, "cannot be explained by material factors alone" (25–26). But if we are truly to take Geertz at his word about cultural systems, as I want to do, then it is necessary to go beyond simply asserting that capitalism is cultural (which is essentially all Appleby has done, important as that recognition is). Cultural systems in Geertz's thinking, after all, are systems of symbols that convey meaning for social actors, a crucial perspective.

I will begin this consideration of Geertz, not accidentally, with a review of his classic "Religion as a Cultural System," since I have employed an epigraph that argues for religion's replacement by capitalism in the West. Geertz writes that he is interested in the "cultural dimension" of religion (1973, 89). I mean here not simply to substitute Geertz's "religion" for "capitalism" but also to show how a cultural system that has become as powerful and pervasive as capitalism is, in fact, a *system*, with its own logic and symbols, its own independence relative to any individual.

Geertz, on the subject of sacred symbols, writes that they

> function to synthesize a people's ethos—the tone, character, and quality of their life, its moral and aesthetic style and mood—and their world view—the picture they have of the way things in sheer actuality are, their most comprehensive ideas of order. In religious belief and practice a group's ethos is rendered intellectually reasonable by being shown to represent a way of life ideally adapted to the actual state of affairs the world view describes, while the world view is rendered emotionally convincing by being presented as an image of an actual state of affairs peculiarly well-arranged to accommodate such a way of life. (1973, 89–90)

Useful here is the all-encompassing conception of religion that Geertz captures, the role that it plays in shaping people's attitudes, their ethos, even their aesthetics and mood. He points out, too, religion's evident reasonableness: it seems to explain what people happen to believe. As does today's capitalism.

Geertz's definition of religion, offered with the appropriate caveats, is also instructive for my purposes. Religion, he writes, is

> (1) a system of symbols which acts to (2) establish powerful, pervasive, and long-lasting moods and motivations in men by (3) formulating conceptions of a general order of existence and (4) clothing these conceptions with such an aura of factuality that (5) the moods and motivations seem uniquely realistic. (1973, 90; italics in original)

We can still learn much from this definition: the role played by symbols, which are not isolated but are part of a system. Symbols can shape what people think and feel and play a potent role in promoting ideologies of how the world is, and that it is right that it should be so. And just as there is no mention here of God or gods, since it would be a mistake to confuse (or conflate) religion with the divine in Geertz's thinking, one would similarly err to confuse or conflate capitalism with money or the pursuit of profit.

An important aspect of any cultural system is that it is beyond the control or influence or apprehension of any single individual. Geertz writes that "culture patterns" or "systems or complexes of symbols" are "extrinsic sources of information" in that "they lie outside the boundaries of the individual organism as such in that intersubjective world of common understandings into which all human individuals are born, in which they pursue their separate careers, and which they leave persisting behind them after they die." By "sources of information," he means "they provide a blueprint or template in terms of which processes external to themselves can be given a definite form" (1973, 92).

Geertz elaborated on this point in another classic essay, "Ideology as a Cultural System," in which he writes:

> Symbol-systems . . . are extrinsic sources of information in terms of which human life can be patterned—extrapersonal mechanisms for the perception, understanding, judgment, and manipulation of the world. Culture patterns— religious, philosophical, aesthetic, scientific, ideological—are "programs"; they provide a template or blueprint for the organization of social and psychological processes, much as genetic systems provide such a template or the organization of organic processes. (1973, 216)

Geertz here sounds rather like a Bourdieusian on the subject of the habitus: culture patterns provide pathways, choices, for subjects. Capitalism as a cultural system offers its own patterns, its own programs, about entrepreneurialism, consumption, and much more.

The goal of studying anything as a cultural system is to attempt to apprehend how it shapes people's thoughts, discourses, and practices. As Geertz writes:

> For an anthropologist, the importance of religion lies in its capacity to serve, for an individual or for a group, as a source of general, yet distinctive, conceptions of the world, the self, and the relations between them, on the one hand . . . and of rooted, no less distinctive "mental" dispositions on the other. From these cultural functions flow, in turn, its social and psychological ones. (1973, 123)

Today, capitalism serves as a source of general yet distinctive conceptions of the world, the self, and the relations between them, as well as "mental" dispositions.

I will continue by discussing neoliberal capitalism in terms of its signs and symbols in a kind of Geertzian exploration of capitalism as a cultural system, which contains signs and symbols that communicate meaning to social actors. What are the signs and symbols of our (Western) capitalism that help us understand self-conceptions and other ideologies of today's capitalism? Plenitude, for one (see McCracken 1997): abundance, plethora, excess, surfeit. Beautiful showrooms with shiny cars. Row upon row of fetchingly packaged goods in grocery stores. The ubiquity of digital technologies, from personal computers to tablets to smartphones. A bewildering array of electronic consumer goods in so-called big box stores. And, for that matter, big box stores. Consumer goods that are used to display status or one's belong in a particular social group rather than another. People, too—in particular, stars, megastars who have triumphed in the (capitalist) cultural industries (including sports), which permits them to live lavish lifestyles that are reported on endlessly in the media (now largely owned by international conglomerates that put profits before reporting). People—stars or not—as brands. Instant gratification. Signs of the importance of consumption are ubiquitous, as is the advertising of endless opportunities to shop thanks to digital technologies such as personal computers and cell phones. The cultural system of neoliberal capitalism proffers plenitude, endless goods, now from all over the world, and digital technologies that connect us more readily than ever, even as they come between us, making communication less personal.

What Follows

Music and Capitalism: A History of the Present continues directions that my work has initiated and pursued in the past, around such questions of commodification and consumption of music, but in more general and theoretical terms than some of these earlier writings. But to say "general and theoretical" is not to imply that this book will be an exercise in theory, or simply a rehash of some of my earlier work. As much as Marx and Marxian writings have influenced my thinking about capitalism, I am also a Weberian, someone who insists on the importance of cultural and historical particularity.

The aim of this book is in some ways simple: to add to the small but now fast-growing number of works that have appeared in the twenty-first century on capitalism in an effort to restore it as an important, and, I would say, the most important, site of cultural analysis. The rise of studies of capitalism in the twenty-first century puts into relief the relative absence of studies of music and capitalism, both in and out of the West. This is for a variety of reasons, perhaps foremost among them the continuing belief among many located in college and university music departments that to discuss masterpieces (the term is still largely unproblematized) in relation to such tawdry matters as how musicians make their living somehow runs the risk of cheapening those works, which many students of Western European classical music still hold in great reverence as something quite akin to sacred texts.[3]

The situation is somewhat better in popular music studies, which has exploded in the last couple of decades as part of the cultural studies boom. Capitalism as a theme is much more central. But, while it has been commonplace for decades to describe popular music as a commodity or to write against the music industry, most studies simply assume a capitalist mode of production and the commodity status of popular music, or conflate capitalism with money, instead of viewing it as a social form that profoundly shapes not only production and consumption but also social relations and perceptions.

There have been, however, studies that examine the music industry and, more broadly, what Horkheimer and Adorno famously dubbed the "culture industry" (Adorno 2001; Hesmondhalgh 2013; Horkheimer and Adorno 1990; Miège 1989; Negus 1999). Such studies, while they do not always thematize capitalism in a systematic way, nonetheless offer important insights into the workings of the music and related industries, and I will rely on some of these in what follows.

While it was a little tempting to attempt to write a systematic history going back to the rise of capitalism in the West, I offer something less ambitious but, I hope, nonetheless useful.[4] I have instead organized this book around concepts and cases that show how Euro-American capitalism works, and has worked, with respect to music. Some of these case studies focus on moments when new communications or other technologies appeared that altered people's relationship to music, such as digital recording and playback; other case studies will address questions of marketing and advertising, for these practices are potent in inflecting or even assigning meanings to commodities of all kinds. All of these case studies will help us to understand the ever-changing landscape of European and American neoliberal capitalism.

After this introduction, chapter 1 offers a brief history of music and capitalism in the West before neoliberalism. This chapter is thematically organized, focusing on the changing nature of music as a commodity, the production of cultural commodities, the rise of the artist and the concept of genius, and social class and cultural consumption, particularly the youth market after World War II.

Chapter 2 examines how neoliberal policies and practices have dramatically altered the landscape of the production, distribution, and consumption of music in the last few decades. Record labels, advertising agencies, and music production companies were bought and sold at unprecedented rates in the 1980s and 1990s; many of the people I interviewed in the industry spoke negatively of the changes that occurred in this era, when budgets were reduced as creative matters increasingly took a back seat to financial ones. In a never-ending quest to wring profits from music, marketing and branding have become central. While some musicians for centuries have been masters of self-promotion, the importance of marketing and branding in neoliberal capitalism has grown to the extent that some musicians not only attempt to link themselves with major brands in advertising but attach themselves to major brands in attempts to brand (or cobrand) themselves. The ideology of the genius has largely given way to an ideology of the star, or star-as-brand: the advertising trade press routinely and unironically refers to major musical celebrities and bands as brands. The genius is no longer someone who has risen to the top of a pool of talent but a star who has risen to the top of a market; Aram Sinnreich writes that when he worked as an intern at a major record label, he realized that for the executives he worked for, "the functional definition of 'genius' was simply the capacity to sell a hundred thousand records" (2010, 62).

This chapter also considers the importance of identity-making in the neoliberal era, which is frequently accomplished through the consumption and display of goods, including musical ones. And there is more and more music available to be heard, which means that it has become increasingly important to know how to find what one wants. The relatively new profession of music supervisor is that of the professional music searcher, finding music to be placed in film, broadcasting, and advertising. They and other consumers also rely on various search engines; "search," as the cultural industries call it, has become a multibillion-dollar business. Algorithms are written to help people find more of what they already like, with consumer tastes stored in vast databases. This is part of the commercialization of social relationships, increasingly mediated by technologies, introducing new forms of sociality. The chapter concludes with a discussion of the growing urgency in the cultural industries of debates over questions of art and commerce.

Chapter 3 concerns globalization, in particular, the global proliferation of musical commodities. As countries around the world have become increasingly part of the capitalist system, industries have sprung up that send recordings and musicians to Western metropoles. Non-Western musicians, who only a few decades ago attempted to fashion themselves into the next Madonna or Michael Jackson, are now more concerned with making musics that speak to local, regional, and, occasionally, global concerns, participating in diaspora-wide musical conversations and in conversations with globalized social groups such as youth (see Appert 2012). As Amkoullel, a Malian hip-hop musician, said to a group of students at my university when he visited the United States in the early 2010s, "We in Africa don't have an American dream. We have an African dream." This chapter also considers Western stars as they represent themselves as connoisseurs in order to curate and collaborate with world music artists. It surveys the career of the Beninoise musician Angélique Kidjo, who has successfully navigated the complex field of production of world music for several decades. The chapter concludes by discussing increased contestations over ownership of music, and UNESCO's establishment of the designation of "masterpiece of the intangible heritage of humanity."

Chapter 4 considers questions of new technologies and the changes they have introduced in neoliberal capitalism with respect to music. Digital technologies have made it possible to produce music alone in high-quality home studios. Many of my interlocutors in my history of music and advertising (Taylor 2012b) lamented the fact that they rarely played with other musicians, and feared that the synergy that resulted from a group of musicians in the studio has been lost, leading to a uniformity of sound. It is also possible to alter recorded music, that is, remix it, which greatly complicates notions of authorship and creativity, even conceptions of labor, as the line between producers and consumers becomes blurred in some arenas of cultural production. For workers in the cultural industries, these new technologies have also resulted in people working longer and harder, as their bosses or clients have learned that even major alternations are possible at the last minute with digital tools.

And, of course, most people today acquire or rent their music via various digital delivery systems, whether iTunes or Spotify or Pandora or others, removing music as a tactile object from their lives. Physicality and tactility—the sound of the cellophane, the smell of the cardboard liner, the feel of the disc, whether digital or analog—are gone. Listeners have found various ways to re-objectify, in the literal sense, their recordings; some listeners have gone back to the long-playing record for the physical connection to music they believe it to offer, and the vinyl LP is currently the fastest-growing sector of the music industry. And a small independent label in southern California has played an important role in revitalizing the cassette tape.

Given the ubiquity and influence of capitalism today, chapter 5 considers those musicians who labor on its fringes. This chapter is based on numerous interviews with independent record label founder/owners and independent musicians (that is, independent from the major labels in the mainstream music industry, which enjoys a near monopoly on most music produced and sold today). Most of these musicians ignore the mainstream music industry, preferring to make their own music and consume music by their friends and fellow musicians in the same scene, which can be increasingly delocalized because of the Internet and social media. Many make music that would not be seen as commercial by the mainstream music industry (broadly understood in these pages as a complex of industries including the recording industry, music publishing, concert presenters, and more), whether because it is viewed as too esoteric, too idiosyncratic, or derivative. These musicians, including some in the mainstream music industry, struggle to ensure that the non-economic values they nurture and protect for their musics are not overwhelmed by economic values, even as some attempt to make a living from their music.

The concluding chapter examines the growing income inequality in the United States with the continuing consolidation of the hegemony of neoliberal capitalism. It seeks also to argue that capitalism is not a monolithic, slow-moving behemoth but can behave nimbly, because it is made of people—it is a social form. Some people in the cultural industries can move quickly to incorporate independent or marginal sounds or musics into the mainstream, though sometimes this takes a good deal of work, shifting music in one regime of value into an economic regime. Neoliberal capitalism might be commodifying more and more goods, but people continue to make and find meanings in them that are not always economic.

A Brief History of Music and Capitalism
before the Rise of Neoliberalism

In offering a brief history of music and capitalism before neoliberalism, I would like to emphasize, as I did in the introduction, that earlier forms of capitalism—indeed, earlier modes of production more generally—have not disappeared with the rise of neoliberalism in the last few decades. This sometimes makes it difficult to discern just what exactly is new about neoliberal capitalism. The cultural industries still produce commodities, though they might be advertised with bigger marketing budgets than in the past, or appear in different formats, or travel more widely. There is no clear demarcation, and there has not been a break with the past. Noncapitalist modes of production still exist, as do earlier capitalistic modes of production. Every historical form of capitalism thrives on previous forms, as well as on whatever non- or precapitalist modes of production remain (Tsing 2013). One thing is clear, however: today's capitalism seems to move faster and operate on a larger scale than earlier capitalisms.

There is therefore no clear entry point or road map for the following discussion. Capitalism so massively shapes the thoughts and practices of those who toil in it that there are a number of avenues of approach. But at the same time, capitalism is not some kind of wave that uniformly engulfs everything in its path. Its progression is neither linear nor total. While it is possible to offer a historical narrative, there are so many different threads one must examine that it makes more sense to tackle the subject thematically. I will thus begin, as does Marx in *Capital*, with a consideration of the commodity.

Production of Musical Commodities

The exchange, capitalist or not, of money for music has a long history, though such exchange in capitalism is relatively shorter. While Marx never explicitly theorized cultural commodities as commodities, he understood how cultural goods could become commodities. In his era, music could only be commodified in two ways, through sales of tickets to concerts (if, as Marx pointed out, a musician engaged with an impresario to generate large volumes of sales [1990, 1044]), or through publishing, which, again, required large-scale sales. "Milton, who wrote *Paradise Lost*," writes Marx,

> was an unproductive worker. On the other hand, a writer who turns out work for his publisher in factory style is a productive worker. Milton produced *Paradise Lost* as a silkworm produces silk, as the activation of *his own* nature. He later sold his product for £5 and thus became a merchant. But the literary proletarian of Leipzig who produces books, such as compendia on political economy, at the behest of his publisher is pretty nearly a productive worker since his production is taken over by capital and only occurs in order to increase it. (1044; emphasis in original)

Marx never really goes beyond these sorts of assertions about the production of cultural commodities.

Just as Marx offers little help in understanding cultural commodities as commodities, he also doesn't help with understanding their production, having written in several places that the maker of a musical instrument is engaged in productive labor (labor generating surplus value for capitalists), while the player of a musical instrument is not (see 1973 and n.d.).

> It may seem strange that the doctor who prescribes pills is not a productive labourer, but the apothecary who makes them up is. Similarly the instrument maker who makes the fiddle, but not the musician who plays it. But that would only show that "productive labourers" produce products which have no purpose except to serve as means of production for unproductive labourers. Which however is no more surprising than that all productive labourers, when all is said and done, produce firstly the means for the payment of unproductive labourers, and secondly, products which are consumed by those who *do not perform any labour*. (Marx n.d., 180; emphasis in original)

Since Marx's writings, technologies of sound recording have arisen, beginning in the late nineteenth century, marking a new way that music could be both objectified and commodified.

We can consider music to exist in different regimes of commodification, all of which are still with us, though some are residual, some dominant, and some emergent: music as a published score, music as live sound at a public concert, and music as recorded sound in the form of player piano rolls or audio recordings in many other formats, analog or digital. Let me take these developments in order.

The commodification of music as a published good began at the end of the fifteenth century with the invention of movable type for music by the Italian printer Ottaviano Petrucci, who petitioned the Venetian government to protect his invention in 1498. Petrucci published his first collection in 1501, a collection not of religious music but of mainly textless arrangements of chansons aimed at a middlebrow audience. This collection of "fluff," concludes the musicologist Richard Taruskin, was important to the future of making music from scores in the West (2010a, 542). It is less a question of the nature of the music, however, than of the fact that it was published and disseminated, which created new markets, new musical forms, genres, and techniques, and new composer-entrepreneurs—all subject to the vagaries of the new capitalist market.[1]

While live music in the form of the performers' labor could be a commodity before recording, the possibility of massive profits from ticket sales wasn't fully realizable until the growth of cities, the rise of concert halls, the emergence of an apparatus of press and publicity, a transportation infrastructure that made travel easier and more efficient, and, later, the rise of a recording industry that could popularize recorded music in the absence of live performers. The rise and spread of publishing created a "public" for music in the seventeenth century, though the musicologist Lorenzo Bianconi (1987) cautions that this "public" was multivalent with respect to music in this era, and could refer simply to music in the home for a small group or in a larger venue for a paying audience. This latter manifestation, paying admission for concerts, arose at the end of the seventeenth century, first in England—one of the places where capitalism gained its first foothold—and then later in the rest of Europe. It wasn't until the late eighteenth century, however, that "public" could refer to something outside of aristocratic salons. With the rise to dominance of public subscription concerts in this era, the patronage system of aristocratic support for musicians was effectively over; now the demand for works was created by listeners, and those works were judged by a new class of critics (Taruskin 2010b, 639). It is necessary to remember, however, that a public concert isn't necessarily a capitalist enterprise unless it can be repeated and occurs on a fairly large scale.

Concerts could serve to increase sales of published sheet music, just as, later, they could influence sales of recordings. But the continuing rise of publishing wasn't greeted favorably by everyone. The German composer, writer, and critic Johann Friedrich Reichardt wrote in 1782 of what he viewed as the decline of art:

> I think the most important thing is that that beautiful natural necessity [that is, the spontaneous creation of folksongs] has become art, and art nothing more than a trade. From the prince's Oberkapellmeister down to the beer-

fiddler who brings operetta into the farmer's tavern, virtually everyone is now an imitative manual laborer for the market rate. Most unfortunately, there are so many of them that there can never be competition among the buyers, but always among the sellers. Therefore, then, even the highest goal of today's so-called artist is this: to satisfy the greatest quantity of his payer's follies at once. And this has so generally fatal an influence on the entire people that when anyone—whether ruler or tenant—once lets a happy human feeling well up, he no longer has enough direct, untroubled sense to express it from himself and according to his own nature; the ever-ready *Spielmann* sings forth from him instead. (Gramit 2004, 89; bracketed passage adapted from Gramit)

This is a rather stunning passage that articulates Adorno's fears in a later era—that mass culture would render its consumers mute, unable to articulate their own feelings, thereby compromising their individuality.

And finally, there is sound recording, which was greeted with similar consternation by some. Americans accustomed to making music for themselves at home or going out to hear it live were slow to purchase the player piano and the phonograph, new recording technologies introduced near the end of the nineteenth century. Thomas Edison's list of potential uses for the phonograph published in 1878 included recorded music, but after he had enumerated several other uses: dictation, books, and education. Considering music, Edison wrote:

The phonograph will undoubtedly be liberally devoted to music. A song sung on the phonograph is reproduced with marvelous accuracy and power. Thus a friend may in a morning call sing us a song which shall delight an evening company, etc. As a musical teacher it will be used to enable one to master a new air, the child to form its first songs, or to sing him to sleep. (Taylor, Katz, and Grajeda 2012, 35)

That Edison didn't conceive of his device as one that could play professionally recorded music wasn't surprising, for he lived in an era when music was still something one made for oneself or heard live. The idea that one would pay for previously recorded music was foreign to most people, and indeed Edison resisted entering the business of selling prerecorded music, though he ultimately acquiesced, as he and others slowly became accustomed to the idea that musical sound was something that could be purchased. Such shifts required a great deal of persuasion, mostly in the form of advertising, which I will discuss below.

While one could trace the development of important music technologies from the player piano and the phonograph in the late nineteenth century through radio in the 1920s to the Sony Walkman in the 1980s to the latest iPod or smartphone, I would not say that these represent different regimes in the commodification and consumption of music, important as they are from a technological standpoint. They are significant socially, in playing a role in shaping or reshaping people's relationships to music, but none marks what one might consider to be a new form of the commodification of music as sound in the broadest sense.

These various means of the commodification and consumption of music still exist, but they experience historical moments of being dominant, residual, or emergent (Williams 1977): some older recording formats such as the cassette and the vinyl LP have recently experienced something of a renaissance (to be discussed in chapters 4 and 5). The music publishing industry isn't what it was at the height of its influence in the late nineteenth and early twentieth centuries, for example, having been affected by the recording and broadcasting industries beginning in the 1920s (though it remains quite lucrative in terms of licensing copyrighted material). Attendance at live events was up in 2011 (Pham 2011), but the function of concerts has arguably changed, for the long-established role of most concerts as a means of promoting the sale of recordings is becoming increasingly residual as recording sales today generate less income for the music industry as a whole, with concerts emerging as more of a source of income for many musicians.

The commodification of music as sound is a central and recurring theme in Theodor Adorno's work. If one reads Marx, it is clear that questions of commodity fetishism and reification (which is not a term Marx used himself but was introduced later, by György Lukács [1971]) are minor concerns; Anthony Giddens's classic *Capitalism and Modern Social Theory* (1971), which introduced him to new generations of scholars, doesn't mention commodity fetishism and reification at all. But in Adorno's and others' hands, commodity fetishism became a key concept. Adorno more or less assumed the commodity status of popular music, about which he was entirely dismissive. His main concern with respect to the question of commodification was that the classical works that he revered were also being commodified. Radio, the phonograph, and sound film made possible the easy repetition of works—not so easily reheard if one could only hear them live or perform them oneself—which, Adorno feared, could be a form of commodification of these great works. A mode of listening to music promulgated by the radio and phonograph in which listeners were encouraged to listen to musical themes as tunes rather than as building blocks in a philosophical argument or social critique was leading to a form of "commodity listening" (Adorno 2009a and 2009b), a relationship to great music that was not intellectual but was shaped by that music's commodification and treatment as a commodity in the capitalist marketplace. Music was beginning to be produced like any other commodity, which for Adorno meant that music itself was changing: *"The commodity character of music tends radically to alter it."* Music, he thought, "has ceased to be a human force and is consumed like other consumer goods," which "produces 'commodity listening,' a listening whose ideal is to dispense as far as possible with any effort on the part of the recipient—even if such an effort on the part of the recipient is the necessary condition of grasping the sense of the music" (Adorno 2009b, 137; emphasis in original).

It is in statements and assumptions like this where Adorno gets into trouble, at least for those of us who would like some sort of historical or ethnographic or other empirical basis for such claims. It is easy enough to point to how many (but not all) types of music emanating from the mainstream recording industry are increasingly industrial products. But without examining consumption practices, which can vary widely, we don't know how people actually are listening to or finding meaning in the products of the mainstream music industry. It is for these (and other) reasons that the Birmingham School offered a more "bottom-up" perspective, concentrating on the vantage point of cultural consumers rather than lofty critics like Adorno.

Some authors have offered distinctions between types of cultural commodities, especially between cultural commodities and other sorts (e.g., Miège 1989), but it seems to me that this is an unproductive exercise (and it is noteworthy that Raymond Williams doesn't address this question at all in his consideration of cultural production in Williams 1981).[2] Viewing cultural commodities as somehow special or different from other sorts of commodities is a form of fetishism of them in the non-Marxian sense, a romanticization of them. If something is produced for the purpose of exchange, it is produced for the purpose of exchange. Such commodities can be invested with all sorts of meanings and interpretations, of course, including interpretations that attempt to isolate cultural commodities from the notion that they are, in fact, commodities. One could argue that cultural commodities could be considered to be special since they potentially convey, or evoke, sorts of meanings that might be deeper or more profound or more compelling than other commodities, and this position is somewhat convincing, but only up to a point. There are plenty of cultural commodities that aren't compelling to large swathes of audiences, after all, and as commodities aren't appreciably different from a coffee mug or toaster oven. And we all own plenty of noncultural commodities that we invest with special meanings, such as the clothes one wore when getting married or a family heirloom (on the latter, see McCracken 1988, chapter 3; and Pels 1998). Rather than theories that sanctify cultural commodities, we need ethnographic and historical studies that show

how commodities and other sorts of goods exist in regimes of value that are meaningful for particular groups of social actors in particular places and times; I will examine one such case in chapter 5 (see Myers 2002 for another).

CAPITALISM AND MUSICAL PRODUCTION

With respect to the production of commodities, at least in the realm of artisanal production, not much has changed over the years. Composers may compose at an electronic keyboard instead of an acoustic piano, and they may notate their scores (or at least the final version) digitally rather than with pen and paper. Perhaps one of the most interesting shifts in cultural production with the rise of new inventions and technologies was the advent of what Raymond Williams called "group production" (1981, 113–14). While this mode of cultural production has a long history, it becomes more complex under capitalism with its division of labor and its class system. Division of labor in cultural production occurs, and cultural production can take on class divisions itself. In my study of the advertising music industry, for example, it was quite clear that composers tended to possess higher amounts of educational and cultural capital than producers, and likely came from backgrounds of higher financial capital as well. Or there is the music producer in the popular music field, whose profession began for some in engineering and for others in music arranging or another such musical subfield, but who is increasingly an auteur, with George Martin and the Beatles as perhaps the first well-known example (see Taylor 2007a).

Capitalism also shapes cultural production in ways that one could call social. Producing in and for a market in large-scale fields of cultural production or one's peers in restricted fields (Bourdieu 1993) is not the same thing as writing to please a patron in the feudal era. There are many examples that one could point to, but I will stick to just a few observations.

First, let us look at Beethoven, specifically at what musicologists call his late style, which audiences in his time tended to find daunting or even bewildering. According to Beethoven's first scholarly biographer:

> When Beethoven's friends called they usually reported to Beethoven about the performances of his works. One day Gerhard von Breuning found that a visitor had written in the Conversation Book: "Your Quartet which Schuppanzigh played yesterday did not please." Beethoven was asleep when Gerhard came and when he awoke the lad pointed to the entry. Beethoven remarked, laconically, "It will please them some day," adding that he wrote only as he thought best and would not permit himself to be deceived by the judgment of the day, saying at the end: "I know that I am an artist." (Thayer 1921, 300)

This statement, rich with its then-new assumptions about the positionality of the artist, is usually interpreted as an explanation for Beethoven's adoption of challenging musical idioms that few of his contemporaries could understand; it implies that he was writing for posterity. But there is another way of reading Beethoven's claim—what if he, as the first major composer to have a viable career in the capitalist market of the postpatronage era, was voicing an understanding of the production of his music for the purpose of exchange? That is, I am arguing, Beethoven articulated the notion that his published music wasn't simply for consumption by his contemporaries but, as a commodity, could have a life beyond him, a new idea at the time. He wasn't writing for a more sophisticated future audience as much as for a future market.

In essence, Beethoven seemed to have some conception of exchange value as later theorized by Marx. Following Marx, Rudolf Hilferding extended the concept of exchange value in an influential book on finance capital published in 1910 that examined the importance of banks and the banking industry to capitalism. He believed finance capital to be globalized, aiding in the rapid expansion of capitalism, and thus perpetuating itself generally. This expansion of capitalism organized all of the wealthy in the service of finance capital (1981, 365). Hilferding characterizes finance capital as capital that industrialists do not own but are able to obtain through banks. At the same time, banks must invest increasing amounts of their capital in industry, becoming more and more industrial capitalists. As far as the owners of capital are concerned, capital always remains money. It is invested as money, accrues interest, and can be withdrawn as money. But, Hilferding writes, the majority of capital invested in banks is transformed into industrial or productive capital. He argues, "An ever-increasing proportion of the capital used in industry is finance capital, capital at the disposition of the banks which is used by the industrialists" (225). Simply put, finance capital is capital that is owned by the banks that is available to be used by industry, giving banks massive influence and power.

What is of interest to those of us concerned with cultural production is the expanded role played by exchange value in Hilferding's thinking. After rehearsing Marx on exchange value, Hilferding makes a case for the increased importance of exchange value in the era of finance capitalism:

> The distinctive feature of commodity exchange trading is that by standardizing the use value of a commodity it makes the commodity, for everyone, a pure embodiment of exchange value, a mere bearer of price. Any money capital is now in a position to be converted into such a commodity, with the result that people outside the circle of professional, expert merchants hitherto engaged in the trade can be drawn into buying and selling these commodities.

The commodities are equivalent to money; the buyer is spared the trouble of investigating their use value, and they are subject only to slight fluctuations in price. Their marketability and hence their convertibility into money at any time is assured because they have a world market. (1981, 153)

A few pages later, Hilferding writes, "For the capitalist only exchange value is essential" (167).

The rise of finance capital was in part produced by, and also helped produce, new urban attitudes that were brilliantly diagnosed by Georg Simmel in his classic essay published in 1903, "The Metropolis and Mental Life," which in a way is a treatment of his present moment in which ideologies of finance capital had begun to circulate (see also Jameson 1997). Simmel considers the well-known form of individualism, but his urban denizens are not just individuals but rational beings. Exchange value dominates, reducing "all quality and individuality to a purely quantitative level" (1971, 326). Relationships between individuals become relationships about numbers, so that "the modern mind becomes more and more a calculating one" (327).

The rise to dominance of finance capital could not be without cultural ramifications. The US sheet music industry became an industry in the late eighteenth and early nineteenth centuries, but the era of the late nineteenth and early twentieth centuries provides clear illustrations of the emphasis on the exchange value of songs. The industrialization of the production of sheet music in this later era occurred principally in New York City, where Tin Pan Alley songwriters worked in what the *New York Times* described in 1910 as "song factories," churning out goods that were "manufactured, advertised, and distributed in much the same manner as ordinary commodities" (Suisman 2009, 41).

Irving Berlin, one of the greatest songwriters in American history, offered this songwriting advice, as recorded by the journalist Frank Ward O'Malley in 1920, advice that was as much about the market as the craft of songwriting:

First—The melody must musically be within the range of the *average voice* of the average public singer. The average-voice professional singer is the song writer's salesman, the average-voice public his customers. The salesman-singer cannot do justice to a song containing notes too high, too low, or otherwise difficult to sing; and the customer will not buy it.

Second—The title, which must be simple and easily remembered, must be "*planted*" effectively in the song. It must be emphasized, accented again and again, throughout verses and chorus. The public buys songs, not because it knows the song, but because it knows and likes the title idea. Therefore sacrifice lines you are proud of, even sacrifice rhyme and *reason* if necessary, in order to accentuate the title line effectively.

Third—A popular song should be *sexless*, that is, the ideas and the wording must be of a kind that can be logically voiced by either a male or a female singer. Strive for the happy medium in thought and words so that both sexes will want to buy and sing it.

The fourth criterion concerns the song's "heart interest"; the fifth, originality; the sixth, "ideas, emotions, or objects" known to everyone; the seventh, easily singable lyrics; the eighth, simplicity; and finally:

Ninth—The song writer must look upon his work as a *business*, that is, to make a success of it he must work and *work*, and then *WORK*. (O'Malley 1920, 242; emphases and uppercase in original)

Clearly, much of Berlin's attention and acumen were directed at making a song something that could be desired by, and performed by, audiences as broad as possible. As much as an art or craft, Berlin viewed songwriting as a business, the business of producing songs to sell, songs as exchange value.[3]

Once written, these songs were heavily promoted by "song pluggers," employed by Tin Pan Alley publishers to pitch songs to stage singers, who would sing the songs to their public, who could in turn purchase the sheet music for themselves. Charles K. Harris, one of the most successful Tin Pan Alley songwriters, vividly described the business around the turn of the last century:

Daily in Tin Pan Alley . . . the song pluggers, from early morning until late at night, stood in front of their respective publishing houses waiting for singers to come along, when they would grab them by the arm and hoist them into the music studios. There was no escape. Once the singers entered the block, they left it with a dozen songs crammed into their pockets and the singers' promises ringing in the pluggers' ears,—promises to sing the newly acquired compositions. Each song plugger had his own clientele of friends who would stand by him through thick and thin, until some more enterprising plugger would offer them more money, which, naturally, would switch their allegiance.

These song pluggers not only worked day and night but operated in the streets.

It was a common sight any night to see these pluggers, with pockets full of professional copies, stop the singers on the street and lead them to the first lamp-post, where the plugger would sing a song from a professional copy. It mattered not how many people were passing at the time. "Anything to land a singer" was their motto.

Publishers evidently spared no expense in wooing singers.

They certainly had a good time of it, as the pluggers and the publishers fed them up with cigars, drinks, and food of all kind *gratis*. In order that a firm's song might be heard in different cities, many a singer's board bill was paid and many a new trunk, together with a railroad ticket, was purchased by the particular firm whose song the singer was exploiting. The publishers spent their money freely, their slogan being, "Anything and everything to land a hit." There was no system, no set rules, no combination of publishers, no music publishers' association; simply, do as you please, everybody for himself, and the devil take the hindmost. (Tick 2008, 364–65; italics in original)

Song pluggers thus brought the art of selling published music to new heights.

A more subtle but nonetheless important shift in cultural production began to occur around the same time as the heyday of Tin Pan Alley with the rise of what I will call an ideology of exchangeability that grew out of the new importance of finance capital. The rise of the ideology of exchangeability meant that composers, and everyone else, could begin to conceptualize other cultural forms, other things, more and more in terms of their exchangeability. With the rise of modern consumer cultures in the West in the same period, music was increasingly thought of as something to be consumed, something that composers could appropriate to incorporate into their own music. For composers and other artists, the ideology of exchangeability, coincident with rapid urbanization, meant that cultural forms stylistically or generically foreign to the artists' own could be appropriated, imported into the artists' own work. Composers borrowed music before the rise of finance capital, of course, but in this period, for the first time, composers began to appropriate music that was remote to their own experience, music from far away, or music from peasants in their own or neighboring cultures. And such appropriations became commonplace in the late nineteenth and early twentieth centuries, in the music of Igor Stravinsky, Claude Debussy, Béla Bartók, Charles Ives, and others, as well as in the visual art of Pablo Picasso, Georges Braque, and others in that field. This is one reason, as I have argued elsewhere, that composers who had access to non-Western musics in the nineteenth century seldom quoted them, but began to do so in the period of the rise of finance capital and the ideology of exchangeability in the early twentieth century.[4]

Last in this section, I would be remiss not to mention the relatively new and fast-growing literature on cultural production (e.g., Caves 2000; Hartley 2005; Hesmondhalgh 2013; Hesmondhalgh and Baker 2011; Miège 1989); this literature tends not to thematize capitalism, though considerations of capitalism are by no means absent. Nonetheless, with its interest in cultural production as a form of industrial production, this literature is greatly expanding our knowledge of cultural production in the last couple of decades.

Artisans, Artists, Geniuses

As composers slowly shifted from being church functionaries or employees of the aristocracy in the feudal system to capitalist entrepreneurs in a market system, their roles in society changed. The transition was not so drastic as to force them to sell their labor in a wage-labor system; they continued to work as artisans, even if they could increasingly rely on concert and publishing infrastructures, as well as new laws such as copyright, introduced in the late eighteenth century, to protect the products of their labor in a capitalist market. Even today, not all that much has changed in terms of the production of music, in the sense that it is still made by individuals or small groups in much the same way that it was made in the past, though now frequently with newer technologies such as computers.

Yet the major developments in the history of capitalism reveal important shifts in the modalities of how composers earned their livelihoods and coped with the pressures of a market that is unstable and ever-changing. Composers had to become adept at appealing to the market, even attempting to create market demand. Music history is filled with stories of how composers dealt with market pressures, though these stories are frequently presented in professional music history as anecdotes or as fragments of history that are ancillary to what is thought to matter the most, "the music itself."

Beginning in the nineteenth century, composers increasingly became public figures, working as critics (such as Robert Schumann, who cofounded the *Neue Zeitschrift für Musik* in 1834), authoring memoirs (such as Hector Berlioz's from 1865), or opining on politics and other things. It was perhaps Richard Wagner who was most proficient at self-promotion, writing on a variety of subjects (see Vazsonyi 2010) and keeping himself constantly in the public eye, in part to be able to fund his grandiose projects (Adorno once referred to him as a "genius at borrowing money" [2009a, 207]).

Composers who were also performers could cultivate public personae that could aid in the reception of their music—and increase ticket prices and sales. Probably Franz Liszt was the most famous at this in the nineteenth century, known for his flamboyant performances and self-displays (see Metzer 1998). Liszt was a savvy entrepreneur, adept at manipulating the press to his own ends (see Gooley 2004). No less an observer than Heinrich Heine observed in 1844, "No one in this world knows how to organize his success so well, or much more, their *mise-en-scène*, than our Franz Liszt" (Gooley 2004, 145). Today, many, even most, artists do much the same thing, though increasingly under the rubric of brands and branding, which I will discuss in the next chapter.

Inevitably, then, the social status of artists shifted once they and their works entered the marketplace. Composers increasingly became thought of as important in their own right. Instrumental musicians were permitted to be more individualistic in their displays in new genres in the eighteenth century such as the concerto (see McClary 1987). The concept of genius was born by the early nineteenth century (see Battersby 1989), so that by the end of the nineteenth century some composers were thought to be geniuses who could justifiably demand more and more of their listeners—more of their time, so pieces got longer, and more of their attention, so pieces became increasingly complex.

Composers thus became artists (as summed up succinctly by Jacques Attali, "The artist was born, at the same time his work went on sale" [1985, 47]). This development was, as Pierre Bourdieu notes, part of the rise of the idea of "art for art's sake," first put forward, tellingly, by Adam Smith (see Smith 1980 and Taylor 2007a).[5] This ideology gave the world the great artist, a new kind of social personality who did not have to adhere to bourgeois norms (Bourdieu 1996, 111). To this day, the idea that the artist and her work somehow stand apart from society remains strong in the realm of classical music, and it is present in rock and jazz, even though this is an ideology that was produced as a result of music's entry into the marketplace as artists both tried to make a living and at the same time show the world that the fruits of their labors were somehow divorced from the messy business of making a living. And discourses about art and commerce in the cultural industries today are apparent in practically every publication, blog, or conversation (see Ortner 2013 and Taylor 2012b).

Such developments were part of a larger shift in historical capitalism, the rise of the notion of the unique, autonomous individual. The growth and spread of this ideology are tied to other phenomena as well, such as the Protestant Reformation, which can be seen as a culmination of earlier ideas about the individual, but capitalism played an important role in inculcating in many Europeans the belief that they were unique individuals rather than parts of a collective. But no social type embraced—or was allowed to embrace—this ideology more than the artist.

This belief in their separateness from society meant that many composers, like other artists, fought to keep market forces at bay even as they hoped to earn their livelihoods from the market. They proclaimed themselves to be artists while struggling to make their works autonomous from market forces in order to service their inspiration. One must remember that artworks were not naturally autonomous, as they are frequently taken to be in music studies; rather, autonomy, as we learned from Pierre Bourdieu (1993 and 1995), was a hard-fought goal, allowing some artists to believe themselves to enjoy a vantage point from which to critique their societies as they stood above them, the belief held, and championed, by Adorno.

An example of the complex processes by which capitalism as a "structure" in the practice theory sense shapes cultural production and is shaped by it, let's consider briefly the rise of opera, which occurred in part as a response to European colonialism, the enormity of which, I once argued (Taylor 2007a), necessitated new systems and forms of representation such as tonality in music that could grapple with the "discovery" of peoples and places previously unknown to Europeans, who could then put them in their place.[6] Lorenzo Bianconi observes that the rise of opera also produced a new kind of musician. Composers were subjected to market forces, with all the market's risks and potential successes, the changing taste of the public, competition with rivals, and much more. But musicians in this era rarely had a financial interest in the operatic enterprise; they were contract workers. Composers were just suppliers of music, much the same as the others involved with operatic production, though composers were paid less than the famous virtuosi in the performances, and not always even named in libretti and scores (Bianconi 1987, 82–83). Operatic and other composers responded to their changing circumstances quite creatively, striking deals with publishers, competing for operatic audiences, and in still other ways (see Weber 2004).

Every genre, every form of music-making, has its own shifting relationship to the marketplace, and thus its own expectations and requirements of musicians. With the rise of what can be called a modern, industrialized music industry in the late nineteenth and early twentieth centuries, music produced for the purpose of exchange has become dominant, influencing musical production increasingly and, particularly with the introduction of digital technologies in the 1980s, reducing the differences between different kinds of musical production.

The principal refuge for composers, at least in the United States, has been the university, where most composers could continue to write music in a field of increasingly restricted production, that is, mainly writing for each other and perhaps a few others. But restricted production isn't what it used to be, as art becomes progressively deautonomized with the encroachment of the fields of power and economics (Bourdieu 1996 and 2003), also increasingly employing marketing and advertising strategies borrowed from the promotion of popular culture (see chapter 2). And, of course, secure university positions are becoming scarcer, at least in the United States.

Social Class, Markets, and Cultural Consumption

I am concerned here with questions of class and cultural consumers; I will not consider the social class of cultural producers. This latter question is difficult to generalize, for the class position of cultural producers can vary, and even within the cultural industries, seemingly similar occupations might be held by those from different class positionalities (on this point see also Adorno 1976, 56–57).[7] This is nowhere clearer than in different forms of group production, where the individual who is permitted to assume the mantle of auteur varies considerably, even in fields that may appear to be similar. For example, in television, the auteur is the showrunner, the person who oversees the day-to-day production of the program and probably is one of the writers, whereas in film, famously, the auteur is the director. Thus, this question, perhaps more than most others, requires empirical investigation into particular fields and cases.

But questions of class positionality are more generalizable with respect to cultural consumption, for, as Bourdieu writes, "nothing more clearly affirms one's 'class,' nothing more infallibly classifies than taste in music" (1984, 18). Most studies of social class that bother with music focus on questions of cultural consumption: Which social groups listen to which musics? Questions of cultural consumption, while complex, become more so in a consumer culture in which some have the power to promote their tastes to others, as I will discuss below. For now, let me simply concentrate on cultural consumption and class. A good deal has been written about the nature of attendance at classical music concerts and how it reveals class stratification and mores. The sociologist Tia DeNora's study of Beethoven argues that while aristocrats continued to play a leading role in music affairs in Vienna in the late eighteenth and early nineteenth centuries, the nature of their leadership changed, from quantifiable expenditures to demonstrations of "good taste" and an increased emphasis on "greatness," which is where the idea of master composers comes from. All of this was a way for aristocrats to remake themselves as "aristocrats of taste" (1995, 48).

Important works on the subject of music consumption by William Weber (1975 and 2008) explore the growth of concert attendance from 1830 to 1848 in Europe, a period in which classical music concert attendance practices and behaviors were standardized, associated increasingly with upper classes. Much the same transpired at the same time in the United States, where social elites sought not only to bolster their standing but also to demonstrate it by sacralizing high culture (see DiMaggio 1986).

The rise of bourgeois concert attendance was coupled with a mode of behavior at concerts that increasingly venerated composers. Concert halls were designed to be almost churchlike, and attendees' behavior was expected to mirror that of the acolyte (see Small 1987). The furor over a cell phone ringing during a performance of Mahler's Ninth Symphony by the New York Philharmonic in 2012 shows just how sacred the concert experience is still thought to be, and just how ostracized are those who fail to observe the expected reverential norms.[8]

With the rise of the modern advertising industry in the late nineteenth and early twentieth centuries, along with the various industries that are now lumped under the term "culture industry" (Horkheimer and Adorno 1990; Adorno 2001) or "cultural industries" (Hesmondhalgh 2013), the so-called developed countries began a slow shift toward increasing consumption, which continues into the present. In my history of music and advertising (Taylor 2012b), I discussed three regimes of consumption in American culture: the first one, which emerged in this period of the late nineteenth and early twentieth centuries, buttressed by the new advertising industry and culminating with the rise of radio broadcasting, which proved to be a potent medium for advertising (see McGovern 2006); a second regime, following the end of the Great Depression and World War II, aided by television, another powerful new medium for advertising (see Cohen 2003); and a third regime, beginning in the 1980s with the rise of neoliberal policies and supported by new digital technologies, particularly the World Wide Web as yet another powerful advertising and marketing tool (see Lee 1999 and Slater 1997).

In all regimes, music, musicians, and sound reproduction technologies were all aggressively advertised, though to varying degrees. Some sound reproduction companies, whether player piano manufacturers or phonograph companies—perhaps most famously the Victor Talking Machine Company and, later, RCA Victor—used advertising as a potent tool to insinuate their product into the homes of American consumers, particularly the middle class (see Suisman 2009).

Convincing people that to purchase recorded music was preferable to making it themselves was a slow and arduous process. Persuading the public, long accustomed to making their own music and hearing music live, to purchase a player piano or a phonograph (or, later, a radio) took several decades of promotion by the recording and broadcasting industries. Consumers at first had to be assured that they weren't surrendering agency, that they were bringing their interpretive powers to the "performance" of player piano rolls. And they were told that, regardless of how good they might be as pianists, they could purchase more piano rolls of works than they could ever learn for themselves. An advertisement for the Gulbransen player piano in the *Saturday Evening Post* from October 17, 1925, read:

The Biggest Thrill in Music is playing it *Yourself*

And now even untrained persons can do it.
You can play better by roll than
many who play by hand.
And you can play *ALL* pieces while
they can play but a few.
(reproduced in Roehl 1973, 23; emphases and uppercase in original)

This sort of advertising was quite common, telling consumers that they could have great music in their homes easily.

Once player piano technologies advanced to the point that they could "record" the great musicians of the day, consumers were told that they could have the master's fingers on their own pianos at home (see Taylor 2007b). Great performers captured on audio recordings were sold in similar fashion (see Suisman 2009). The efforts of sound reproduction technology manufacturers were aided by powerful advertising campaigns that emphasized how listeners could hear the great composers play their own works, as well as performances by the greatest pianists of the day. Such campaigns were also bolstered by sympathetic journalists and other writers who covered new recording technologies positively and who helped spread a powerful ideology of the democratization of access to what was thought to be great music.[9] "Even an Alaskan nowadays," wrote the influential music critic and composer Deems Taylor of the player piano in 1922, "can hear the masterpieces of piano literature played by great artists" (1922).

Selling the phonograph adopted the same strategies, employing ideologies of democratization of access to Great Music, and selling the artistry of the recorded pianists and composers on the player piano, and artists of all kinds—especially opera—on the phonograph. In a 1918 pamphlet published by the Empire Talking Machine Company, a Mr. Ames laments the lack of live musical entertainment after a nice dinner in the summer. "It's too bad, mother, that you never learned to play the piano," he says. Like many American middle-class families in this era, the Ameses had a piano that was under- or unused; daughter Dorothy is too nervous to play, and brother Will's playing of ragtime did not find favor with father. Mr. Ames opined:

> "This is too peaceful and beautiful an evening to be disturbed like that. . . .
> You know . . . I have thought several times of buying a talking machine—a
> phonograph."
> "Yes, canned music," sneered Will.

"No, my boy," returned Mr. Ames. "Not canned music, as you call it, but the accurately recorded performances of the world's greatest artists. With the modern methods now employed for making records it's just the same as having, say, [Italian tenor Enrico] Caruso come into this house and sing for you. The same voice, the same songs, for which's paid thousands of dollars a night. It's really Caruso himself—or [soprano Geraldine] Farrar—or [Irish tenor] John McCormack—whomever you choose to hear." (*Dorothy Decides* 1918)[10]

Advertising campaigns such as this helped produce the new musical consumer, which, in Adorno's estimation, was a form of musical Babbittry (2009a, referring to the title character of Sinclair Lewis's 1922 novel *Babbitt*, whose main concerns in life were material success and the leading of a respectable bourgeois existence).

Early studies of the musical preferences of US consumers were mostly conducted by radio networks, or commissioned by them, beginning in the 1920s. More informal information on audience preferences was gathered by the burgeoning radio press of the 1920s and after, which conducted its own surveys or held contests, asking readers to write essays on their favorite radio star. An early polarization emerged between "classical" music and "jazz," though "classical" usually referred to middlebrow works, and "jazz" usually referred to white musicians' dance bands, such Paul Whiteman's, the most famous of the era. And the radio press also frequently discussed such terms as "middlebrow," "lowbrow," and "highbrow," which became increasingly urgent questions as music became more easily available, and as the growing consumer culture created an ever more complex landscape of what Thorstein Veblen famously called "conspicuous consumption" ([1899] 1994).

All the studies of radio listeners from the late 1920s on show a clear and predictable pattern of higher-income groups preferring classical music of various kinds and lower-income groups gravitating toward types of "lowbrow" music, though the earliest studies sometimes classified listeners not by income group but by region (e.g., Starch 1928) or simply audience preference (e.g., Grunwald 1937). By the early 1930s, studying music listening preferences by income group became the norm. Socioeconomic class was classified first by using an "ABCD" scheme, with A being the highest-income group (e.g., "Boston Survey" 1930), though this quickly was complicated by the addition of more class groups (e.g., Columbia Broadcasting System 1934). One of the better of these early surveys with respect to musical taste makes the class preferences for music clear (table 1.1): Orchestral programs such as the Philadelphia Orchestra broadcasts were clearly more popular with higher-income

TABLE 1.1. Ranking of Most Popular Classical and Semiclassical Musical Programs by Income Level (from Beville 1940, 202)

Classical and Semiclassical Music	Total Rating	Income Group Indices[1]			
		A (highest)	B	C	D (lowest)
Ford Sunday Evening Hour[2]	13.9	157	129	90	62
General Motors Symphony[3]	11.7	172	107	92	76
Palmolive Beauty Box Theater[4]	10.1	145	113	95	80
Cities Service Concert[5]	10.1	148	114	87	95
Lawrence Tibbett[6]	9.9	160	122	92	62
Voice of Firestone[7]	9.9	137	111	102	64
Andre Kostelanetz[8]	7.9	154	128	91	72
A & P Gypsies[9]	7.2	122	125	93	72
Philadelphia Orchestra[10]	5.8	233	114	79	81
Contented Program[11]	5.8	162	116	90	81

1. "Income group rating adjusted for amount of listening of group and related to total rating as 100" (Beville 1940, 202).

2. Beville describes this in his earlier publication as "the Detroit Symphony Orchestra, under the baton of guest conductors such as Jose Iturbi, Eugene Ormandy and John Barbirolli in a program of symphonic music featuring guest stars from the concert and opera stage" (Beville 1939, Appendix, 4).

3. "Program of symphonic music, with full symphony orchestra conducted by Erno Rapee, and featuring guest stars from the concert and opera stage" (Beville 1939, Appendix, 5).

4. "Outstanding musical operettas with orchestra directed by Nathaniel Shilkret. The leads are played by such outstanding singers as Helen Jepson, James Melton, Gladys Swarthout, supported by large singing and dramatic cast" (Beville 1939, Appendix, 10).

5. "Semi-classical and popular music program featuring Jessica Dragonette, soprano [later replaced by Lucille Manners]; Robert Simmons, tenor; Rosario Bourdon directing the Cities Service Concert Orchestra. Each fall Grantland Rice joins the program during the football season to give football news" (Beville 1939, Appendix, 3).

6. "Musical program featuring the Metropolitan Opera baritone with Don Voorhees's orchestra, offering a variety of musical selections ranging from operatic arias to current popular numbers" (Beville 1939, Appendix, 13).

7. "Program of classical and symphonic music presented by the Firestone Orchestra, conducted by William Daly [later replaced by Alfred Wallenstein]; Margaret Speaks, Nelson Eddy and Richard Crooks soloists (the two men alternate)" (Beville 1939, Appendix, 14).

8. "Musical program of the classical and semi-classical type featuring the music of Andre Kostelanetz with Lily Pons, Nino Martini and Rosa Ponselle, of the Metropolitan Opera Association, as soloists" (Beville 1939, Appendix, 7).

9. "Program of light classical concert and popular music played by Harry Horlick and his orchestra with guest artists" (Beville 1939, Appendix, 1).

10. "Program of symphonic music with the Philadelphia Symphony [sic] conducted by Leopold Stokowski or Eugene Ormandy and a guest speaker; a prominent national figure speaking on business conditions" (Beville 1939, Appendix, 11).

11. Beville provides no information on this program.

audiences, while more middlebrow and lowbrow programs such as the *Contented Program* (which was probably *The Carnation Contented Hour*, a music variety program) appealed more to lower-income groups.

More recent sociological studies of cultural consumption beyond the world of the most prestigious classical music show clear links between class positionality—or more finely, amounts of educational and cultural capital—and taste in music. Bourdieu's landmark study showed clear preferences for more abstract, instrumental classical music (J. S. Bach's *Well-Tempered Clavier*) by those possessing the most cultural and educational capital ("higher-education teachers, art producers" and "secondary teachers"), while George Gershwin's *Rhapsody in Blue* was the most popular among people in the middle ("technicians"), and Strauss's *Blue Danube* waltz the most popular among "manual workers," "domestic servants," "craftsmen, shopkeepers," and "clerical and commercial employees" (1984, 17). In the United States, links between social class and tastes in country music are well known and have been well studied (see Fox 2004).

In the last couple of decades, however, various sociological studies in the United States (e.g., Peterson 1990, 1992, and 1997; Peterson and Kern 1996; Peterson and Simkus 1992) and Europe (e.g., Coulangeon 2003 and 2004; Donnat 2004; van Eijck 2001) have shown that the cultural tastes of elite groups have become less connected to the fine arts and increasingly eclectic, leading some researchers to posit a change from "univore" tastes for high culture to more "omnivore" tastes in the last few decades (Peterson 1992; Peterson and Kern 1996). Peterson's study shows a decreasing interest in classical music among elite groups; only 30 percent of his survey respondents in the most elite group said they preferred classical music to other kinds of music, and only 6 percent said they preferred opera. Peterson reasoned that 64 percent of the highest-status group no longer fits the model of the "aesthetically exclusive snob" (1992, 248). Peterson and other sociologists who have studied the same phenomenon explain the trend toward omnivorousness in taste for cultural goods by crediting the rise of the sophistication of the mass media since the 1960s (Gans 1985), better and more widespread public education (Gans 1985), and the rise in white-collar service jobs (Ehrenreich and Ehrenreich 1979; Gans 1985; Lash and Urry 1987). Others argue that the baby boomers, unlike previous generations, did not (re)turn to classical music as they aged, but continued to listen to their music from their youth (Peterson 1990, 210–13; see also van Eijck 2001). I have a different interpretation of this shift that I will discuss in the next chapter.

Studies of the consumption of music are still rather rare in music studies (though studies of cultural consumption are less rare in other fields). I remember well the befuddlement-leading to-disapprobation that I faced from my senior colleagues when I first taught a graduate seminar on the consumption of music at my former university in the early 2000s, a course that was probably the first of its kind in a music department. Yet if music is more an object of consumption than production for the majority of people today, as it has been for decades, consumption as the primary relationship that most people have with music must be taken seriously.

YOUTH

As Marx and Engels famously pointed out in the *Communist Manifesto* and elsewhere, capitalism attempts to find its way out of crises by conquering new markets and seeking ways to exploit old ones (1964, 13). Perhaps the best example of this in the twentieth century is the "discovery" in the 1940s of youth, who quickly became viewed as a new market by capitalists (see Palladino 1996), particularly with the rise of the baby boom generation after World War II.

A 1956 article in the *Wall Street Journal* argued that the sixteen million teenagers in the United States comprised a market that merchants and advertisers were increasingly paying attention to, since teenagers spent between $7 billion and $9 billion annually (Kraar 1956, 1), and the number of teenagers was expected to grow by 70 percent in the following decade. Teenagers were seen as having influence on family purchases and family habits. One advertising man told the *Wall Street Journal* that he "'was all ready to watch an old movie on television until daughter Linda decided on the Hit Parade, on another channel'" (1). Teenagers became closely studied consumers, so much so that one such student of teenage behavior, Eugene Gilbert, authored a syndicated newspaper column entitled "What Young People Think" and in 1957 published *Advertising and Marketing to Young People*. His overall argument was simple: "Today's teenager is an independent character.... The fact is, he can afford to be" ("New $10 Billion Power" 1959, 78). The music industry was well aware of the potential of this market. Dick Clark's *American Bandstand*, which he had begun to host in 1956, was suffused with commercials aimed at teenagers. According to Clark in 1957, "It's been a long, long time since a major network has aimed at the most entertainment-starved group in the country. And why not? After all, teen-agers have $9 billion a year to spend" ("Challenging the Giants" 1957, 70).

Once a (predominantly middle-class) subsection of this market coalesced as the countercultural movements of the 1960s, drawing in members older than the postwar baby boom generation, one of the most powerful social movements in American history took form. Yet this social movement was less a push for civil rights—except, of course, for those portions of it dedicated to civil rights for African Americans and women—than a reaction against the postwar conformity suffered by this group's parents, particularly their mothers, confined to the home after having served their country by working outside the home during the war. This countercultural movement was anticonsumption in orientation, hoping to chart a path toward greater social freedoms and equality.

And it was accompanied by a soundtrack by some of the most memorable and enduring popular musicians of the last century, whose music tastes were decried by those who viewed rock and roll as decadent and threatening, but whose listeners were also endlessly catered to and marketed to by the music industry. The music of the counterculture, rock and roll, produced bountiful profits for the record industry, even as many musicians represented themselves as antiestablishment, or even anticapitalist, just as artists in restricted fields proclaimed their autonomy from the market. Simon Frith (1983) has written what remains in my view the most insightful treatment of the rise of rock music and how, though rooted in folk music and African American musics, rock managed to artify itself and give itself a form of autonomy akin to that of art, allowing it a position from which to critique society.

This critique was part of a broader indictment of postwar capitalism, a critique that Luc Boltanski and Eve Chiapello have called an "artistic critique" (2005). The substance of this critique was against the conformity and blandness of postwar capitalism, what I called "gray-flannel capitalism" elsewhere (Taylor 2012b). Boltanski and Chiapello observe that midcentury capitalism "offered itself both as a way of achieving self-fulfillment by engaging in capitalism, and as a path of liberation from capitalism itself, from what was oppressive about its early creations," though they later argue this liberation was just another form of slavery, with people reduced to consumers in thrall to production (2005, 425, 427).

Consumption proffers a form of liberation in today's capitalism parallel to "liberation via the commodity." For them, the "archetypal form" of this liberation concerns music, "listening to a recording when one wishes, to the kind of music that one wants to hear precisely now, at this instant, and for a chosen length of time, as opposed to going to a concert" (Boltanski and Chiapello 2005, 438). Consumption, as many have written, has thus become a way of self-definition, of self-construction, of making fantasies, experiencing nostalgia. This was perhaps best summed up by Arjun Appadurai, who writes that people practice consumption daily, bringing together nostalgia and fantasy in a landscape of commodities (1996, 82).[11]

Music has long been one of the consumer goods by which people have constructed identities, perhaps exemplified most clearly in the 1960s, when popular music became an integral part of many of the social movements of the era. Decades later, it has become impossible to think of that decade without a soundtrack of music by Joan Baez, Bob Dylan, Janis Joplin, Jimi Hendrix, and many others. Listening to certain artists, songs, or bands today is no less important in defining one's identity, though I would also argue that the ideology of the hip and the cool has been extended to certain consumer goods as well as cultural goods, so the device one listens to music with has become perhaps as culturally significant as the music itself. Steve Jobs didn't just make good products or make products look good—he made them seem to be cool.

And coolness was what neoliberal capitalism began to seek, and manufacture, following the "artistic critique" of capitalism in the 1960s (see Frank 1997 and Taylor 2012b). Internalizing this critique, the cultural industries, and, increasingly, every other industry, have sought to appropriate whatever is thought to be cool, even manufacture what is thought to be cool, in order to sell ever more goods. I will consider this more in the following chapter.

Conclusions

I have refrained from attempting a chronological history of capitalism and music in the West because this has not been, and will not continue to be, a linear history. The spread of capitalism in the West has been neither an inexorable nor uniform conquest, though it has indisputably become hegemonic. It is the most potent force in the lives of everyone in the West, and is increasingly becoming so elsewhere on the planet.

But as the following pages will show, there are differences between hegemonies and totalities. Capitalism is not total, even in the West, and hegemonies, as we have learned from Antonio Gramsci (most famously in Gramsci 1971) and those following in his wake, leave plenty of room for alternatives and resistances and insurgencies, other regimes of value that are not economic. While much in the following pages details just how neoliberal hegemony works in the West with respect to the production, distribution, consumption, advertising, marketing, branding, and consumption of music, it also pays plenty of attention to all the ways that people attempt to make neoliberal capitalism work for them, allowing them to do what they want in it.

And yet hegemony is hegemony. The hegemony of capitalism has meant a radical altering of just about everything. Capitalism as a social form is made by people, but it also shapes people, their thoughts and practices. To noneconomic or noncapitalist systems of value comes a new sort of value, exchange value. Goods such as music increasingly become produced and consumed under a capitalist rubric. Production as Marx understood it—the myriad ways that we interact with each other, a "complex set of mutually dependent relations among nature, work, social labor, and social organization," in Eric Wolf's words, becomes increasingly a capitalist mode of production (1982, 74). Workers are alienated from their labor, and the products of their labor can be produced and distributed and consumed on so vast a scale that those products can seem to take on lives of their own.

All this does not sound much like a system anyone would willingly participate in. And yet it continues, becoming even more widespread and virulent in the last few decades. As we will see in the following chapters.

Neoliberal Capitalism and the Cultural Industries

This chapter begins by considering the concept of neoliberal capitalism as I use it in this book, then continues by tracing what this has meant for the production, distribution, advertising, marketing, branding, and consumption of music and musicians. It is clear that much has changed in the last few decades: capitalism has become more present across the globe, less regulated, commodifying and commercializing voraciously, and is increasingly present in laws, helping the rich become richer and the poor poorer. But older forms of capitalism remain.

While I have learned much from the literature about neoliberalism, many of the writings tend toward the economistic, which is insufficient to understanding how neoliberal—or any—capitalism shapes, and is shaped by, the cultures in which it finds itself; Michel Foucault once observed that one cannot understand capitalism simply in terms of the "economic logic of capital and its accumulation" (2008, 164). In other words, I am arguing that many of the accounts of today's capitalism are rather too Marxist in their assumption of an economic base, and are not Weberian enough in their attention to culture, with one self-proclaimed exception (Boltanski and Chiapello 2005). But most accounts of today's capitalism don't advance our thinking on how capitalism shapes culture. David Harvey's offhand reference in his primer on neoliberalism (2005) that he examined the cultural effects of neoliberalism in an earlier book (1989)—a book published sixteen years earlier, before most people even in the West had a personal computer or Internet access or a cellular telephone—serves as an example.

Ideologies of Neoliberal Capitalism

The changes wrought by neoliberalism in the last few decades are profound. Even if capitalism hasn't changed that much (as some have argued; see Doogan 2009), the world has. What we need, rather than rigidly economistic analyses that tell us that not much has changed—which we already knew anyway, since the rich are still rich and, at least in the United States, becoming richer as the poor continue to get poorer—is analyses that tell us not only what has changed, but why. Thus, while I require studies of today's capitalism that emphasize the economic, I am more concerned with how neoliberal ideologies and policies have influenced the culture, particularly in the United States, as well as having shaped the production and consumption of cultural goods.

Since neoliberalism is an ideology, a mode of governance, and a set of policies (Steger and Roy 2010, 11), it profoundly shapes any culture in which it finds itself, a point I made in the introduction but now want to consider in some detail (see also Brown 2005). This is an issue Foucault spent some time with. For him, in the United States in particular, liberalism (and, presumably, neoliberalism) is not simply a set of governmental and economic policies and practices; it is, rather, a culture, a "whole way of being and thinking," "a type of relation between the governors and the governed much more than a technique of governors with regard to the governed" (2008, 218). Thus, he argues that American neoliberalism generalizes the "economic form" of the market throughout society, including those portions where monetary exchanges didn't normally occur (243). Foucault was observing the positions promoted by Milton Friedman ([1962] 1982) and others, in which every problem in society was thought to have an economic solution. Foucault's critique is of particular interest, since I am concerned not simply with how capitalism in general and neoliberalism are cultural(ized) but with what this means for the production, distribution, advertising, marketing, branding, and consumption of culture.

Today's neoliberalism has produced a new type of economic person, someone, according to Foucault,

> who accepts reality or who responds systematically to modifications in the variables of the environment, appears precisely as someone manageable, someone who responds systematically to systematic modifications artificially introduced into the environment. *Homo œconomicus* is someone who is eminently governable. Far from being the intangible partner of *laissez-faire*, *homo œconomicus* now becomes the correlate of a governmentality which will act on the environment and systematically modify its variables. (2008, 270–71)

Foucault's thinking on neoliberalism is not simply an economic system but an organizing ideology that shapes thoughts, practices, and self-conceptions.

One of the most powerful weapons in this ideological arsenal is the trope of freedom. Pierre Bourdieu and Luc Boltanski set out to understand the new dominant ideology in France in the 1970s, arguing how the idea of liberation or freedom of expression and sexual relationships emanating from the student movement of the 1960s and superficially May 1968 in France led to a generalized trope of "freedom," a theme that was retained from May 1968 but had been emptied of anything subversive (1976, 44, note 9). Bourdieu wondered elsewhere if this "ethic of liberation" was "in the process of supplying the economy with the perfect consumer"—*Homo œconomicus*, perhaps—"whom economic theory has always dreamed of" (1984, 371).

Today's ideologies of neoliberalism, drawing in part on writings by Friedman ([1962] 1982) and F. A. Hayek ([1944] 1994) and others, employ this trope of "freedom" to attack what are seen as the interfering and regulatory practices of the state, helping elites to regain their position (Harvey 2005). This was accompanied by an ideology of freedom in other arenas, such as consumer choice, and also lifestyles, and a host of cultural practices (Harvey 2005, 42). The trope of "freedom" has become a kind of free-floating ideology that can be used to attach itself to whatever its bearer wishes. Harvey argues that the ideology of freedom gave the dominant group in New York City the impetus to open up the cultural field, so that exploring self, identity, and sexuality became the norm in bourgeois urban culture (47). Artistic freedom was an important component of this, which led to what Harvey calls the neoliberalization of culture (47). The influential proto-fascist political right in the United States attacks almost every policy emanating from the Democratic Party, whether the Affordable Care Act (Obamacare) or gun control, as an assault on freedom.

The social effect of all this "freedom"—in particular, I would say, the freedom to believe oneself to be the sole author of one's individuality—has been the rise of social incoherence, which is extremely difficult to counteract. Harvey views the rise in interest of morality and religion, whether evangelical Christian or New Age or the neglected religion of one's forebears, the revival of old forms of politics such as fascism and nationalism, and the rise of new social groupings as attempts to combat this social incoherence (2005, 80–81). And, I would add, "identity" becomes more important, identity as something that one fashions, mainly through consumption of particular goods and not others, which give one entrée into a particular social group. Identity is a way of attempting to find stability, or at least a sense of stability, in an anomic social universe increasingly disrupted and fragmented (see Castells 1997 and Taylor 2007a), and I will discuss identity at greater length presently.

Another effect of neoliberalism in urban cultures has been the decline of the public, and the infiltration of the private into the public, perhaps best represented by the now common headphone- or earbud-clad individual, cocooned in her own sonic world. This new mode of listening privately in public began in 1979 when the Sony Walkman was introduced, marking a revolution in people's relationship to recorded music. The previous revolution was wrought by the phonograph in the late nineteenth century and, even more importantly, the radio in the 1920s, which in its early days broadcast almost everything live: people could listen to recorded or live music at home. They could listen to music that they once would have had to leave their homes to hear as part of a public, at home. With the Walkman, they could listen to music privately, in public. It would be impossible to overstate the importance of this device. Music—one's own music, on demand—became much more portable (see Hosokawa 1984), and the public space became increasingly populated by private listeners.

We should remember that early radios, some of which were (barely) portable, could only be listened to with headphones. And the pocket transistor radio, which became immensely popular in the 1960s and 1970s, frequently had a jack for a small earpiece, mainly so one could listen to the ball game or the latest rock hit under the covers and not be caught by one's parents. People seldom used these earpieces in public—the idea that one would go out in public and listen to music privately didn't make sense in the 1960s and 1970s in a culture where public was still seen as public. But by the 1980s, when music had become not only an object of consumption but a mode of self-definition, of identity-making, and neoliberal ideologies had further emphasized the importance of the individual and the waning support for the idea of the public (whether in the form of parks or libraries or schools or something else), the idea that one could listen to private music in public began to be socially and culturally accepted. And many more today, as MP3 players and cellular phones are nearly ubiquitous (see Bull 2005). Such usages of these devices demonstrate the hyperindividualism in the culture of neoliberal capitalism.

Yet, since any capitalism always has contradictions, it is clear at the same time that communications technologies can be used to create new publics, or counterpublics, as evidenced by the circulation of Ayatollah Khomeini's sermons on cassette in the 1970s before the Iranian revolution (Hirschkind 2009) or the use of social media in the Arab Spring and other more recent social movements.

Last in this section, I need to note a transformation of intimacy associated with neoliberal capitalism. According to Martin Stokes, the relationship of the citizen to the state in Turkey increasingly employs intimate representations of identification with the state (Stokes 2010, 13). As a result of neoliberal transformations, urban Turkey is undergoing a shift to a "new regime of intimacy and urban civility" (182), and music is not aloof from this shift.

The Cultural Industries as Industries

Nothing in the West has been left untouched by this latest phase of capitalism. Beginning with this section, I will explore the various aspects of the production, distribution, advertising, marketing, branding, and consumption of music that have been affected by the neoliberal shift, beginning with the cultural industries. Let me make it clear that my concern is with the cultural industries, and what follows may sound rather top-down and depressing to anyone interested in the possibility of resistance, or hoping to create forms of capitalism that are less rapacious. I will discuss some of these strategies in chapter 5.

A major feature of neoliberalism has been the growth of conglomerates of unrelated businesses as a result of antitrust regulation (Centeno and Cohen 2010, 81–82), and the cultural industries have not been immune to this trend. General Electric, for example, has owned the National Broadcasting Company since 1986. This trend has resulted in the increased corporatization of the cultural industries, held much more to the bottom line than they were in the past, in part also because of the increasing ownership role played by managers, who through the mechanism of stock options began to think of themselves more as owners with a responsibility to stockholders. One of the people I interviewed discussed what he characterized as a "game of Wall Street mergers and acquisitions" in the 1980s (Backer 2004), which greatly affected that industry, as well as the other cultural industries: all the major television networks and movie studios have been acquired by multinational corporations, as have most of the major record labels.

Many people I interviewed in my history of music and advertising (Taylor 2012b) spoke, often with some bitterness, of how the business changed after all of these mergers and acquisitions and the rise of these modern managers. Testing of advertisements became increasingly important, with a concomitant decline in trusting the professionals who wrote and performed the music. As Anne Phillips, a composer and singer in the realm of advertising music, wrote in an unpublished article from the early 1980s when this change was beginning:

Thirteen years ago when I started writing commercials everything I wrote went on the air. I'd get a call from an agency, compose the music, get immediate approval, orchestrate it, record it and generally within a few weeks I'd hear it. Pepsi, Campbell's Soup, Kent, American Gas Association, Sheraton and many, many more won awards and stayed on the air because they worked, they sold the product. . . . All these campaigns were created and beautifully executed by talented professionals who knew their business and whose judgment was respected. There was quality. . . .

Then something began to happen. More and more campaigns began to mysteriously die somewhere between creation and broadcast. Those of us who work freelance weren't close enough to the business end of things to hear such words as "quantitative" and "risk-reduction" but we did learn about "testing." Soon it seemed that the people who once got excited about new campaigns had gotten knocked down so many times by the numbers that they just couldn't believe in or fight for an idea anymore. It's like falling in love and getting hurt too many times. Some people get to a point where they are afraid to invest too much of themselves to really commit themselves to anything. . . . And that's a terrible way for any creative person to live. Today if I write 30 commercials and one finally makes it through the maze of client presentations, marketing analysis, legal, testing, etc., I consider it a miracle.

Can you imagine how that affects me as I sit down at the piano to compose a piece of music? Here I am, writing better than ever, yet I can't help having the feeling that no matter how good the piece of music, it stands little chance of ever seeing the light of day. . . .

But those of us who care about excellence can't stop caring. So we keep knocking ourselves out turning out quality and often getting no response at all. Sometimes I feel as though I might as well have sent over a sack of potatoes. Hardly anyone on the agency end is going to say, "Hey, this is great!" and go to bat for it. What's the use? Their opinion isn't worth anything.

It's as though the rug of basic pride in our work and faith in our experience, talent and professionalism was slowly pulled out from under us. The basis for decision, if you call what is in truth non-decision, "decision," is no longer one's wisdom and ability to make sound judgments. It is numbers. (Phillips n.d.)[1]

In this article, Phillips interviewed others in the fields of advertising and commercial music and found many of the same sentiments. I will quote several of her examples, for voices from the time of this transition are rare, and these excerpts capture well the disenchantment and feelings of demoralization that workers in the cultural industries felt in this period as they faced the increasing rationalization of their workplace.

An ad agency senior vice president copywriter-producer said:

Sometimes I wonder why I ever wanted to be more than a secretary—at least I could cover my typewriter and go home without this gnawing feeling of apprehension. I haven't produced anything I've really felt good about in so long I begin to wonder if I still can. I rack up my old reel [collection of previous work] now and then just to reassure myself that we once did produce that quality.

Someone Phillips describes as "a top executive at one of the largest record companies which has been run for the last 15 years by accountants and lawyers in the presidency," told her, "I'm a puppet. I know what has to be done. They let me speak at meetings and then they turn back to the numbers. I resent it, I'm a pro and I know about profit and sales figures but there's more to it than that."

A New York City record producer, publisher, and songwriter said, "I just told my wife I thought I'd get out my horn and take a quartet into the local Holiday Inn. At least I'd get some satisfaction and be happy."

A studio musician said:

This business used to be fun, I don't know what's happened. I go into a session, play my notes, pack up and go home. There's no joy, no spirit in the room. Nobody tells you it was good; in fact nobody tells you it was bad. There's this feeling of nothingness and I think it shows in the music. It hasn't got any spirit either.

And an advertising agency art director said:

I just produced a commercial and they put it into test—it scored a little below average, so they put it into a different test and it scored fantastically. They put it back into the first test again and this time it scored above average. They didn't know what to do so they didn't do anything. I guess it's dead. It's depressing; it was a good commercial.

The trend toward monopolization has occurred in the radio industry as well, which is an important way that potential consumers of music hear it. The passage of the Telecommunications Act of 1996 has created a near-monopoly situation in which the biggest four media companies have 48 percent of the listeners, the top ten have nearly two-thirds of the listeners, and only fifteen formats comprise 76 percent of commercial programming (DiCola 2006, 5, 7). This has resulted in the streamlining and standardizing of playlists, which in turn has made it much more difficult for musicians to receive radio airplay since there are fewer different songs being broadcast. And getting a record deal is increasingly difficult as the major labels concentrate on a few blockbusters rather than cultivating a variety of musicians.

Since early in the second decade of the twentieth century, capitalism in the realm of cultural production has thrived on stars, though the cultural industries once supported those who shone less brightly. Major record labels' former practice of subsidizing moderately profitable musicians through their most successful musicians has given way to a system of seeking to land and market only the best-selling musical (or whatever) b(r)and, using increasingly rationalized means of testing and market research and publicity. Today, we are in a relatively new phase in which stars, or potential stars, are even more important. In today's music industry, 80 percent of revenue is derived from 20 percent of inventory (Seno 2007, 32). Computer software designed to analyze songs and predict hits has been developed (Sherwin 2006; Sydell 2009; Werde 2004) (though such software is one of many such technologies developed out of an uncritical, utopian belief in the possibly of a technological solution to every problem).[2]

But, despite the occasional successful blockbuster, the record industry is struggling, largely because of the rise of the digital distribution of music, which makes it easy to share music as high-quality digital files. The record industry has endeavored to find ways to entice the growing number of fans who believe music to be free to pay something for it, whether as an inexpensive (usually ninety-nine cents) download from iTunes or through a streaming subscription service such as Spotify or Rdio.

In their emphasis on blockbusters, the cultural industries have thus become increasingly like the manufacturer of any other commodity, no matter how quotidian or mundane. As *Advertising Age* (the main chronicle of the advertising industry in the United States) observed in 2010 of Disney's films: "Each release [has] become more and more like the launch of a package good from Procter & Gamble" (Hampp 2010, 27), though blockbusters can nonetheless be quite meaningful to many.

And musicians in the broadcasting, film, and advertising industries are pressured to produce music ever more quickly, sometimes in a single day. Until fairly recently, film music composers could count on six weeks to compose their scores; today, they are lucky to have four weeks. The assembly line has speeded up. (I will discuss this more in chapter 4.)

In the record industry, the move toward consolidation and monopolization has altered the retail side of the record business as well. The rise of big box stores that have largely destroyed smaller mom-and-pop shops has greatly changed the landscape of music retailing in brick-and-mortar outlets. Manufacturing does not drive trading nearly as much as it once did; beginning in the 1980s and continuing to the present, factories, through global supply chains, were increasingly linked to massive retailers such as Walmart. Decisions are increasingly determined by lowest cost (Centeno and Cohen 2010, 48).

For many Americans, the only physical places left to buy sound recordings are Best Buy, Target, and Walmart. The music distributor that supplied Walmart used to be independent but was acquired by Walmart, and this company distributes to Best Buy as well. Jeff Castelaz (2012), cofounder of the independent label Dangerbird (and since September 2012 the president of Elektra Records), told me that the distributor informed its customers of the maximum they would be willing to pay for a current CD. "That comes straight from the top," Castelaz said, "yet my costs for staff don't go down."

And, of course, these stores don't carry that much stock, only that which will be most likely to sell. Bill Nowlin (2012) of Rounder Records told me that stores like Best Buy once bought a lot of their releases,

> but then it turned out that a lot of them really didn't sell that well to their market, and so massive returns started to come back, and it created a crisis throughout the whole industry—everybody manufactured all this extra stock and then couldn't sell it. It came back as returns, and you just had to eat it, so to speak.

For this reason, Nowlin spoke at some length about the demise of retail, and he wasn't simply referring to digital piracy but to the disappearing independent record store: "I think one of the areas that's changed considerably for us is that with the demise of retail, we've turned down lots of artists that we would have signed and whose music we would have released, because we didn't see a way to make it work."

In the realm of film and television, the business began to change dramatically in the 1980s as well. A strike by the American Federation of Musicians in 1980–81 had the effect, among other things, of closing studio music departments, which had handled orchestration and copying and of course obviated the cost of an outside studio. At the same time, new digital technologies began to put some musicians out of work. This effectively meant the end of this system of producing and recording orchestral music for television, a system in which composers wrote scores that were arranged, orchestrated, copied, and performed by world-class professionals. In this system, the average cost of a sixty-minute prime-time television film score in 1979 was about $35,000 (almost $113,000 today), which covered all costs: the composer's fee, arranging and orchestration, the musicians' fees, studio fees, union benefits, and payroll taxes.

But the AFM strike failed, in that the union did not achieve its key demand, a piece of the residuals pie ("Tentative Pact Reached" 1981; see also Malnic 1981). That and the rise of digital technologies created an opportunity for studios to cut costs, and not just by closing their music departments. Enter Mike Post, a composer famous for many television theme songs, from *The Rockford Files* to *Hill Street Blues*. Post, along with agents Mike Gorfaine and Sam Schwartz, cut a deal with two of the most powerful producers in the industry, Stephen J. Cannell and Steven Bochco, to produce television scores for them for roughly half, if Post were allowed to retain the rights to his music. Post would receive a package deal for each program, out of which he would pay the musicians and other needed personnel and all fees, and keep the rest for himself. The immediate result was that music budgets for television programs were cut by around 50 percent, and composers were, and are, much more likely to try to do everything themselves with electronics rather than hiring live musicians. And it wasn't long before other composers were offering to charge less and less. Today, the average price of a television score for a sixty-minute prime-time program averages about $14,000. "The package" has become the standard practice in the industry, and Mike Post became the highest-earning television composer of the last forty years.[3] This kind of entrepreneurialism, fostered and even necessitated by neoliberalism, has become the norm (see also Guilbault 2007).

Film and studio musicians who once played multiple gigs daily have lost a fair amount of work, as these jobs are increasingly outsourced to Eastern Europe. Many of the working musicians I have interviewed complained bitterly about this. All believe that the quality isn't as good as what can be had in Los Angeles and London. But it is cheaper to record in Eastern Europe. Costs are saved in other ways, too. Music editor Craig Pettigrew explained (2012):

> When the score is recorded there the producers own it; there are no repayments to the musicians, as there are in Los Angeles. See, when they record here, there are repayments when the film and/or the film's music is sold to other markets. So musicians here have been getting these one-time payments every year for scores that they worked on that have been sold and distributed to other markets, so they get paid again. I know people who worked very hard for many years and now depend on those payments, because they're over fifty and they're not being called to do session work nearly as much. That's been a big bone of contention for a long time, and they've set up low-budget payment scales, a, kind of a tier payment arrangement for scoring. So if I wanted to score a low-budget film, union, here in Los Angeles, there would be a special provision to pay the musicians less, but it's still more expensive than going to Prague or Bratislava or Budapest. Now, I prep composers to go to Prague and I don't even go anymore—they'll no longer pay for me to go. So I make all

these streamered QuickTimes [video files with visual cues for the conductor] with clicks [that indicate tempo] and Pro Tools sessions, and I prep everything as I would normally; I just upload everything to a server for the recordist in Prague to download. And I just tell them, "Pray that everything goes right, because if the machine breaks down, or if something goes wrong with the file, I'm not there to fix it so you run the risk of not getting your session, your music recorded, because I'm not there." Unfortunately, I'm diligent, so I make sure everything works, so I'm screwed out of a trip now. So that's just another cost that they've managed to take out of the budget.

Pettigrew believes that all the money saved goes upward, to the producers.

BRANDS AND BRANDING

Brands and branding have a long history, originating in the late nineteenth century as manufacturers attempted to differentiate their products on the shelf through different styles of packaging (see Moor 2007). I would argue that branding has become a more intense, frequent, and dominant strategy in neoliberal capitalism. Every commodity in neoliberal capitalism is treated as a brand or potential brand, for this is the only way a consumer economy knows how to introduce products to mass audiences and manage them; Jean Baudrillard was not mistaken when he called the brand "the principal concept of advertising" (1988b, 17). Today, it has become a central concept in neoliberalism more generally. Brands aren't simply names of objects, but objects that carry meaning for people as things that make sense to them and communicate their sense of who they are to others. As one study of brands puts it, "Brands are . . . an example of capital socialized to the extent of transpiring the minute relations of everyday life, to the point of becoming a context for life, in effect" (Arvidsson 2006, 13).

Music and musicians have not been left unaffected by branding processes and brand management. Scott Lash and John Urry (1994) discussed the rise of the branding of cultural producers, and it is clear that major musicians (such as Michael Jackson in the era they were writing) were attempting to brand themselves, and were sometimes brand-effects of their labels. While what we call the branding of musicians today has a long history in earlier practices in the creation of distinctiveness (see Samples 2011 for a history), today's branding practices are not only marked by their ubiquity and pervasiveness but are also bolstered by massive amounts of research into consumer demographics and behaviors. Today, it is routine to read *Advertising Age* and see major musicians referred to as brands. And how-to guides for budding professional musicians published in this century frequently offer advice on how to brand oneself (e.g., Gordon 2011; see also O'Reilly, Larsen, and Kubacki 2013).[4]

I want to spend some time with the question of branding, for I have come to think of it as a central force in American life, a result of the outsized role played by advertising in American culture. Sociologist Celia Lury views the brand as a kind of new media object, "a platform for the patterning of activity, a mode of organising activities in time and space" (2004, 1). For her, the brand is not an object but a relationship, "*a set of relations between products in time.*" (2; emphasis in original). She sees the brand as "an example of *a specific market modality or market cultural form*; for her, "*the brand mediates the supply and demand of products through the organisation, co-ordination and integration of the use of information*" (4; emphases in original).

Sarah Banet-Weiser similarly emphasizes the social role played by brands, writing that branding today is an ideology that both draws on and produces social and cultural relations (2012, 4). Thus, for example, the ideology, discourse, and language of branding now powerfully shape considerations of musicians' sound and image. For the purposes of brand recognition, conformity to conceptions of a musician's brand can be more important than sound or genre. Musicians still care about sound, style, genres, and the fields in which they operate, of course, but those who represent them might well override their desires.

Lury, in a later book coauthored with Scott Lash, extends her arguments about the brand in an examination of the global cultural industries. In a discussion that juxtaposes global cultural production with cultural production in a way that implicitly chronologizes the two, they contrast commodity production, which is the work of the cultural industries, with brand production, the work of the global cultural industries. Commodities in their thinking are single, discrete products, while brands are sources of production that are employed in a range of production activities (2007, 6). In short, for Lash and Lury, the commodity is an industrial product of an earlier capitalism, while brands are emblematic of today's capitalism creating a regime of power that produces "inequalities, disparities and deception" that were rare in the earlier regime (7). While I largely agree with this characterization of cultural production today, it is not the case that commodity production by the cultural industries has disappeared and given way to brands. The industry still makes commodities as it cultivates brands. Earlier capitalisms, earlier ways of producing value, are still with us.

It is also useful, and telling, to examine the advertising and marketing industry's own discourses on the question of branding, for it reveals how powerful they believe the practices of branding to be. Alina Wheeler, as is common in the industry, refers to central concepts without articles; thus, her book opens with a consideration of "What is brand?," a question she answers thus:

> As competition creates infinite choices, companies look for ways to connect emotionally with customers, become irreplaceable, and create lifelong relationships. A strong brand stands out in a densely crowded marketplace. People fall in love with brands, trust them, and believe in their superiority. How a brand is perceived affects its success, regardless of whether it's a start-up, a nonprofit, or a product. (Wheeler 2009, 2)

Wheeler continues by noting that brands have three primary functions: helping consumers navigate in a crowded marketplace, reassuring them of the quality of the product and the correctness of their purchase choice, and engaging them with "distinctive imagery, language, and associations to encourage customers to identify with the brand" (2).

Wheeler contrasts "brand" with "brand identity":

> Brand identity is tangible and appeals to the senses. You can see it, touch it, hold it, hear it, watch it move. Brand identity fuels recognition, amplifies differentiation, and makes big ideas and meaning accessible. Brand identity takes disparate elements and unifies them into whole systems. (4)

The last of Wheeler's major concepts is "branding," which she defines as

> a disciplined process used to build awareness and extend customer loyalty. It requires a mandate from the top and readiness to invest in the future. Branding is about seizing every opportunity to express why people should choose one brand over another. A desire to lead, outpace the competition, and give employees the best tools to reach customers are the reasons why companies leverage branding. (6)

There are, it seems, types of branding: cobranding, which is "partnering with another brand to achieve reach"; digital branding, designed to increase Web commerce; personal branding, "the way an individual builds their [sic] reputation"; cause branding, aligning a brand with a cause; and country branding, which concerns efforts to increase tourism and attract businesses (6).

It is clear that for Wheeler, branding is a complex process that involves interpellating consumers emotionally. Branding is a way of inserting a product into the culture and people's consciousnesses, not just the market. One of the many quotations that suffuse her book, by Marc Gobé, makes this point: "Emotional branding is a dynamic cocktail of anthropology, imagination, sensory experiences, and visionary approach to change" (Wheeler 2009, 6).[5] The goal for many in the industry is to make a brand seem to possess the characteristics of people, so that the brand can become akin to a trusted friend. This is referred to as "brand personality," defined by Jennifer Aaker as "the set of human characteristics associated with a brand" (1997, 347); elsewhere she writes, "Brand personality is conceptualized based on the way that observers attribute personality characteristic to people during everyday interaction" (Aaker and Fournier 1995).

As a sign of just how powerful a force branding has become in American culture, I note that a veritable explosion of "personal branding" books occurred around the beginning of the second decade of this century, with titles such as *What Is Personal Branding?*, *How to Create a Memorable & Powerful Brand that Sells YOU!* (Kukral and Newlands 2011), *Be Your Own Brand: Achieve More of What You Want by Being More of Who You Are* (McNally and Speak 2011), and many, many more. There is even (or perhaps predictably), *Personal Branding for Dummies* (Chritton 2012). As people are increasingly thought of not as people but as "human capital" (Friedman [1962] 1982), necessitating what Foucault (2008) called a kind of entrepreneurialism of the self, branding seems to be the main way that this entrepreneurialism is realized, as a project of what Alison Hearn (2008) has called the "branded self."

Additionally, while once manufacturers of commodities attempted to attach themselves to musicians or a particular song to attempt to make their goods seem cool or desirable, it now seems to be increasingly the case that musicians will try to link themselves to a brand in processes of cobranding.[6] Hip-hop musician Common, for example, engaged with Microsoft in the late 2000s; Microsoft sponsored his tour and displayed him in commercials (example 2.1). Common's justification for working with Microsoft reveals that he seems to view himself as a brand, speaking of himself in the third person:

> Microsoft is classy, it's a timeless brand, and it means something to the world, internationally, and I felt like that's the direction of what I want Common to be, to be honest. I want to be timeless, I want to be international and those are the things I feel like I'm working toward now. I was able to team up with them for some of those reasons. . . . I liked creatively where they wanted to go. (Moran 2008, 22)

And Intel named Will.I.Am of the Black Eyed Peas director of creative innovation in 2011. Intel's vice president for creative marketing described the musician's function, which sounds deeper than a cobranding relationship, the musician becoming ever more implicated in the cobranding process:

> I don't want him to be the promo man. This is not meant for him to say, "Here's the latest and greatest product from Intel and go buy it." There's an overlapping

creativity, understanding, desire and expertise that he brings with him. While he may go out and talk about some of the products we'll be coming up with, it was clear to both of us that he needed to be an employee and at the center of these products' creation. (Hampp 2011, 10)[7]

A Pepsi commercial from the fall of 2011 entitled "Music Icons" shows the evolution of the cobranding process clearly, employing excerpts of past Pepsi commercials that featured famous musicians: Michael Jackson, Ray Charles, Britney Spears, Mariah Carey. Kanye West is shown wearing the red, white, and blue hues of Pepsi's logo, the colors bleeding off as he walks, Pepsi in hand, conveying the message that there is no difference between West and Pepsi: cobranding consummated. The commercial asks, "Who's next?"—the next music icon—before displaying the tagline, "Where there's music, there's Pepsi," which articulates quite baldly Pepsi's long-standing strategy of employing popular musicians in its advertisements (example 2.2; according to Pepsi's chief marketing officer, Global Consumer Engagement, "Pepsi has always been at the center of music and pop culture and is known for featuring top talent in its campaigns"). Pepsi chose the song "Tonight Is the Night" by Outasight to accompany the commercial, "because it perfectly captures the spirit of music today. This spot is about re-igniting the timeless connection between Pepsi and iconic pop music," a connection Pepsi is happy to tout ("New Pepsi Television Ad" 2011).[8] This trend is only heightening; Jay-Z's 2013 album *Magna Carta Holy Grail* was described by Gawker as "not so much an album as a co-branded multimedia content delivery platform, Presented By Samsung™ Galaxy™" (Chen 2013). Samsung spent $5 million to purchase one million albums; users (it doesn't seem to right to write "listeners") could obtain a free copy of the album before its official release if they downloaded a special app (Sydell 2013).

And some brands are getting into the music business. Converse, the sneaker company, has built a recording studio that records bands at no charge. Brands are starting labels, seeking talent, and paying for it. Red Bull and Mountain Dew have record labels. Musicians don't mind, since it's a way to generate income. Bethany Cosentino of Best Coast, a Los Angeles band, says, "Music is everywhere now, and if you have it tied to a brand, there's nothing wrong with that" (Sisario 2010, 10). She released a single through a headphone company, then made a recording for Converse. Nima Kazerouni (2014), who is the lead singer of the Echo Park, Los Angeles–based band So Many Wizards, also made a recording using Converse's facility; he described it as a great studio and a great experience overall, and praised Converse's generosity. All this is part of chasing the hip and the cool; if a brand can be the purveyor of the latest indie rock song, it makes them look good. According to Josh Rabinowitz, director of music at a major advertising agency, "Indie-inflected music serves as a kind of Trojan horse. Consumers feel they are discovering something that they believe to be cool and gaining admittance to a more refined social clique" (Sisario 2010, 10).

Today's processes of branding musicians have made fans' interactions with their branded idols a kind of entertainment. A marketing professor at the Berklee College of Music says that to entice fans with snippets of information about an upcoming album release or other music commodity is a way of creating buzz around those commodities; the old strategy of engaging with the gatekeepers has been replaced by attempting to circumvent the gatekeepers and market directly to fans (McKinley 2013, C1).

There is another way to understand cobranding, however, and that is branding as a process that is undertaken by corporations, marketers, musicians and bands, and fans themselves. This is the subject of a study by Nicholas Carah, who pursued the question of "how brands are created as a series of social relations" through popular music (2010, 2). The making of meaning is conceived by corporations but authored by young fans whose activities add value to brands. The hosting of live events by brands such as Coca-Cola creates an enjoyable space for fans to listen to musicians they like; Coca-Cola gets to act as the benevolent host of enjoyable experiences for young people, experiences that seem to be authentic and cool, which reflects well on Coca-Cola (35).

Branding and marketing have become perhaps even more jarringly apparent in the world of classical music, since this music was for so long aloof from such things. Keith Negus has written of the increased use of portfolio management techniques in the record industry in the 1980s and 1990s, which meant that marginal "genres" such as classical increasingly were expected to be profitable and were thus no longer subsidized by sales in other divisions. According to Negus (1999, 49–50), this pressure to be profitable has resulted in composer's greatest-hits compilations, exploitation of stars (such as Andrea Bocelli), creation of ensembles such as the Three Tenors, and the employment of popular music marketing methods for classical musicians.

This trend began in the 1990s. Perhaps the most spectacular example in that decade was the cover of a 1996 recording of Bach's violin partitas by Lara St. John, which showed the midtwenties St. John nude from the waist up, her violin covering her breasts. Sales of her album nearly reached the ten thousand mark—huge for classical music—whereas another of her recordings released by the same label were under one thousand (Marks 1996, 58). But it was controversial among classical music lovers: one music director at a classical station returned the album without playing it; the buyer for Tower Records in Seattle did not carry it; a commentator in Canada referred to the recording as "jailbait Bach" (58). St. John claimed that the cover was intended "to do something unusual and perhaps break down some of this elitism stigma that is inherent in classical music today. And perhaps demystify to become more innovative and to make things more interesting and less highbrow" (St. John 1996). Other women musicians in the classical realm have also been shown to be sexy and desirable on cover art, whether violinist Anne-Sophie Mutter or pianist Hélène Grimaud. According to the person who oversees classical music marketing for Universal Music in the United States, "Hélène is attractive, and that makes a difference. Her covers can compete against the pop records that are on the home page of iTunes" (Max 2011, 60).[9]

And some women musicians who have attempted to cross over from classical to more popular kinds of music have found themselves marketed in similar fashion to St. John, sometimes even more salaciously. Perhaps the most notorious case remains that of violinist Vanessa-Mae Nicholson, who is frequently photographed in sexy poses. One photo from the mid-1990s when Nicholson was sixteen years old resulted in her record company having to fend off charges that they had exploited her (Stewart 1995, 1). But their strategy worked, for the single with the problematic cover climbed to number 16 on the UK Top 40 singles chart, and the album debuted at number 11 on the Top 40 albums chart—the pop charts. Youth and beauty—marketability—have become almost as important, perhaps as important, as musical ability and skill in determining the success of a classical musician. And classical composers, no less than performers, in the last few decades have become increasingly adept at self-marketing, employing websites, blogs, provocative titles of works, and attention-getting musical devices to attempt to capture the public's attention (see Taylor 2002).

Baudrillard's comment on branding in advertising is now apt to describe the cultural industries—even the culture—more generally. The cultural industries and their retailers, whether brick-and-mortar shops or online ones, require that goods be displayed in places that are accessible to consumers, who want to know where to find what they want, but also want to find more of what they already like. Thus, the cultural industries treat cultural products in generic terms, working assiduously to genericize new musics or groups of musics. Within some "genres," the logic of branding can take hold, as I will discuss in the next chapter with respect to "world music."

For workers in advertising, marketing, and related industries, branding is even a way to create value, which is conceptualized in noneconomic terms that are nonetheless made to be almost immediately commensurate with economic ones: "Image and perception help drive value; without an image there is no perception," says Scott M. Davis, who is chief growth officer at a company called Prophet (Wheeler 2009, x). Probably the best example is Apple Computer, whose products are deliriously supported by its many fans, some of whom are willing to wait all night long in a queue to be among the first to purchase a new product. Wheeler identifies value as one of the goals in the creation of brand identity, defining value thus: "building awareness, increasing recognition, communicating uniqueness and quality, and expressing a competitive difference create measurable results" (31). She later writes, "A brand is an intangible asset—brand identity, which includes all tangible expression from packaging to website, upholds that value" (48). In other words, the creation of a brand identity through diverse practices of advertising and marketing adds value to the brand, value that is not necessarily economic but that can help a brand compete better in a crowded marketplace.[10] Value in this literature is usually described as something noneconomic and economic simultaneously; it is a sort of cachet that a good might have, which is convertible to economic value.

Organizational theorist David A. Aaker writes in *Building Strong Brands* on the question of value. It is not enough for a product to be good and sell: its brand needs to generate value.

> One role of brand identity is to create a value proposition. The value proposition, which usually involves a functional benefit, is basic to brands in most product classes: If the brand does not generate value, it will usually be vulnerable to competitors. The value measure provides a summary indicator of the brand's success at creating that value proposition. (1996, 326)

Aaker continues by arguing that "brand value" can be calculated by asking whether the brand provides good value for money and whether there is a reason to buy one brand over another (326); hardly scientific measurement, but this is the kind of argumentation that is the norm in this literature. It is clear enough that certain products, certain brands, do enjoy a kind of cachet that allows their producers to charge more. Doubtless some of these increased charges are the result of the labor of those in the marketing and branding industries, but only some.

Conferring value in this way is more difficult for cultural commodities, which enjoy widely variable amounts of promotion and promotion expenditures. It is clear, however, that, at least in the realm of film, the promotion budget can now exceed by far the cost of production as a result of increased competition and the shortened amount time of theatrical release (Ulin 2009, 397), which is a fairly new development. In music, marketing budgets have

also risen from about 10 percent of expected album sales to around 20 percent at many firms, though marketing support has dropped since the early
2000s as the industry began to experience difficulties (Wikström 2013, 130).
Nonetheless, according to the International Federation of the Phonographic
Industry in 2012, marketing and promotion are the biggest expense in introducing a musician to the public, which creates a fan base and opportunities
for merchandising and touring. It costs roughly $1 million to break an artist,
with an estimated $200,000–$500,000 of that cost spent on marketing (IFPI
2012).

While all of these assumptions about value seem arbitrary, corporations
have begun to represent them as actual assets. Melissa Aronczyk and Devon
Powers write that in the late 1970s, corporate owners of brands began to look
for means by which to list the value of brands in their accounting practices.
Brands were beginning to be seen as forms of capital, however intangible
(Aronczyk and Powers 2010, 5–6; Arvidsson 2006; Lury and Moor 2010),
what Robert Foster characterizes as a "historically particular way of convert-
ing use values into exchange value" (Foster 2013, 45). The idea that something
other than a commodity—in this case, a corporate complex of representations of a commodity—could possess value is far from Marxist and other
conceptions of value in capitalist cultures. But if companies and people adopt
practices that assume the value of a brand, and if those assumptions can now
be legally quantified and counted as a company asset, then that value must be
considered to be real.

The Conquest of Cool—and the Culture

The response of capitalists to what Boltanski and Chiapello (2005) call the
"artistic critique" of capitalism (along with McGuigan 2009 and Frank 1997,
whose title is reflected above) was to attempt to co-opt what was thought to
be cool and hip and edgy (see also Taylor 2012b), to seek out the hip and the
cool, or trying to manufacture it. Music and musicians are frequently at the
center of what is thought to be hip and cool (see Ford 2013).

This "conquest" has had enormous cultural and social consequences. The
authors discussed in chapter 1 whose empirical research has led them to conclude that taste among elite groups is becoming increasingly eclectic have
tended to miss the changing nature of the cultural industries themselves. In
part—a large part, I would argue—these shifts in tastes have been driven by
the advertising industry. Advertising has become the most important arbiter
of the hip and the cool. These terms are never defined, but the former seems
to be more baby-boomer-oriented and ironic, and the latter more youth-

oriented and now. Advertising agencies and music production companies select music that is cutting-edge before it has become a hit, acting rather as influential disc jockeys once did. The industry is saturated with the pursuit of the cool, as Thomas Frank (1997) and others have written (see also Gladwell 1997), or even the manufacture of cool, attempting to turn a brand into a cultural icon through a strategy that Douglas Holt has called "cultural branding" (2004; see also O'Reilly, Larsen, and Kubacki 2013). As the president and chief executive at a major advertising firm said about Burger King:

> We want the pop culture dialogue to include Burger King. . . . The mission is not about generating awareness of Burger King . . . because everyone knows Burger King. We want to make a connection. We want to make Burger King the kind of brand people would want to wear on a T-shirt (Elliott 2005, C4).

A common description, which appears across the cultural industries and not just the advertising industry, is "edgy." My interlocutors for my history of music and advertising (Taylor 2012b) used the term with some frequency. Josh Rabinowitz (2004), for example, of Grey Worldwide in New York City, told me, "I think the marketers certainly always want to attach themselves . . . certain products want to attach themselves to what they consider to be hip, edgy, cool—'cutting-edge' is always the word people use".[11] And the anthropologist Sherry B. Ortner's study of the production of independent film revealed the same ubiquity of the term "edgy" in that cultural industry (2013). Thus, on the production side, edginess is valued above all else, "edgy" in the sense that it disrupts norms and expectations of the mainstream. This is construed as hip or cool by others in the cultural industries, such as the advertising industry—if, that is, it receives enough buzz and doesn't escape notice.

The culture industry's identification of, and creation of, what is thought to be hip, cool, or edgy is just one example of how capitalism is able to absorb critiques (see Boltanski and Chiapello 2005), to adapt and survive, even flourish. Youth and popular culture have become not just important to the reproduction of capital but essential.

NEW SOCIAL CLASSES: THE NEW PETITE BOURGEOISIE

The emergence of a new phase of capitalism means that the class system must be changing—the middle class is getting squeezed, as many have observed and discussed (e.g., Packer 2013). With respect to cultural production, it is members of a new class who find what is hip, cool, and edgy and who both promulgate this ideology and employ it to sell anything from commodities to Obamacare. In *Distinction* (1984), Bourdieu analyzed the way that tastes for cultural goods were arrayed along social class lines, but he was also concerned with changes within the dominant group: Would it be supplanted by a more technocratic, commercially oriented sector? The battle for legitimacy in the dominant group, between a traditional bourgeoisie and the newer technocratic wing, was fought in part over culture, which, as Bourdieu writes, is one of the arenas where battles for legitimacy are waged (93). It seems clear now that these technocrats, armed with neoliberal ideologies, have prevailed. But they were aided, as I have argued elsewhere (Taylor 2009), by some members of the new petite bourgeoisie, who also desired to wrest some degree of legitimacy from the more traditional bourgeoisie by destabilizing traditional cultural hierarchies with ideologies of the hip and the cool.

Bourdieu argues that this new (technocratic) bourgeoisie is "the initiator of the ethical retooling required by the new economy from which it draws its power and profits, whose functioning depends as much on the production of needs and consumers as on the production of goods." This new economy (Bourdieu was writing before the term "neoliberal" was common) requires a social world that judges people by their "capacity for consumption," their standard of living, their lifestyle. And this new economy relies heavily on advertising and other cultural mediation to spread its message. This economy's "new taste-makers" offer a "morality" or program that is nothing other than an "art" of consumption and enjoyment (Bourdieu 1984, 310–11).

The ascendance of this faction of the dominant group has meant that ideas of what counted as legitimate culture within the dominant group as a whole have begun to shift: knowledge of the fine arts has become less important, and knowledge of the hip and the cool more important. In other words, this is a form of cultural capital that has emerged and seems to be moving to dominance. To be sure, knowledge of the fine arts was probably never as important in the United States as in France, and the American political class not as well educated or intellectually oriented. If the older dominant group based its conception of cultural capital on knowledge of the fine arts, today's dominant group's notion of cultural capital stems from knowledge of the hip and the cool, and is no less exclusionary and no less contemptuous of those farther down the ladder. Those who don't know what is hip and cool are just as despised as those, in the earlier scheme of things, who didn't know the works of Shakespeare or Beethoven. Knowledge of the hip, the cool, the edgy is much more ephemeral than that of the fine arts, which, safeguarded in canons, seldom change very much over time, though these fields of cultural production have their own trends. Today's cultural capital is less knowledge of particular works than of whatever is thought to be imbued with the ideology of the hip and the cool, whether objects such as the newest iPhone or the latest flat-screen television, or cultural forms such as the recent, obscure independent film or indie rock band.

Bourdieu argues that today's economy

> can appear as an *economy of intelligence*, reserved for "intelligent" people (which earns it the sympathy of "hip" journalists and executives). Sociodicy here takes the form of a *racism of intelligence*: today's poor are not poor, as they were thought to be in the nineteenth century, because they are improvident, spendthrift, intemperate, etc.—by opposition to the "deserving poor"—but because they are dumb, intellectually incapable, idiotic. (2003, 33; emphases in original)

"Intelligent" in quotation marks refers less to knowledge of Shakespeare than to knowledge of indie film: it is a question of hipness, of the volume of cultural capital as measured by one's knowledge of the hip and the cool, which is lurking in Bourdieu's analysis though not nearly as prominent as what I am arguing for.

Bourdieu also notes that opposing commercialized cultural production is difficult because the cultural industries seek the favor of the general public, in particular young people, and partly because mass-produced cultural forms are more accessible, require less cultural capital, and, he says, "are the object of a kind of *inverted snobbery*" (2003, 70; emphasis in original). Bourdieu argues that this is the first time in history that the cheapest commodities are seen as chic. Jeans, Coca-Cola, and McDonald's have not only economic power on their side but also symbolic power that accrues from these and other corporations' targeting of children and adolescents, supported by advertising and the media. The big cultural production companies exert an extraordinary and unprecedented hold over contemporary societies, which, he argues, find themselves infantilized (71). But children and adolescents aren't only targets—they are sources, the sources of the hip, the cool, the edgy. Their tastes, practices, and consumption habits are relentlessly and ruthlessly studied and marketed back to them. And everyone else.

Increasing Commodification

One of the most remarked-upon effects of neoliberal capitalism has been that certain arenas that were once uncommodified were increasingly commodified, including, as we have seen, classical music. Education, healthcare, and more have also increasingly become commodified and subjected to the rules of the market; as one former Enron employee said, "We could commoditize anything" (Frank 2002, 20).

With the increased ambit of commodification has come increased consumption, another tenet of neoliberal ideologies: consumption drives the
economy, and increasing consumption raises profits for those who own the
means of production. Much has been written about the growth of consumption in the twentieth century, including its latest phase, initiated in the United
States by Ronald Reagan and by Margaret Thatcher in the United Kingdom,
sacralizing consumption, as George Lipsitz (1998) has argued, a project bolstered by the increasing sophistication of advertising, including the rise of
MTV in the early 1980s.[12] From 1990 to 2006, per capita household consumption in the wealthy countries grew at an annual rate of 1.8 percent (Centeno
and Cohen 2012, 94). Today, 70 percent of all US economic activity depends
on consumption (Harvey 2010, 107).

CONSUMPTION AND/AS IDENTITY-MAKING

If virtually everything is a commodity, the growth of consumption must have
cultural effects. What I want to focus on here is a particularly salient effect of
neoliberal capitalism, the rise in discourses and practices of identity. There
have long been conceptions of national identity, cultural identity, ethnic identity, and still more, but "identity" as a personal conception of one's individuality that can be managed and displayed is a relatively new phenomenon. The
increase in conceptions of personal identity has been the neoliberal version of
divide-and-conquer strategy in the labor force, exploiting every conceivable
conception of difference to divide the labor force to prevent it from organizing (Harvey 2010, 104) and has been supremely successful.

Grant McCracken (1997) writes of his study of the personal ads over some
decades in the *Village Voice*, which changed from rather straightforward
"man seeking woman" to far more complicated searches of, say, a bisexual
African American woman seeking a partner. Clearly, conceptions of identity
as a personal(ized) conception of selfhood have exploded in the last few decades, in large part a result of the continuing rise of this consumer culture, a
culture of such plenitude (McCracken 1997), so suffused with signs (Baudrillard 1981), that the ideology of identity has become a potent way for many to
attempt to ground themselves and to differentiate themselves from others.

The emergence of this personal concept of identity can be traced to Erik
H. Erikson's *Childhood and Society*, published in 1950, an influential book
that introduced the concept of identity (and "identity crisis," a term coined
by Erikson) into the public vernacular. Earlier folk conceptions of selfhood
in American culture—"character" in the Victorian era, slowly replaced by
"personality"—were, to varying degrees, essentialist in that one simply pos-

sessed them, though "personality" was something that could be worked on if one cared to purchase self-help books that proliferated early in the twentieth century (see Susman 1984). "Identity," however, is constructed by the social actor, though there can be a strong essentialist underpinning of racial or ethnic or sexual orientation. I am in general agreement with Manuel Castells's definition of today's conception of identity: "I understand by identity the process by which a social actor recognizes itself and constructs meaning primarily on the basis of a given cultural attribute or set of attributes, to the exclusion of a broader reference to other social structures" (Castells 1996, 22), though I would emphasize that its construction is not always based on a "given cultural attribute" but is importantly dependent on consumption. Identity is a process of recognition and construction. It is not a natural condition.

Forms of identity in earlier capitalisms were organized around nationality, or culture, or language group, or other factors. Today, however, it is a "personal" conception of identity that is constructed by individuals, though they can frequently draw on earlier conceptions of identity. Douglas Holt believes that in the United States, consumption is an "open-ended project of self-creation" (2000, 65; see also Warde 1997). This is accomplished through the consumption of particular commodities and not others, and the consumption of certain means of communication and not others, ensembles of commodities and not others, as in that brand of shoes, that brand of shirt, that style of haircut, that brand of cellular phone—that is the primary means of fashioning identities today.

The consumption of music is part of this project of identity construction, and for some social groups, particularly youth, a potent part. "Style," broadly understood to encompass clothing, manner of dress, and hair treatments, usually has a soundtrack. Youth associated with one social group don't listen to music associated with another. As one young woman told the author of one study:

> It's not like going out and buying CDs because somebody very well could have the same sort of CDs but it's not. . . . It's just like what just represents me and my taste in music really. Nobody else in the world is going to have the same line-up of tunes in the bag, it's just me. (Nuttall 2009, 218; see also Shankar, Elliott, and Fitchett 2009)

It is not, however, only the consumption of goods that individuals employ to fashion themselves but also the consumption of other identities, positionalities. Grant McCracken writes of the penchant in today's culture for trying on new identities, for constant self-transformation in a culture of what he calls "expansionary individualism" (2008, 293). McCracken posits what he calls "transformational routines," by which he means "set of conventions by which an individual is changed" (xxii), which he loosely historicizes into four periods: traditional (traditional rites of passage), premodern or status ("processes by which individuals change their social standing"), modern (making the self mobile in personal and public space), and "postmodern" (transformations that "open up new kinds of multiplicity and fluidity to the individual") (xxiii). It is the last of these that interests me here, since it corresponds historically to the rise of neoliberal capitalism, though McCracken is clear that one regime does not replace another but that regimes should be seen additively; that is, even in today's world, all of these modes of transformation operate.

McCracken doesn't begin his book chronologically, however; instead, he offers examples from popular culture (which he had previously characterized thus: "Popular culture has become culture" [2008, xvi]). From pop stars to Martha Stewart, McCracken shows how celebrities of all sorts have transformed themselves, sometimes repeatedly, and sometimes purposefully, as part of their public displays in today's popular culture. These sorts of selves, and transformations, have become common, McCracken believes, arguing for many characteristics of these "postmodern" transformations of self, including:

- The self is porous, and even encourages excursions in and out of the self. Today's culture is preoccupied making vehicles for these excursions.
- The world is also porous, which in a way is similar to the fluidity and open boundaries of traditional societies, in which members, as people today, could move across categories of time, space, and cultures.
- Individuals believe themselves to be able to create and narrate themselves.
- Individuals claim the right of cultural creation, the right—and ability—to alter the cultural categories that define them.
- Individuals are made up of many selves, favoring exploration of these selves over the authenticity or essence of any one of them.
- Transformation of the self is motivated by a variety of factors, some free, some forced. (2008, 306)

In a long chapter McCracken identifies new types of self in the postmodern era, some of which can combine to form composite selves. He concludes by wondering if a new "global self" is emerging, which is

> curious and catholic in searching out new definitional options, credulous in trying them on, mobile in its incorporation of diverse and improbable materials, adroit in its embrace of several at once, skillful in managing the portfolio of selves that is the result, and sturdy enough to live with the ideational and emotional turbulence that must ensue. (2008, 293)

For McCracken, the global self is imperial above all: "The global self is a pre-sumptuous self, seeing itself as a master of its own fate, as the author of its own circumstances, as the rightful inventor of the self. It claims all experience as its province, all definitions of the self as its domain (294).

This "global self" seems to me a supremely agential self that is not available to those who aren't from the middle class and above. Members of the middle class may well believe themselves to possess the sorts of qualities Mc-Cracken ascribes to this new self, whether or not they actually possess them, but given the middle class's role in cultural production, representations of those who act out of the belief of such a self are common. But those with less economic capital might find it much more difficult to create and narrate themselves, alter cultural categories, and perform others of the transforma-tions McCracken lists.

McCracken reserves a consideration of the origins of this new "expansion-ary individualism" until the final few pages of his book. Useful as his earlier arguments are, at least for the middle class, his explanation is rather too brief. In part, he says, this new expansionary individualism is a result of the earlier forms of self-conception before the postmodern era, and also in part a result of the social movements of the 1960s. McCracken writes that this expansion-ary individualism is cultural, that it emanates from the culture that it opposes (2008, 304). But one would think that to declare this expansionary individual-ism cultural is a premise to an argument, not an argument about the cultural and historical origins of this new self.

I thus return to my earlier discussion about consumption (which, strangely, plays only a small role in McCracken's book, even though he was one of the founders of the modern study of consumption in the 1980s): one consumes goods to make oneself; one even consumes other modes of self-hood to make oneself as a way of demonstrating one's agential selfhood to oneself and others.

Plenitude

One of the most noticeable and remarked-upon features of today's capitalism is the seemingly limitless supply of commodities, including cultural com-modities such as music. It is easier and easier to hear or view virtually what-ever one desires. This, of course, isn't just a result or producer of globalization but a potent indicator of how much digital technologies have contributed to our sense of plenitude, for these technologies purvey not only music or films by stars but cultural forms from afar. Even on small devices such as mobile telephones, there is enough memory to contain more songs than one would ever be able to listen to.

With the easy availability of cultural forms from all over, it has become increasingly difficult for consumers to navigate through them to find what they might want and not just for consumers, but for professionals in the cultural industries as well. In this section, I'll discuss not only this new plenitude but also the appearance of new workers in the cultural industries whose labor consists of sifting through the massive amount of recorded music.

MUSIC SUPERVISORS

The easy availability and portability of music from everywhere, due in no small measure to the rise of digital technologies and globalization, has given rise to new intermediaries, professional consumers: these are those members of the new petite bourgeoisie whose jobs are to find music for use in advertising, broadcasting, and film, and who rely on new forms of the databasing and searching of music to find what they want. These people, and recommendation systems, are thought to be necessary in order to navigate through the vast numbers of digital music files now circulating. Broadcasters, advertisers, and filmmakers want to find music that they believe fits in their work, and retailers such as Amazon.com and rental companies such as Netflix want to maximize profits by helping consumers easily find more of what they already like.

Plenty of nonmusicians have performed somewhat similar functions of finding new musicians and bringing them to the attention of a broad public. These are music supervisors, whose profession emerged after the massive success of the soundtrack of *The Big Chill* in 1983.[13] The record industry realized that such compilations were lucrative and so sought to place prerecorded popular songs in films in order to increase sales. This new profession of music supervision began to take off in the 1990s. Chris Douridas (2013), perhaps the first music supervisor, describes how the profession emerged out of his time as a disc jockey at station KCRW in Santa Monica. He was receiving telephone calls from various producers and directors, including Michael Mann, wondering what it was that he had just played on the air. Douridas finally told Mann that he could hire him as a consultant, which Mann did, for the film *Heat* (1995) with Al Pacino and Robert De Niro. Douridas said that he was one of the first DJs at KCRW to do this kind of work; he didn't know it was called "music supervision" then. He also said that every piece of music in *Heat* had been played on his radio show. Douridas professed to be exited about the opportunity to reach a broader audience.[14]

Music supervisors have become, in the words of *Business Week*, "Hollywood's new power players" (Lowry 2006, 80). Music supervisors can act as the new A&R (artist and repertoire) people, a function once performed by record label employees. They are a new kind of manager posited by Boltanski and Chiapello, people with a "talent for sniffing things out" (2005, 444).[15] Said one music supervisor:

> If your band is successful locally and you are playing a great gig that gathers a large crowd, and you look out into the audience and ask yourself if there might be someone in that audience who might help your career, it's more likely that a music supervisor is out there scouting than a record company executive. (Levine 2007a, 82)

He also said:

> What will work for me and my film will also work for those artists in their careers. Obtaining a film placement or a television placement is a very valuable and positive step in a live musician's career. It's kind of like what getting on the radio meant in 1955. . . .
>
> [A] lot of [television] shows are music driven. A huge percentage of the people who are of record-buying age buy their music based on what they've seen on television. The people who are selecting music for television shows are trusted; their taste is trusted by the watchers of those shows. So in a weird twist of fate, I am able to function in much the same way that, say, Wolfman Jack did back in 1970—by finding songs and helping people discover new music. (80)

At an audition for the undergraduate ethnomusicology program at my university, the applicant, an articulate young woman, answered the question "Why do you want to study ethnomusicology?" by saying that she wanted to be a music supervisor, and she believed that familiarity with different kinds of musics would be an advantage. A few years ago, my university's extension arm offered a class on music supervision for $415 for eighteen hours of instruction that introduced students to music industry personnel, including, of course, music supervisors.

Music supervisors are part of the growing ubiquitization of popular music in every realm of life (see Kassabian 2013), not just in the sense that it is always instantly available through one's cell phone but that it is increasingly heard in television programs, films, commercials, and in public places through the licensing of popular song tracks (see N. Klein 2009 and Taylor 2012b) for use in many different ways.

SEARCH

Music supervisors rely on their own sense of taste and familiarity with popular music, but they also employ the same tools as everyday users to find music that they might want to listen to: YouTube, iTunes, and online recommendation systems. "Search," as it is called, has become extremely important, a way for consumers to navigate an ever-growing marketplace. Google, the most popular search engine on the Internet, is worth many tens of billions of dollars. *Advertising Age* magazine regularly reports on search, which is responsible for a significant chunk of online advertising spending, growing from $13 billion in 2009. Marketers in the United States are projected to spend over $103 annually on search, display, social media, and e-mail marketing by 2019, with about $45 billion of that on search and "organic optimization" (i.e., unpaid search results). Interactive advertising is expected to surpass television advertising in 2016 (Sullivan 2014).

Because of the importance of search, a number of algorithms have emerged that have been designed to help people find what they want, whether a film on Netflix, a book or recording on Amazon.com, a kind of music similar to what they already like, a kind of music to suit the listener's mood, and more. Most if not all of these recommendation systems, as they are known, stockpile consumer preferences in vast databases and use this data to recommend more items to a user, or to other users who purchased or rented or streamed the same thing. These systems are playing a role in changing the music business.

I have discussed these systems at some length (Taylor 2014c) and will not recapitulate that discussion here, though I will mention a few of the older services and some new ones. One of the first music services that didn't simply offer a vast, searchable database but permitted users to find their way through it based on their own criteria was Pandora, which was launched in 2005. Based on the "music genome project," songs are given a number of identifying tags. Listeners can say that they like or dislike a particular selection, and these preferences are stored and used to help zero in on what a particular listener likes. This is the only service of which I am aware that is based on formal qualities of songs, and in my experience it can be hit-or-miss. For example, as a Bach lover but not someone fond of the sound of the harpsichord, if harpsichord music pops up, I "dislike" it, and am frequently given more harpsichord music by Bach. But if one keeps at it, one can develop a precious playlist. A friend told me that his brother had honed his Pandora playlist of music to listen to while doing yoga to something truly special and had passed it on to him, speaking of it as though he had been the recipient of a cherished family heirloom.

Perhaps because of experiences like mine, other services have appeared more recently. Some are based on mood, because many people tend to use music in their daily mood management; one of these is Moodagent, a plug-in for Spotify, a popular music streaming subscription service. More recently,

Songza appeared. Songza offers music to listen to while performing certain activities. When one visits the website or launches the app, Songza will display something like: "It's Wednesday afternoon. Play music for: An Energy Boost / Brand New Music / Exploring Obscure Sounds / Doing Housework / Creating a Cool Atmosphere." Pressing any of these virtual buttons leads to more buttons, and pressing one of those leads to a playlist.

The most popular trend as of this writing, and one that seems to be gathering considerable steam, is to combine recommendation systems with social networking. The first attempt was the launching of MySpace Music, which appeared in 2008. *Billboard* magazine claimed, "Years from now, when the pundits talk about the turning point for digital music, they will point to the launch of MySpace Music" (Bruno 2008, 10). MySpace teamed with the music industry to give musicians a platform and to allow users to find what they wanted to listen to. The CEO/chairman of Warner Music Group said in a press release, "This venture may provide a defining blueprint for this next important stage in the evolution of social media, benefiting consumers, artists and music companies alike" (10). MySpace didn't live up to this hype, but other music and social networking sites have continued to appear. In the fall of 2010, Apple launched Ping, a service that would let users of iTunes share their opinions on songs. Steve Jobs introduced this service by saying, "It's like Facebook and Twitter meet iTunes."[16] But Ping didn't fare well either; Apple shut it down in September 2012 and integrated connections to Facebook and Twitter through the iTunes store on the iTunes application.

More promising seem to be the streaming audio subscription services such as Spotify, Rdio, and Google Play, which contain vast databases of recorded music. Users can link their Spotify account with their Facebook account, and elect to have their Facebook friends notified of what they are currently listening to.[17] Within Spotify, one can view one's friends' playlists and what friends have recently listened to. Of course, this is a boon to advertisers. *Advertising Age* reported that embedding Spotify and Netflix in Facebook not only allows people to use such services in Facebook and share what they're watching or listening to in real time with their friends—they can also be targeted by advertisers based on what they watch or listen to using these apps ("Facebook Unveils" 2011). As one person in the industry said, "Anything that increases engagement on Facebook, and captures more user data, will drive up ad revenues" ("Facebook Unveils" 2011). Spotify CEO Daniel Ek said that the integration of his app into Facebook was a coup for the music industry, for it fairly compensated the industry. "Social discovery on Facebook is bringing people back to paying for music," he said ("Facebook Unveils" 2011). They're paying very little, however, as I will discuss in chapter 4.

Today's systems are extremely sophisticated. Brian Whitman, founder of Echo Next, describes how his system works:

> We crawl the web constantly, scanning over 10 million music related pages a day. We throw away spam and non-music related content through filtering, we try to quickly find artist names in large amounts of text and parse the language around the name. Every word anyone utters on the Internet about music goes through our systems that look for descriptive terms, noun phrases and other text and those terms bucket up into what we call "cultural vectors" or "top terms." (Leonard 2014)

SOCIALITY

All this is part of the commercialization of social relationships, as Duménil and Lévy (2004, 2) have argued. A 2002 article in the *Wall Street Journal* reported that Amazon.com's recommendation algorithms had begun to rival the author's music-lover brother for advice on what to listen to (Frangos 2002). Face-to-face modes of social relations are slowly attenuating as electronic modes rise, which themselves are increasingly conduits to new forms of the commodification of social relationships, music, apps, and various forms of hardware.

It will come as no surprise that new services have arisen that attempt to replace live sociality with computer-mediated forms. Purveyors of various online listening venues and apps are well aware of the social aspects of listening, building into their software various ways of sharing one's music with others. Spotify, for example, shows a user's Facebook friends who are online with Spotify, allows users to share music by dropping a link of a playlist or a track into an e-mail or via Facebook and Twitter, and Spotify provides a mailbox so that one can look to see what music has been shared. Other applications or websites similarly socialize the music listening process. SoundTracking, an iPhone app, allows one to see what songs are popular in a particular city or neighborhood. Songza permits users to make and share playlists of music organized around a particular task or activity, such as falling asleep, reading in a café, and more.

And an online service called Turntable.fm, along with WahWah.fm, Outloud.fm, and Listening Room, is trying to re-create, virtually, the experience of listening to music with friends. According to the *New York Times*, Turntable.fm's fans like the service because of its focus on group listening and the selection of songs to play based on the mood of people in the room (Wortham 2011, B1). One fan said, "It's not just me playing what I want to hear. It's me playing music based on what other people are listening to" (B1).

Increasingly, artists are employing Turntable.fm during live shows. Billy Chasen, Turntable.fm's cofounder, says, "I think artists love Turntable because it gives them an intimate way to interact with their fans. It's like showing up at a small venue and surprising everyone with a show, except they get to chat with everyone during the show. It turns fans into super-fans" (Watercutter 2011). Before each show, fans can congregate in a Turntable room that is projected on the wall of the venue where the show is occurring. Those attending the venue live can DJ by using Turntable's iPhone app, and listeners at home can serve as DJs for the crowd, allowing them to feel like they are participating even when not present live (Watercutter 2011).

Sociality in today's neoliberal capitalism can take many forms. In Los Angeles, as in other cities, the silent disco is becoming popular. Dancers listen to one of two DJs on wireless headphones, which are designed so that they can toggle between the two channels. If they find someone on the dance floor with whom they want to dance, they switch channels if necessary so they can dance in synch.[18] A club owner in Santa Monica said that the silent disco "is becoming one of our signature parties," and that participants like the "voyeuristic passerby factor." A participant said, "On a normal dance floor, everyone stays in their little circles." At a silent disco, however, strangers seem to interact more. "It's almost like because everybody has got the headphones on that we all have something in common" (Levin 2011, D16).

Yet face-to-face sociality still matters. Some of the Burger Records musicians I interviewed for chapter 5 discussed it. Kyle Thomas of the band King Tuff describes the world of Burger Records musicians as a family, and this metaphor is apt enough (Thomas 2012). Musicians in the Burger scene attend each other's shows and purchase or trade each other's cassettes and LPs. Even Burger artists who are not in Southern California, where Burger is located, are still intensely local. Cathy Illman (2012a), whose stage name is Veloura Caywood, spoke of the dearth of venues for live music in Lansing, Michigan, where she is based, but said that there were a lot of house concerts, and also told me that she tended to purchase recordings by musicians she knew in her local scene.

It is this sort of sociality that is overlooked by Theodor Adorno and others who decry the effects of the music industry on everyday listeners. But it seems to me that "hidden musicians" (Finnegan [1989] 2007)—amateurs in the literal sense of the term—shouldn't be left out of pessimistic considerations of the State of Music Today. The music industry has its pernicious tendencies, but one part of it, musical instrument sales, seems to be growing (Simmons 2012). There are plenty of people who still want to make music for themselves and people they know, whether Irish traditional musicians with whom I regularly play, church choir members, or many others.[19] Sociality matters, or else capitalists would not try to commodify it.

Art and Commerce

Before concluding, I would like to consider what has become a salient discourse in the cultural industries in the last few decades, the discourse concerning art and commerce, or art versus commerce. As the cultural industries increasingly become part of multinational corporations whose only goal is profit, questions about the nature of their products has become more and more urgent. Can the cultural industries still make art if what they produce is more and more obviously made for profit, if their products are more and more blatantly commodities?

First, let me address the largely false nature of this opposition. It is frequently assumed that "art" is a form of cultural production that is ancient and stands apart from the messy world of commerce. But the concept of art is a fairly recent European invention, emerging when artistic producers entered the marketplace in the late eighteenth and the nineteenth centuries, and has since become a confection shot through with metaphysical subtleties and theological niceties. "Art" is neither real nor illusory: it is a historical construct that powerfully shapes perceptions and practices in cultures where it has taken hold. To maintain whatever degree of autonomy it has sometimes had from the market requires a great deal of continual work by individuals, groups, and institutions.

There have long been debates in the cultural industries about whether popular cultural forms could be considered as art. Especially with the rise of rock music, attitudes from the field of artistic cultural production found their way increasingly into the field of commercial cultural production. Rock since the 1960s, as Simon Frith (1983) has pointed out, has long relied on the "rock ideology," the notion that rock music should be autonomous from market forces, as high art is thought to be, even though, of course, the most successful rock musicians can earn many millions of dollars. Many rock musicians nonetheless believe that their music is apart from the messy world of commerce; many fans hold this notion no less fervently.

But as neoliberal capitalism increasingly affects cultural production, the question of art and commerce has become more fraught. The cultural industries have responded in various ways. The rise of independent film in the 1980s (Ortner 2013) was one reaction, an attempt to make less commercial films; indie rock exemplifies much the same tendency (see chapter 5).

The world of advertising is perhaps where the discourse of art and commerce is obsessed over the most, because advertising is generally assumed

to be closer to the realm of the commercial than the other cultural industries, though, of course, the other cultural industries are every bit as profit-
oriented. As the advertising industry plays an increasingly powerful role in
the production of culture as commonly referred to in the industry as "the
convergence of commerce and content," the discourse of advertising-as-art,
or not, has heightened. Older advertising producers were well aware of their
role, and they warned against viewing advertising as art (e.g., Teixeira 1974;
Harris and Wolfram 1983).

Today, advertising industry musicians more frequently view their activities as artistic, though it is art-for-hire, and they often make comparisons to
musicians-for-hire of the past. Some composers see what they do as commissioned art, and as such, not that different from artists and composers had
been asked to do centuries ago in Europe; several of my interviewees mentioned this. The advertising music composer Bernie Drayton (2009), for example, says that in the past, "the product was still the king and you came and
performed your thing in the context of what the king wanted . . . what the
king needed and what the king's story was. That's why I always called it the
last vestige of commissioned art."[20] Fritz Doddy (2004), a composer and former creative director in a major New York City music production company,
made much the same argument in our interview.

> This industry that we're in is really one of the last places for great commis-
> sioned art in terms of music. And we have a long history, I mean it goes back
> to Joseph Haydn—that's how far back it goes in essence. And not just music
> for advertising, but commissioned art, in that way. That's how I look at it. He
> was given an assignment: "Well, you know, the Grand Duke of Soviet Georgia's
> going to come in and we need an entrance theme for him—whip up some-
> thing for him." And that's what he did.[21]

It is clear that workers in the film and television industry view their labor
in much the same way: they write commissioned music, and their goal is not
to realize their own creative vision but to serve the director's. As film music
composer Sharon Farber (2012) told me:

> In film music, you cannot have any ego. It's not about your music (of course
> you want to write the best music you can so you are proud of every note; and
> hence the reason for me to also compose concert music, where I am free to
> compose with no artistic restrictions), it's about the vision of the director. Your
> job is to take what you know—your inspiration, your talent, and your skills—
> and use it as a vehicle to bring the director's vision to life.

In the world of commercial music, broadly understood, very few people
are permitted to serve their muse; for this reason, Farber and other film and

television composers strive to maintain side careers as composers of what they call concert music, that is, contemporary classical music. And even those musicians who do enjoy some authority in the industry nonetheless must compromise constantly, whether with record producers or record labels or film directors or fans.

ADVERTISING AS HARBINGER OF THE PRESENT

Pierre Bourdieu, like Horkheimer and Adorno before him, identifies advertisers and advertising as the root of the problem of the decline of the autonomy of cultural production and the rise of the profit motive, because advertisers can force the adoption of "norms and constraints linked to the requirements of the market" and because advertising promulgates the ideologies of the strongest forces in today's world—economic forces (1996, 345–46).

Cultural production in general is increasingly like the production of advertising, which is usually believed to be the antithesis of artistic production; *Advertising Age* magazine introduced a section early in the new century called "Madison & Vine," referring to the intersection of Madison Avenue, symbol of the advertising industry, and Vine Street, the corner (at Hollywood Boulevard) that represents the music industry (see Donaton 2004). For Bourdieu, something entirely new is happening in the developed world: the autonomy that cultural production had gained from the market is being threatened "by the intrusion of commercial logic at every stage of the production and circulation of cultural goods" (2003, 67). Cultural goods under neoliberalism are even more conceived and produced for exchange than they had been in the past.[22]

In *The Rules of Art*, Bourdieu writes of the growing threat to the autonomy of the artistic fields (1996, 344). Part of the problem as he saw it was that artists and intellectuals were being excluded from public debate, partly by choice, partly due to lack of opportunity. Bourdieu believed that those cultural producers who were most insulated from market forces, most autonomous, were never in such a precarious position or so weak (2003, 81).

But the autonomy of cultural production that remains is in jeopardy now as commerce increasingly makes inroads in the neoliberal world. Bourdieu writes of this in the most dire terms.

> At the present time, [there] is the destruction of the economic and social bases of the most precious cultural gains of humanity. The autonomy of the worlds of cultural production with respect to the market, which had grown steadily through the battles and sacrifices of writers, artists and scientists, is increasingly threatened. The reign of "commerce" and the "commercial" bears

down more strongly every day on literature, particularly through the concentration of publishing, which is more and more subject to the constraints of immediate profit; on literary and artistic criticism, which has been handed over to the most opportunistic servants of the publishers—or of their accomplices, with favour traded for favour; and especially on the cinema. (1998, 37)

Bourdieu fears that since the conditions of art are being destroyed, art itself will soon die.

While I share some of Bourdieu's concerns, I don't think that artistic fields were as autonomous as Bourdieu makes out; artists, once released from the feudal patronage system, had to make a living, after all; they weren't divorced from the market. "It took painters nearly five centuries to achieve the social conditions that made a Picasso possible," Bourdieu writes, not admitting the wealth and privilege the late artist enjoyed as a result of selling his work (2003, 71). Bourdieu contends that everything the fields of cultural production have achieved is threatened by the reduction of artworks to commodities, products (71–72). But they have been commodities as long as they have been in the market, since it was their entry into the market that created the category of art with all of its accompanying ideologies. In the neoliberal world, they are simply more obvious as commodities, and less obvious as gifts or other sorts of noncommodities. I am not saying here that cultural commodities are "more" commodified than in the past, but that their nature as commodities is more apparent than in the past, their exchange value more dominant.

While there are those who continue to worry about questions of art and commerce, a concern brought about by the growing commercialization of cultural production after the mergers and acquisitions in the last few decades, there are also those who have made a kind of peace with it. Georg Bissen and Victoria Gross (2004), two young advertising music composers I interviewed in New York City in the mid-2000s, meditated on the question. Bissen said, "You've got to put aside your frame setup. Is music art? Is it not art? It's not relevant, really. Basically you're just providing a product, and trying to help somebody else sell their product better." Gross responded by saying:

> But at the same time, it does become your own signature sound, and your own style, and your own flavor, so that a company, an agency, would come back to us and be like, "Oh, we thought that piece that you wrote for that Jell-O commercial was magnificent and we'd really love to have something that's just you guys, your style, specifically you." So that it becomes our art, our trait.

In a historical moment when production in the cultural industries is ever more driven by the pursuit of profit, perhaps this is the best that one can hope for—making one's own work. Even if it is made to order.

3

Globalization

Once in a while a term emerges that seems to capture people's conception of their present better than any other. In the 1920s, the adjective was "modern," and its noun, "temper." In our own period, perhaps no term is employed more often to explain the present, especially its ills, than "globalization." Globalization is used as an unqualified explanation for almost anything—the poor economy, or poor recovery, or lack of jobs, or outsourcing of jobs, or immigration problems, and more. As Pierre Bourdieu once observed, the term "operates both as a password and as a watchword" (2003, 74–75).

Yet, as I have argued repeatedly (see at least Taylor 2007a), our world, the world of the last few decades, is not newly globalized but globalized in new ways, since peoples and their cultures have been circulating as long as there have been peoples and cultures. "Globalization" as a term that describes the global (or near-global) movement of people and commodities isn't new but rather, as a global system, goes back to the beginning of the seventeenth century, when trade and cultural intercourse had been penetrating vast swathes of the globe (see, most famously, Wallerstein 1974 and Wolf [1982] 1997). And Anna Lowenhaupt Tsing has usefully reminded us that all cultures have been shaped by "long histories of regional-to-global networks of power, trade, and meaning" (2005, 3).

It is nonetheless evident that "our" globalization does seem to be different from earlier ones, just as our capitalism is different, though both demonstrate some continuities with the past. It is important to understand the most recent form of globalization as just that, the most recent form of globalization, the latest among many global regimes of interconnectedness, some of which do not supersede each other but compete. It is a measure of capital's success that its latest conception *of* the world and its operations *in* the world have both become so normalized and naturalized that the agents of capitalism as the primary cause for making much of the world the way it is has been rendered invisible except to some few observers.[1] Globalization, like today's capitalism, has come to be seen as inevitable (Bourdieu 1998, 30).

Globalization should be understood neither as a new phenomenon nor merely as an effect or harbinger of neoliberal capitalism. Today's globalization is both: the extension of neoliberal policies and ideologies through the exploitation of new technologies, accelerating global trade in the last few decades (see Centeno and Cohen 2010). Geoffrey Ingham makes a similar point, arguing that our globalization is the result of the efforts of the US government, multi- and transnational corporations, and, especially, Wall Street investment banks (2008, 211). Similarly, Bourdieu writes that globalization "is merely . . . the imposition on the entire world of the neoliberal tyranny of the market and the undisputed rule of the economy and of economic powers" (2003, 9).

Yet this imposition is not uniform. James Fulcher notes that capital doesn't really circulate globally but moves among a small group of rich countries; that capitalism isn't organized globally, for capitalism has local varieties; that nation-states are still important in the activities of transnational corporations; and that global capitalism isn't integrating the world but is, in fact, dividing it (2004, 103). That is, just as the members of wealthy social groups get richer and poor, poorer, so, too, with nations. The five richest countries in the world in 1820 were three times as rich as the five poorest; by 1992, they were seventy-two times as rich (98). According to Duménil and Lévy, in today's globalized, neoliberal capitalist world, each country is supposed to play its own role in an international division of labor. Countries such as China are expected to provide cheap commodities to the economic centers and offer opportunities for profit to investors (2011, 324).

Information technologies play a critical role in the extension and reach of the metropoles. David Harvey writes that information technologies are more useful for the activities of financialization than improving production, noting that the failure to improve production has been masked by the hype over how these new technologies are changing the cultural industries and the marketing of new products (2005, 159).

One way of understanding "globalization" is to view it as the spread of capitalism to other places—that is, outside the West. There has also been a rise in transnational corporations, which invest in operations abroad, in particular the construction of manufacturing plants that exploit cheap labor. Yet these corporations still remain tied to their nations of origin. Other work conducted abroad includes telecommunications such as call centers. Tourism has increased as well. And trading in foreign currencies has risen. One cannot conclude that, even though it is the dominant economic system in the world, capitalism is equally globalized, for it is not. Likewise new technologies; capitalism has always sought new productive forces, so, in this sense, the new digital technologies to be discussed in the next chapter are nothing new in the long history of capitalism.

There is more to say about neoliberalism capitalism and globalization, but I will proceed to the next section and make further arguments as I consider various aspects of the production and consumption of music.

Globalization, Neoliberal Capitalism, and the International Music Industry

Perhaps the main symptom of globalization in the cultural industries has been their growing internationalization as parts of multinational corporations; the music industry has been part of this trend, increasingly bringing Western music to the West's Elsewheres, and bringing musics from Elsewheres to western metropoles under the rubric of "world music."

A couple of publications have chronicled the development of the music industry in the last few decades, showing how this industry took root in small countries (Wallis and Malm 1984), and how the Western industry became increasingly internationalized (Burnett 1996). Neither of these books situates these developments in shifts in global capitalism (few authors were doing so at the time of the publication of these books), but they are instructive in providing the empirical data to do so now. It is clear that the music industry in the era these authors discuss was becoming just as corporatized as the music industry discussed in the previous chapter.

During the period chronicled by Wallis and Malm, mainly the 1970s and early 1980s, most of the transnational music industry did not have much of an interest in marketing local or regional musics internationally. The major labels largely acted as purveyors of major Western musicians to the rest of the world, as well as recording local musicians in places around the world for local and regional distribution. But the presence in local markets was haphazard and variable, highly dependent on governments and local infrastructures of recording and distribution. The major labels would come and go. When present, they would generally be on the lookout for a musician or band that might just make the leap into the international market, as Bob Marley was able to do in the 1970s.

Wallis and Malm summarize a fair amount of data in a table, which I reproduce below in highly truncated form, focusing only on the question of the ratio of foreign and local musics and exports of local musics (table 3.1). From this it is clear that, save for reggae, local musics that happened to be recorded seldom escaped their region in this era, except when conveyed by listeners themselves.

Wallis and Malm emphasize that the transnational labels were profit driven, but the unpredictability of the market made it difficult for the labels to know where to concentrate their efforts in small countries. The major labels watched the smaller and/or local and regional independent labels to see if what they attempted to record would find an audience. The authors write of a case in 1982, when the record label Virgin invested in an East African group based in Tanzania, the Orchestre Makassy. CBS waited eagerly to launch its own East African groups if the Virgin recording performed well in the UK (Wallis and Malm 1984, 105).[2]

But the difficulty of finding a hit musician or band or song in non-Western markets was daunting. EMI's international manager, Richard Lyttleton, put the problem facing the major labels this way:

> EMI has local companies in 32 countries. Obviously if you do no local record-ings, you're not going to pick up the major talent from each country. If they do too much local recording, they might go bust because the local market can't take it. My own view is that if each territory could break even on its local output, then you'd get sufficient spread for one of them to pick up the ABBA, the Baccara or the Boney M. I would never criticize the manager of a local company for breaking even or better. I think if you go into a loss it becomes arguable about the advisability. And you might argue that you need 28 compa-nies in loss to get two big hits. I think CBS have some of that philosophy—I'm not quite sure if I subscribe to it. I think you need the commercial discipline. (Wallis and Malm 1984, 107)

Clearly, for most record labels, with the occasional exception of the less risk-averse CBS in this era, it was not thought to be economically viable to scour small countries looking for a promising musician who might sell enough re-cordings in the major markets to justify the expense of production, market-ing, and distribution.

While Wallis and Malm found that most of the major transnational la-bels had varying to negligible commitments to small countries as potential markets, it was only CBS in this era that was dedicated to recording local musicians wherever it could. The president of CBS Records, Dick Asher, con-firmed this:

> Well, as you probably have noticed we believe in having a record company any place where it is possible to have one. If it is viable to have a record company

TABLE 3.1. Aspects of the International Phonogram Industry, 1981–82 (adapted from Wallis and Malm 1984, 112–13)

Situation in the phonogram industry, 1981–82	Sweden	Jamaica	Trinidad	Wales	Tanzania	Kenya	Sri Lanka	Tunisia	Chile
Ratio of local/foreign music	App. 40/60	App. 40/60	App. 50% Caribbean (20% Trinidadian), 50% non-Caribbean	Mainly English-language pop	Local music on the radio; some foreign programs played at discos	East African music dominates (mainly Zairian and Tanzanian)	50/50 (foreign music Western or Indian)	60/40 (foreign music mainly Egyptian and French)	30/70 (70% mainly other Latin American music)
Exports of local music	ABBA dominate by far (mainly via license deals)	Much reggae exported, often via tapes to London	Some calypso exported in small quantities	Some to expatriates in Canada, Australia, etc.	Unofficially via Kenya	Some to West Africa; more to Central and Southern Africa	Cassettes to migratory workers in Middle East	Via Athens to Tunisians working in Europe (mainly in France)	Some Chilean artists released in Latin America; many in exile

in a country, even though maybe it's a very small country, we try to have one. And as you also probably know, every place we have a record company, as soon as it gets going a little bit it begins to record local artists. We believe very strongly in local recordings and developing local artists. And then we try to spread it around to other parts of the world. Obviously with different degrees of success depending on the accessibility of the music. For example, we have recently opened a company in India. To my ears Indian music doesn't sound like we will ever sell a great deal of it very quickly in the US, although I hope some day we will try at least. And maybe we will. I could be wrong. (Wallis and Malm 1984, 283)

The major labels' interest in supplying their international products to small markets varied from time to time and place to place frequently depending on local realities, and whether or not there were reliable subsidiaries. In times of recession, the impetus to market international music locally tended to increase (Wallis and Malm 1984, 105).

A major shift discussed by Wallis and Malm was the rise in the distribution of the resources for making recordings, represented by an increase in the number of both quality studios and factories that stamped out discs. All of the countries they studied, with the exception of Tanzania, had such facilities by 1983 (1984, 277). This development, along with the quick rise to ubiquity of cassette technology in the late 1970s, gave access to the means of musical production to musicians in small countries, which were at the same time increasingly exposed to music from beyond their borders.

Wallis and Malm's important contribution chronicles the rise of a music industry in four "small countries"—Tanzania, Tunisia, Sweden, and Trinidad—during the immense and rapid changes that overtook the global music industry in the 1970s and after with the introduction of cassette technology, a format more durable than vinyl in hot climates. The authors identify concentration and integration as the main means by which the major record labels attempted to establish or strengthen their influence in small countries. A transnational label purchased a smaller, regional label in order to own its content, and frequently closed a regional factory to centralize production (Wallis and Malm 1984, 76). The major labels and other media corporations were increasingly becoming parts of larger and more diversified multinational conglomerates in this era, and Wallis and Malm provide some data: EMI had 32 subsidiaries in 29 countries and 28 licensees in the same number of countries; Polygram had 48 operations in 30 countries and 182 other labels working for them as licensees globally (81).

But while the products of the music industry spanned the globe, this didn't mean that the transnational industry was present everywhere on earth. Cassette piracy discouraged many transnationals from setting up shop in certain countries, or caused them to pull out altogether. Wallis and Malm write of the difficulties the local music industry had in Trinidad, provoking a calypso by Willard Harris (Lord Relator), which they quote:

> We throw away the franchise
> We no longer monopolize
> We're treating calypso like some prostitute or whore,
> So now she pack up she grip and gone
> She's disenchanted with this place where she was born.
> Since the local recording industry in a total mess
> I use let you know, Madame Calypso
> Just changed she home address.
>
> For Calypsonians to make a record
> They now have to go abroad
> It's a fact of life but it is sad.
> No records are made here in Trinidad.
> The music that they jump to and play mas today
> Is now mass-produced in the USA
> It is a bad blow
> For Trinidad and Tobago.
>
> In case you don't know
> We're now importing we own calypso.
> Calypsonians in trouble, no studios available
> Mankind making horror, Barbados and New York making stampers
> Tax and import duty cannot be denied
> Because the records are manufactured outside.
> Recently, you know, we closed down a pressing plant
> It's a real pity our record industry is non-existent. (Wallis and Malm 1984,
>   84–85)

For major labels in this era, it was necessary to sell around half a million copies of an album to break even, moving increasingly toward the blockbuster model that currently reigns in the major media conglomerates. In the United Kingdom in the last quarter of 1978, it cost roughly £100,000 per album to market sixty-six albums on television, a form of marketing that had become increasingly necessary. Wallis and Malm quote a trade press report in which an EMI general manager for A&R said, "It's just about impossible to make a major deal profitable in the UK alone, so we sign acts we can develop world-wide." Another executive emphasized the importance of maximizing sales in new markets (1984, 88).

In the meantime, small markets tended to be ignored. Technologies such as the bar code, which gained popularity in the 1970s, made niche marketing increasingly possible, but the major cultural industries were moving more toward the blockbuster model. Wallis and Malm write of the experience of Decca in Wales: Decca had about fifty recordings of Welsh music to offer Welsh customers, but the company, after being acquired by Polygram (one of the major labels of the era), eventually decided to delete its Welsh catalog. For a company of its size, selling fewer than fifteen hundred copies of a recording a year did not offset the cost of warehousing the unsold recordings. An independent label continued to supply some Welsh recordings to that market. A Decca/Polygram producer said that Polygram couldn't record "ethnic material":

> That's something we can't get involved in. They are talking in terms of one, two, or three thousand. We're talking in terms of 30 or 40 thousand per item. . . . Polygram is a company with wide international interests. I doubt whether we would make a particular record just for one particular market. It's too expensive. (Wallis and Malm 1984, 89)

The question of whether or not to record musics from outside the West was a somewhat different matter, it seems. An EMI executive touted his company's ability to attract African musicians, for big labels were known for paying royalties reliably, unlike small firms.

> That's why Africans go to the European companies rather than their brothers. One would think that if the big producer was a member of their tribe then they would flock to him. But they don't, 'cause they know they'll get screwed. That's really why the CBSs, EMIs and Polygrams survive. At least they're honest. (Wallis and Malm 1984, 92)

But, as Wallis and Malm continue, EMI's experience in establishing a subsidiary in Kenya in the late 1970s was less than satisfactory for the company, despite positive indications and the presence of Polygram in Kenya already. EMI lost several hundred thousand pounds, due, it seems, to inept management in Nairobi. CBS tried soon thereafter, hoping to tap local talent to sell in East Africa more than to sell its products in Africa. CBS's strategy was to partner with a local studio owner, who was awarded 30 percent of the shares. This endeavor seems to have been successful, mainly because CBS was able to please people on different sides of various issues and was sensitive to local concerns.

Globalization in neoliberal capitalism has largely meant the abandonment of local music markets by the major record labels, as discussed by Wallis and

Malm, a process that was beginning when they were conducting their study. By the mid-1990s, the major entertainment industries derived over 50 percent of their income from foreign markets (Burnett 1996, 11). The mergers and acquisitions in the advertising industry discussed in chapter 2 affected the other cultural industries just as much. The cultural industries shifted to a model of seeking to find and promote blockbusters that they can market around the world rather than cultivating local or regional artists.

MTV found its way to Europe in the late 1980s, then India in the late 1990s and elsewhere on the planet, and found that it could not simply export American culture around the world; local musics needed to be aired in order for the network to have a chance of survival. But local musics frequently owe much to Western pop and rock. And these musics are frequently employed in marketing campaigns. Local rock music, for example, is used to promote a rising consumer culture in India through the sponsorship of festivals by multinational brands (Coventry 2013).

The Rise of "World Music"

Those few recordings of musics from outside of Western metropoles by major labels, along with imports of recording by small labels, slowly began to awaken interest in what has become known as "world music." While Western popular musics had been exported to non-Western countries for decades, it wasn't until the 1980s that non-Western musicians commonly made popular musics that clearly emulated Euro-American popular musics and that were noticed in the West (though there was the occasional precursor, such as songs by Miriam Makeba or Manu Dibango's "Soul Makossa," from 1972, and the occasional fad for Indian or "Latin" sounds).

It was probably African popular musics that first captured the attention of most listeners. These musics didn't fit in the usual retail sections in record stores or radio formats, and a new term was needed. Thus, in 1987, a group of music professionals gathered in London to confect this new term. After bandying about a variety of labels, they settled on "world music," a term that was already circulating in some ethnomusicological circles. The influential British DJ Charlie Gillett recounted:

> We had a very simple, small ambition. It was all geared to record shops, that was the only thing we were thinking about. In America, King Sunny Adé (from Nigeria) was being filed under reggae. That was the only place shops could think of to put him. In Britain they didn't know where to put this music—I think Adé was just lost in the alphabet, next to Abba. In 1985 [sic] Paul Simon did Graceland and that burst everything wide open, because he created an

interest in South African music. People were going into shops saying: "I want some of that stuff" and there wasn't anywhere for them to look. (Denselow 2004, 10)

Radio formats emerged, mostly on college and public radio, a small critical press appeared, charts were created in *Billboard* magazine beginning in 1990, a Grammy Award was created starting in 1991, specialty record labels materialized, and space was carved out in retail establishments.

World music quickly became the main musical signifier of globalization. But it has never sold much, about the same as classical music. At the same time, however, the educated, middle-class consumers of music have been catered to more and more by the music industry, particularly with the decline of audiences for classical music. World music has increasingly come to occupy the exclusive space, both figuratively and literally (in record shops), once held by classical music. For just one example, BBC Radio 4 now airs world music and jazz, not just the classical music it once broadcast exclusively.[3]

The term "world music" has traveled, for new information technologies have made it increasingly possible to impose the West's notion of cultural production and consumption on the rest of the globe. Local musics become incorporated into the new "genre" of world music, though a good deal of cultural work is required to do this in the form of festivals, placement in retail establishments (whether brick-and-mortar or online), the establishment of charts, awards, specialized magazines, specialized reviewers, and more.[4] This effort to contain a vast number of unrelated musics under a single generic label is part of how today's globalized capitalism operates, attempting, as Bourdieu writes, to universalize through the imposition on other cultures Western cultural traditions in which commercial logic has been fully developed (2003, 75).

Genrefication, as I have argued elsewhere (Taylor 2014a) with respect to world music, is a complex process that is most likely to occur in moments in capitalist cultures when historical regimes of consumption are dominant or ascendant, exerting pressure on purveyors of various commodities to put them in their place, rendering them easily accessible to potential consumers. The rise of "world music" as a genre occurred in just such a moment, when other types of music such as hip-hop and heavy metal were also emerging and becoming genrefied.

Imagine the surprise, or consternation, of a musician outside of the West who discovers that her music with a local genre name actually has a "genre" name applied to it by the Western music industry: "world music." The great Senegalese singer Youssou N'Dour said:

I want people just to say it is good music, not that it is good for African music. It's music that is as relevant on the streets of New York as on the streets of Dakar. If people call it world music they are putting it in a ghetto. I prefer to call it Afropop. I am an African artist and you can hear that in everything I do. But it's more than that. It's music for the whole world rather than world music. (Williamson 2000, 43)

Other musicians profess to like the term, for it gives them a slot in which to place their music in order to market it. Still others have merely made their peace with it. The Beninoise singer Angélique Kidjo said in 2007 that the term "used to make my blood boil." But "now I don't care—I know it's human nature to try to categorise people in order to feel in charge" (Jaggi 2007, 37).

SHIFTING AUTHENTICITIES

One of the most prominent discourses that accompanied the rise of world music in the late 1980s and early 1990s concerned authenticity, one of the most complex ideologies in Western culture. Consumers seemed to want to hear "real" African music or Native American music or something else believed to be real. Concerns for authenticity are not new in Western culture, but this form of authenticity is in part an effect of the suffusion of consumer goods and signs in a commodity-laden culture. Jean Baudrillard argued that one of the effects of the "real" no longer seeming what it was once was is that authenticity becomes a symptomatic discourse of this shift (1988a, 170). In today's Western neoliberal capitalist culture, authenticity has become a kind of floating ideology that is used to animate a variety of other ideologies/discourses.

In *Global Pop* (Taylor 1997a), I identified three forms of authenticity with respect to world music in the late 1980s and early 1990s: authenticities of positionality, emotionality, and primality, all of which I conceptualized as being interrelated. (This parsing of the authenticities at play during this period was an attempt to understand the ideologies through which, or with which, listeners were apprehending world music.) The first type, positionality, refers to expectations that musicians be downtrodden or from a poor or dangerous part of the world. Musicians who were more privileged were viewed as inauthentic, or at least less authentic than those with few advantages. As Angélique Kidjo said:

There is a kind of cultural racism going on where people think that African musicians have to make a certain kind of music. No one asks Paul Simon, "Why did you use black African musicians? Why don't you use Americans?

Why don't you make your music?" What is the music that Paul Simon is supposed to do? (Burr 1994, H28)

Elsewhere she said:

> I won't do my music different to please some people who want to see something very traditional. The music I write is me. It's how I feel. If you want to see traditional music and exoticism, take a plane to Africa. They play that music on the streets. I'm not going to play traditional drums and dress like bush people. I'm not going to show my ass for any fucking white man. If they want to see it, they can go outside. I'm not here for that. I don't ask Americans to play country music. (Wentz 1993, 43)[5]

Authenticity of positionality is no less important in musics such as hip-hop, where musicians must frequently demonstrate their lowly origins in blighted urban areas, or country, where a musician's poor and rural upbringing greatly matters. Authenticity of emotionality refers to the kind of raw emotions that people with the backgrounds just described are thought to possess and express in their music. This is in contrast to the highly produced nature of most Western popular musics. But even with these musics, stars are expected to pour out their hearts in song. And finally, authenticity of primality was meant to refer to Western expectations that non-Western musicians were closer to nature, to the earth, than modern Western musicians. Countless recordings and record labels made reference to the earth, to the supposedly "natural" characteristics of the music purveyed.

But this regime of authenticities shifted fairly quickly after the rise of world music as a label. By the late 1990s, authenticities of positionality and primality had waned to a certain extent, and Western listeners, at least as measured by critical response and marketing language, were more tolerant of non-Western musicians who employed some popular music sounds. I was struck, for one example, at how quickly critical reception to Kidjo's recordings changed. Whereas her earlier albums had been critiqued for sounding too influenced by Western popular music (see Taylor 1997a), by the late 1990s, what was perceived as a hybrid sound between Africa and the West was praised, though the plaudits employed language that continued older ideologies of the authenticity of primality. For example, one reviewer commended Kidjo's 1998 album *Oremi* for balancing the "electronic and organic," the former presumably referring to the Western influences and the latter to African (Robicheau 1998, D15).

A more striking example from the same era is the Cameroonian musician Wes Madiko, who goes by his first name only. Sony Music introduced his 1997 collaboration with producer Michel Sanchez of Deep Forest fame, *Welenga*, thus:

Having written his first traditional album (which only appeared in the USA),
Wes was wary of facile and over-artificial associations, a form of white-gloved
slavery that is at the heart of too many fashionable cross-cultural projects. He
was, however, reassured by the sincere passion of Michel Sanchez, who for
three years gave Wes his time and his know-how. The combination of the two
spirits, the irrational Wes and the virtuoso Michel, was a fusion of fire and
water, the meeting of a wild but fertile root and the gifted loving caretaker
of a musical garden where Wes could flourish. (Liner notes to *Welenga* 1997)

What is noteworthy here—beyond the rather astonishing pseudo-political
correctness and the continuing representations of a non-Western person as
"irrational," "wild," and more—is the continued use of familiar ideologies of
authenticity of primality, but this time subordinated to the ideology of the
hybrid-as-authentic.

Reviews of Kidjo's and other African musicians' later albums have slowly
jettisoned some of the earlier reliance on ideologies and discourses of various forms of authenticity, though they do persist. A review of Kidjo's *Oyaya!*
from 2004 praised the album for "strip[ping] away the Europop affections and
return[ing] . . . to a rootsier sound" ("Angélique Kidjo 'Oyaya!'" 2004, T07).
Kidjo still feels buffeted by different critical reactions, telling an interviewer,
"I've been bashed left and right by people who want to have control. I never
fit those clichés. I grew up listening to all genres" (Jaggi 2007, 37).

All these conceptions of authenticity persist today, sometimes more
strongly or weakly than at the advent of world music, though whatever ideology of authenticity that serves capitalism is subject to change, sometimes
quite quickly.

As a result of the entry of world music and musicians into the Western
market, just as some musicians have become brands, as discussed in the previous chapter, the logic of branding has been extended to certain types of
music, particularly small "genres" such as world music. Branding is another
way of putting something in its place, making it knowable and accessible to
potential consumers and creating an emotional connection to it. Fairly early
in its existence, "world music" was branded as happy, celebratory, unthreat-
ening, symbolized in the packaging of recordings in multicolored artwork
and employing wacky, colorful fonts, sometimes mimicking the fonts of the
music culture's, e.g., "Gaelic" or a South Asian language. This is the "celebratory" aspect of world music, as opposed to the anxiousness about it, as Steven
Feld (2002) has written, anxiousness that reflects a concern for the dynamics
of economics and power around world music (figure 3.1).

I would now argue that the rise of "world music" in the late 1980s wasn't
the beginning of something but a culmination, or at least an important mile-

FIGURE 3.1. Putumayo Presents: *World Hits* (2007), Cover

stone in the ways that Western peoples put their Others in (small) boxes. For almost immediately with the rise of "world music" and the various process of genrefication of it, we saw the conglomeration of some musics into brand categories under what I have elsewhere called the "brand warehouse" of "world music" (Taylor 2014a). It is perhaps "subgenres" or "styles" within world music where this process is clearest. Probably the best example remains "Celtic" music, which frequently has little or nothing to do with traditional musics from the ancient Celtic nations of Ireland, Wales, Cornwall, the Isle of Man, and Brittany, and which usually employs the color green, images of Celtic crosses or standing stones, and/or "Gaelic" fonts; another example is Gypsy music (see Silverman 2012). What branding accomplishes for small bodies of music such as this is that it organizes them into knowable, recognizable categories so that consumers can instantly determine whether or not a particular music is "Celtic" (or whatever) and if it has made an emotional connection. Certain sounds became emblematic, metonymic, of such musical brands, such as the sound of the tin whistle in the "Celtic" brand. Branded

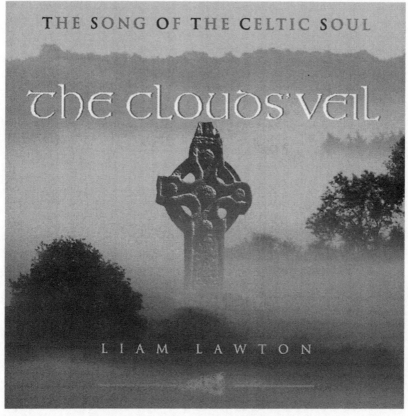

FIGURE 3.2. Liam Lawton: *The Clouds' Veil* (1997), Cover

musics are expected to conform to the authenticity of the brand more than anything else (figures 3.2 and 3.3).

World music is also increasingly produced in studios. Musicians in the commercial music world have had to learn how to make "world music," or at least approximate it. Commercial music composers need to know how to compose in a variety of styles, as they always did, but their brief increasingly includes world music. One commercial music guidebook advises to hire "native" musicians to perform compositions written in a "typical folkloric style," warning that unless the performer really knows the musical culture she or he is playing, "it will not sound authentic" (Zager 2003, 24).

There are also "utility" performers who have sprung up, musicians who can imitate a variety of sounds and styles for use in commercial music. It is simply more economical to hire such a person than to seek out an authentic practitioner of a particular tradition, despite the advice proffered above. Mi-

FIGURE 3.3. *The Best of Celtic Music* (2006), Cover

chael Stern, a recording engineer and music-scoring mixer, told me that Los Angeles boasts many world-class musicians:

> One thing we have in Los Angeles is ethnic specialists. You've got people like Pedro Eustache, who is one of the most phenomenal duduk players in the world, and he will show up to a recording session with 200 flutes, and both legit instruments and things he's made out of plastic tubes, one-of-a kind, unique instruments that he will get incredible sounds out of. You have George Doering who is probably one of the busiest studio musicians in the world who is a phenomenal guitar player, but he'll play bass and all the dulcimers, the Aeolian wind harp, things that you don't even know what they are, and he'll tell you, he'll play lute or oud or whatever is required for the film score, and he'll do it fast, he will be efficient, he will play what is right almost every single time. (Stern 2012)

It is no different for singers today in the commercial music world. Marissa Steingold (2009), a singer who works for commercials and films, told me, "A lot of times they'll ask, 'Can you do this?,' 'Can you sound like a Bulgarian . . . ?' 'Okay,' and I'll just listen to one YouTube example and just sort of make it up. I've had to do a lot of Celtic stuff, just hoping I'm pronouncing things correctly." And she provided an illustrative anecdote.

> I had this gig not too long ago for Coca-Cola. They had this Indian singer who they really liked and so they gave me a recording in advance of her doing some wonderful chanting, and they said, "We want you to sound like her, but it's a Coca-Cola commercial and there are lyrics in English." So I called up my friend from Bangladesh and had her do an impression of an Indian person speaking English who just doesn't speak English that well, and tried to absorb that without being really offensive. It's quite difficult; sometimes I have to be "Asian," and I'm just praying that no one in Asia is listening. There's no time to really work it out.
>
> They need people like me who are not genuine, not genuinely black, or not genuinely Indian, or whatever, because it would be offensive to ask an Indian person to sound less Indian.

Steingold reflected on the range of "ethnic" sounds she operates in, from the Irish New Age singer Enya to Lisa Gerrard, who is famous in the commercial music world for her emotional singing of nonsense syllables that imitate a foreign language (heard in the 2000 film *Gladiator* among other places).

> I think of two singers as a spectrum and one's on each end. Usually on one side you've got Enya, and then on the other side you've got Lisa Gerrard, and she's much more intense. And so often I'm having to play this dance, so if I start to get too intense, earthy, too ethnic then it's got to go to the Enya side. I think part of the reason why she's been so successful is, she's still pretty white. It's an "Other"—it's Celtic, but it's still something that we can handle (Steingold 2009).

Another commercial singer, Randy Crenshaw (2009), told me:

> When you get the call they'll say, "We're looking for someone who can sing authentically in Farsi, are you good at that? Or do you know somebody who's good at it?" So you come preapproved, but once you get called for that you're expected to come in there and really sound quite authentic. I've had to do things where I had to come in and do, you know, Sufi devotional music. I've had to come in and sing things that were in Hindi, or things that were in Sanskrit, or things in Indonesian, where they said, "Okay, we have kind of a gamelan orchestra and we need you to sound authentically like—" and they'll play me samples of stuff.
>
> In a lot of cases producers are still looking for a pastiche thing that has the flavor of it without the genuine article. But in enough cases they're true aficionados of a musical style and when they say they want Bulgarian women, they really do want it to sound just like the record they have of the Bulgarian women. So it's made us be a lot more broadly based eclectic music makers,

instead of what we used to be, which is really highly technically great tone generators.

Crenshaw also told me:

> I have a library of probably three thousand CDs and two thousand LPs, you know, of the vinyl variety that nobody knows about anymore? I still have a wall full of them, and I purposely took samples of virtually every vocal style that's known to exist. I try and actually have a listening library so that when somebody says that they me want to sound like Nusrat Fateh Ali Khan, or whoever it is, I'll say, "Okay, sure," and then I go and listen.

Connoisseurs, Collaborators, Curators

Promoting musicians who don't sing in English to US and UK audiences has always been difficult, no matter how famous those musicians might be in their own countries or regions. Chris Stapleton and Chris May write of the regular flow of African musicians from various countries to Britain, other European countries, and North America; musicians left their homes for lack of opportunity to realize their musical and professional ambitions in their own countries, finding also that they couldn't become influential until they had spent some time in a Western metropole. The prominence of a particular musician could result in new waves of immigration, as in the success of the UK-based Ghanaian/Caribbean group Osibisa in the 1970s, which increased Ghanaian and other West African immigration. Manu Dibango's globally successful "Soul Makossa" from the early 1970s and Miriam Makeba's success inspired more immigration, as did the rise of Sunny Adé (Stapleton and May 1989, 279–80). Yet it remains difficult for musicians not singing in English to break through; the international music industry's conservatism and xenophobia make success even more difficult.

What has helped non-Western musicians achieve some degree of international success is the efforts of a Western star/broker. Beyond the increasing noticeability and availability of what has become known as world music, one of the effects of globalization under neoliberal capitalism has been the increased desire of Western musicians to work with non-Western ones, under ideologies of "collaboration" (Meintjes 1990; Taylor 2007a). When the Western musicians who take an interest in non-Western ones are stars, collaborations commonly take the form of curatorship. Fans are invited to use the Western stars' tastes to follow them to new music.

Paul Simon, David Byrne, Peter Gabriel, Ry Cooder, and others serve as examples of how "globalization" has created awareness of and interest in musics from afar, but their desire to collaborate—a desire that could only have resulted from being in a capitalist culture in which no object, tangible or not, is seen as unobtainable, especially by the wealthy—resulted in complex relationships and negotiations between famous musicians and those less famous but with aspirations toward fame, international recognition, and wealth.

At the vanguard of these new intermediaries, at least in the realm of popular music, were musicians themselves, stars who performed and recorded with little-known musicians from around the world. Early examples include Paul Simon and his Grammy-winning *Graceland* (1986), which featured musicians from South Africa, and his later recording *The Rhythm of the Saints* (1990) with Brazilian musicians. Other such connoisseurs/curators from the early days of "world music" include, most prominently, David Byrne, who founded the Luaka Bop label, which released many recordings by Brazilian and other musicians, and Peter Gabriel, whose record label Real World features musicians from around the world.

A common strategy employed by Western musicians who work with non-Western or other subaltern musicians is to claim affection and longtime familiarity with the music whose makers they are drawn to collaborate with. It is a fundamental expression of connoisseurship: they found this music before it became popular. This is clear enough in Paul Simon's (1986) liner notes to *Graceland*.

> In the summer of 1984, a friend gave me a cassette of an album called **Gumboots: Accordion Jive Hits, Volume II**. It sounded vaguely like '50s rock 'n' roll out of the Atlantic Records school of simple three-chord pop hits: "**Mr. Lee**" by the Bobettes, "**Jim Dandy**" by Laverne [*sic*] Baker. It was very up, very happy music—familiar and foreign-sounding at the same time. The instrumentation (accordion, bass, drums and electric guitars) and the name of the record label (Gallo Records) made me think that **Gumboots** probably hadn't been recorded by an American or British band [boldface in original].[6]

Or David Byrne's comments on working with salsa musicians for *Rei Momo* in 1989: "For years I'd listened to this music and at some point it just seeped into me enough where I felt comfortable enough to say, 'Okay, now I can actually approach the musicians and work with them, and it's not gonna seem like I'm just adding a sound or a texture onto something else'" (Thompson 1988, 44).

These and other Western star musicians employ other common discourses about the musicians with whom they worked and the musics they appropriated or collaborated with. The dominant ideology and discourse are that non-Western musics are a kind of natural resource that is available for the taking, though these acts of appropriation are frequently tempered by the Western star's appearance alongside the non-Western musicians in publicity photographs, on recordings, and in liner notes. Examples from the early days of "world music" are still the clearest, though the ideologies that inform them remain. Stewart Copeland, the drummer for the 1980s band the Police, released a recording in 1985 entitled *The Rhythmatist*, which is a collection of songs utilizing sounds from all over the African continent. The liner notes and iconography point to nineteenth-century notions of the Western explorer entering the untamed jungle. An interior photograph, for example, shows a dressed-in-black, hatted Copeland brandishing a huge, phallic microphone. Here is Copeland's description of the music on the album:

> "Rhythmatism" is the study of patterns that weave the fabric of life; with this speculation in mind a black clad figure is on his way across the so-called dark continent. He meets lions, warriors, pygmies and jungles before stumbling across the **rock**.
>
> This record is a curious blend of musical snatches from Tanzania, Kenya, Burundi, Zaire, the Congo and Buckinghamshire (Copeland 1985; boldface in original).

Paul Simon evinced much the same position when working with Ladysmith Black Mambazo and other African musicians on his acclaimed *Graceland*. Simon's summary of the process of collaboration indicates his overall approach to both *Graceland* and *The Rhythm of the Saints*, invoking the explorer/discover trope: "The act of discovery becomes what the work is about" (*Paul Simon: Born at the Right Time* 1992).

Both Simon and Copeland, when faced with criticisms that they had appropriated black music just as early rock and roll musicians had done, defended themselves by claiming that traditional musics were a resource that belong to everyone. Simon exclaimed, "You think it's easy to make a hit out of [that]?," as though the African musics that appeared on *Graceland* were nothing but raw material awaiting his refining touch (*Born at the Right Time* 1992). For him, other people's culture is natural—he has said, "Culture flows like water. It isn't something that can just be cut off" (Herbstein 1987, 35)—though his own cultural productions are, of course, protected by copyright and lawyers (see Taylor 1998 for my experience with the latter). For his part, Copeland defended his album against the idea that he was plundering or appropriating other people's music, similarly viewing somebody else's culture as a natural resource:

I've recently heard an expression: cultural mining. It's a term of derision, although I proudly assume this term for my own work. Because I think the term itself is only used by intellectual journalists who are very ignorant of the mindset of the indigenous people in exotic places. That mind-set is very open and giving of its culture and proud to have people from across the world listening to it. And appreciating it. The idea that someone goes to an African village, records their music, and takes the tape away—it's not like, suddenly, "Where's all the music gone? Must've been that white guy with his microphone! He stole it and took it away with him!" Nothing could give them greater happiness than the idea that some people in a faraway land are dancing to their beat. (Blank-Edelman 1994, 38)

A somewhat different case of connoisseurship is that of Ry Cooder, whose famous "discovery" of prerevolutionary Cuban musicians resulted in the 1997 hit *Buena Vista Social Club*. This was after several other projects with musicians that could be interpreted as more collaborative than some other famous world music projects (such as *Talking Timbuktu* with the Malian guitarist Ali Farka Touré in 1994). Nonetheless, Cooder was hailed as a discoverer, and participated in this perception himself, telling one interviewer, "Music is a treasure hunt. You dig and dig and you find traces. But there I found it all" (Williamson 1997, 33). And his septuagenarian and octogenarian collaborators were treated as isolated from modernity: "The players and singers of 'son de Cuba' have nurtured this very refined and deeply funky music in an atmosphere sealed off from the fall-out of a hyper-organised and noisy world," said Cooder (Mengel 1997, 13).

But it should be remembered that the relationships of Western stars to their fellow musicians are complex and can seldom be characterized merely by a colonizer/colonized or dominant/subordinate framework. In the case of Simon and *Graceland*, all the musicians wanted something from each other. Simon was clear about wanting to rejuvenate his career, and Ladysmith Black Mambazo was clear about desiring a broader international audience.[7]

Despite the variety of relationships that Western stars have had with the musicians with whom they work, the result is usually taken as an uncomplicated example of collaboration (Meintjes 1990). This interpretation is valorized by the Grammy Awards for World Music, which have tended to go to collaborations, as I noted in *Global Pop* (Taylor 1997a), though this pattern was upset somewhat by the introduction of a new World Music Grammy Award in 1992 for the Best World Music Album, to which another award, for Best Traditional World Music Album, was added in 2004 (this category was jettisoned when the National Academy of Recording Arts and Sciences [NARAS], which oversees the Grammy Awards, eliminated a number of awards in small categories in 2011, merging the two back into the Best World Music Album category beginning in 2012). But the likelihood of a recording that featured a known American or European star fronting non-Western or other subaltern musicians was for a time so great that I entitled my review of *Buena Vista Social Club* "Ry Cooder's Next Grammy" (Taylor 1997b), which would have been prophetic if it hadn't been practically foreordained by the demonstrated preferences of the NARAS.

COLLABORATION WITHOUT COLLABORATORS

Other forms of connoisseurship, curatorship, and collaboration have been accomplished electronically, facilitated first by tape recording technologies and then digital ones. A harbinger of what was going to become a trend within world music appeared in 1981 with the release of Brian Eno and David Byrne's *My Life in the Bush of Ghosts*, a recording that utilized snippets of music and speech from various places (made before the advent of digital sampling, this was accomplished through the cutting and splicing of tape). Eno said that he wanted to make a "fourth world music," which he defined as

> music that is done in sympathy with and with consciousness of music of the rest of the world, rather than just with Western music or just with rock music. It's almost collage music, like grafting a piece of one culture onto a piece of another onto a piece of another and trying to make them work as a coherent musical idea, and also trying to make something you can dance to.[8] (Tamm 1989, 161)

With the rise of digital technologies and sampling, which is now as easy as cutting and pasting in a word processing application, sampling of world music (and other musics) has become so common as to be the norm rather than the exception. The recording that propelled samples of world music into the mainstream appeared in 1992 and was a result of the efforts of two European producers, Michel Sanchez and Eric Mouquet. Their recording, *Deep Forest*, sampled heavily from recorded music by the Baka people of central Africa, representing them as happy, premodern children. The album was so successful that the duo continued with the album title as their "band" name on subsequent albums that repeated the same formula.[9]

Mouquet says that the recording was just for their pleasure at the beginning. "We just put all the feeling that we wanted into this music, and after we saw the success, we were very proud." According to Mouquet, his partner, Sanchez, found some tapes of Pygmy chant recorded decades ago and played them after dinner one night. "It was very quiet, very beautiful," said Mouquet, who then came up with the idea of combining the sounds with their own music. He and Sanchez cut the tapes, mixed them with synthesized music, drum beats and sound effects while keeping as much of the original melody and tempo as possible. Then they took their demos to producer Dan Lacksman, and the songs were entirely reworked. "It was the vocals and the emotion of the songs which attracted me," said Lacksman (Geitner n.d.). These quotations give a good idea of how Others' music is romanticized, treated as natural, raw material to be manipulated in the studio.

The liner notes to *Deep Forest* contain the following statement:

> Imprinted with the ancestral wisdom of the African chants, the music of Deep Forest immediately touches everyone's soul and instinct[.] The forest of all civilizations is a mysterious place where the yarn of tales and legends is woven with images of men, women, children, animals and fairies. Not only living creatures, but also trees steeped in magical powers. Universal rites and customs have been profoundly marked by the influence of the forest, a place of power and knowledge passed down from generation to generation by the oral traditions of primitive societies. The chants of Deep Forest, Baka chants of Cameroun, of Burundi, of Senegal and of Pygmies, transmit a part of this important oral tradition gathering all peoples and joining all continents through the universal language of music. Deep Forest is the respect of this tradition which humanity should cherish which marries world harmony, a harmony often compromised today. That's why the musical creation of Deep Forest has received the support of UNESCO and of two musicologists, Hugo Zempe [*sic*] and Shima [*sic*] Aron [*sic*], who collected the original documents. (Liner notes to *Deep Forest* 1992; names spelled as in the original)

There follows information on how to contribute money to "the African Pygmies": for contributions of five dollars or more you receive a receipt, a "To Save the People" kit, and an original 5½″ × 8″ photograph of a pygmy child.

Taken together, all this constitutes a remarkable text. The names of prominent ethnomusicologists (Hugo Zemp and Simha Arom) are misspelled, and the notes seem to strive to touch all the most revered themes of Western modernity: the mysterious Other, universal cultural practices, the Other's unique, idealized kinship to nature, the totalization of the Other—different tribes from different parts of the African continent become "Pygmies," not to mention the use of the word "primitive" without quotation marks. Sanchez and Mouquet's discussion of the music continues these mythologies. "When we began the project, the idea was just to play the music we want and to preserve the emotion of the music. It was important for us to preserve the tribal voices and not let the music overpower it," says Mouquet (Borzillo 1994, 44).

The source music is construed as raw material, thought to be unpalatable to Western listeners with sophisticated tastes. So it's backgrounded, encompassed, surrounded by up-to-date synthesized magic and drum machines. Most of the source music on *Deep Forest* is unrecognizable; it has been so manipulated, so smoothed over, so covered up by the Western synthesizers, that whatever might be "universal" about the original music is subsumed under a Western totalizing ideology of universalism. The music of the "Pygmies" becomes zoo music: placed into Western meter, undergirded by Western harmony, made accessible to today's Western listener. Evidently the original music has been sufficiently altered so that the two main forces behind the album, Eric Mouquet and Michel Sanchez, are listed as the "songwriters" for each track.

With the success of *Deep Forest* and other such recordings, the sampling of world music sounds has become commonplace. There are a number of sample libraries for composers to choose from, libraries that are variable in quality, often imitating instruments and voices from other cultures rather than actually offering recordings of them. But, as is usual, one gets what one pays for. Higher-priced sample libraries tend to be higher quality, featuring recognizably real instruments rather than synthesized ones. No matter the quality, however, they all tend to be marketed as exotic or wild, allowing their users to fabricate "world music" from a safe distance.[10]

Musicians in the Field of World Music in Neoliberal Capitalism

Neoliberal capitalism and globalization are extremely complex historical processes that are both fragmenting and uniting, exploitative to many and beneficial to some. It is impossible to characterize either without running the risk of oversimplification, or of theorizing at such an abstract level that theory might not even be possible. Thus, as ever, it is important to attend to specificities.

CASE STUDY: ANGÉLIQUE KIDJO

Readers of my earlier work on world music will know my respect for and fascination with Kidjo (b. 1960), a singer from Benin now living in Brooklyn. Kidjo, perhaps more than any other world music figure, has been canny in her negotiations of the ever-shifting (but always sexist, racist, and xenophobic) Western music industry. For that reason, an in-depth examination of her career will help shed light on how difficult the terrain of world music is, and the positions musicians are forced to take in the world music field.

Kidjo and "World Music"

This is the point where I might attempt to situate Kidjo in a field of cultural production (Bourdieu 1993), but this raises the question of what the "field" is. This proves to be a complex issue with respect to world music, which is still undergoing processes of genrefication. In many ways I would nonetheless consider it to be a field since there are forms of capital that circulate concerning musicians' lineages or background, and positions to be taken, about language choice, how much Western pop influences to permit, and more.[11]

Kidjo maneuvers through a complex field that is continually under construction by the music industry, musicians, critics, and others. All fields are never static, but world music is different in that it is constantly being constituted as a genre by the music industry, and this constitution is resisted by some musicians. It is thus less stable than many other genres since it is relatively new and is forced to contain a massive variety of musics, making it sometimes difficult for musicians to know what positions might be available for them to take in the field of world music.

One of the positions Kidjo takes is to resist the field itself. She takes positions to help her escape the confines of the world music field and attract a more mainstream audience, a move that she has in common with some other popular musicians from the African continent and elsewhere. Early in her career, however, Kidjo said she liked the term "world music":

> I like world music. It expresses an open outlook, a lack of musical sectarianism. World music is not a genre, like funk or reggae. It is played by musicians who think that artists—especially in Third World countries that are not overrun by the media—can express themselves in a very contemporary and original way, thanks to the richness of their cultures. The only danger of the world-music label is that of being left out of the mainstream, because this music is given the same weight in the market that the Third World is given on the global economic chessboard. (Aubert 1992, 25)

Only two years later, she had changed her mind:

> World music doesn't mean anything for me. We African musicians are not the world; we are just part of the world. The term is created to categorise music that is not pop or rock, and for me no one has the right to decide what is rock or pop, how the music deserves to be listened to.
>
> The day I will take into account "world music" will be the day I will enter a record shop and where there will be a big sign on which is written "world music" and everything will be under it, from classical music to the music I am doing. Then it will mean something.

> The same people who created the term "Third World" also created the term "world music." (Masterson 1994, 3)

This last statement isn't actually true, but she is right in that "Third World" and "world music" stem from the same kind of classifying and distancing ideology.

Later, Kidjo was even more blunt: "I do not want my music to be put in a ghetto," Kidjo said about the term (Ntone 1999), and blunter still a decade later:

> What is not from a developed country, what is not Western, has to be in a different category—they call it "world music." We share the same planet but we don't have the same rights, apparently. We are not considered mainstream artists because we don't sing in English or in French or in Spanish or in Portuguese." (McDonald 2009, 7)

The trajectory of Kidjo's comments maps the shift of "world music" from an inclusive category that incorporated African music to its clear relegation to the margins of the music industry.

Positions and Forms of Capital in the World Music Field

Even though the world music field is still forming, its relation to the popular music field more generally has bequeathed it positions that are active. There are essentially two main positions: the question of the proximity to sounds that could be considered pop, and the question of the language in which to sing. Kidjo has continually negotiated these in her long career.

The question of the forms of capital at play in this field is more complex. They tend to be ideologies of authenticity that congeal, or are harnessed, as forms of capital, or positions in the field. All forms of capital relate to the authenticity of positionality as I described it in *Global Pop*, such as the musician's origins in a remote or oppressed place or conditions of poverty. Lineage matters, too: if, for example, a West African musician can claim to be a griot (a kind of bardic historian), or descended from a line of griots (the role is hereditary), this can be considered as a form of capital in the field (and griots have been musicians particularly fetishized by Western listeners and critics in the world music field); or if a musician simply comes from a line of famous musicians, or even just a generation or two. In some kinds of music, such as Irish traditional music, winning or faring well in a competition can matter a good deal (there is an extensive system of competitions in Irish traditional music). Studying with a famous teacher can also matter; I derive a fair amount of capital in the field of Irish traditional music from having studied with the well-known Irish flute player Mike Rafferty, for example. If a musician comes from a region famous for music, or famous for producing musicians, or famous for a particularly revered regional style (as in Rafferty's case)—all these can be constructed as forms of capital as well. They can be complicated by musicians' position-takings, or how they attempt to use these forms of capital; abandoning a beloved regional style for more pop sounds is an example.

Another position to be taken concerns the proximity to popular music. World music artists must decided just how much to sound like Western pop stars, and how much of their local, regional sounds to preserve. This is a complex question, since people around the world have been able to hear Western popular musics for decades. Kidjo has always said, and reiterated in many interviews, that she grew up listening to many kinds of popular musics. Fairly early in her career, when she was first becoming known to Western audiences, she singled out James Brown, who "opened our ears to the fact American rhythms did sit alongside those of our own people and could be mixed together in exciting new ways" (Sly 1992). She also cites the Rolling Stones, Aretha Franklin, the Jackson 5, and the Beatles, all recordings brought home by her older brother and covered by his band. "I'd hear my brothers playing modern music inside, and then I'd hear the drums outside, and I was in between both" (Azerrad 1992, 32). Elsewhere, she said, "All the music I heard sounded good to me. Whatever I heard, I found a place for it in the music I was developing" (Sly 1992).

Predictably, however, questions of authenticity crop up frequently in interviews with Kidjo if her music is found to sound too much like Western pop. About *Logozo* (1991)—her first album for Island/Mango, an important label—she articulated her position: "You have to maintain the tradition but expose it to today's realities. My records sound like dance music because that's the only way for Europeans to approach something they don't know" (Romney 1991). As dance music, this album was produced by Joe Galdo, producer for the Miami Sound Machine, who had been chosen by Chris Blackwell, founder of Island Records (Kidjo and Wenrick 2014, 85). *Logozo* included contributions by Branford Marsalis, as well as Cameroonian Manu Dibango, a world music superstar, and keyboardist Ray Lema from Zaire. Galdo's presence elicited disapprobation from some critics for sounding too much like American popular music.[12]

Kidjo has always maintained that she will not accede to what her Western fans might want (at least as their opinions are represented by critics) by performing music that seems to be "authentic," from the bush. She has been taken to task by many a critic for this. In 1993, Kidjo said, "I don't want to deny myself. I don't want to deny my culture or my education and I don't envy the culture of the rest of the world. I just take what I want to take out of it. I take what I think can help me to grow" (Feist 1992, C5).

One journalist contemplated the crossover question and put it to Kidjo, though neither knew just what she had crossed over into: "I'm an African person bringing my culture to the Western world. I am using technology. And rhythm and blues. And jazz. I make it available for you by combining your tools with mine. But then they say it's not pure" (Zwerin 1998, 10).

A later strategy in the face of criticisms that she did not sound "African" enough was to universalize and dehistoricize African musics. In response to a 2006 interviewer's question about her musical influences, she said:

> You are talking about R & B and funk. Where do they come from? They came from Africa with the slaves. The music that I am doing, the roots always go back to Africa. Why should we African artistes be stuck in one genre of music while we have been influencing the music of the world one or two centuries back? ("Music Lets Me See beyond Color" 2006)

Later still, she summed up her position succinctly: "La pureté, ça n'existe pas" (Dunlevy 2007, D5).

The position concerning language choice shows a similar set of negotiations at work. Kidjo has changed her position over time. Early in her international career, she said:

> I talked about the idea of having English lyrics with a few people but we didn't think my music could take it. Take the words out and put in English lyrics and it won't sound the same. It will be completely new. My voice is very rhythmic, like an instrument. Take it away and you're losing an important part.
>
> The people I chose to work with may not have known the actual words but I was confident they would treat the songs carefully. I knew these men could give me the kick I needed on a record, the same sort of big thing that I get in the live show (Sutton 1994).

Later, it became an issue of individual choice. About *Fifa* (1996), which was Kidjo's first album to include English lyrics, when an interviewer wondered if some would think she was selling out, she said, "I do what pleases me. I do the music I like. I don't know if it's going to be English or French or some African dialect. Music is music, it's all about communication" (Brand 1996, G10). Later still, she adopted a position one could perhaps call philosophical: "Music is about expression. It doesn't ask for color or language. I perform music that speaks to me and that is in my heart" (Oppelt 1998, D1).

Asked about singing in different languages in 2006, Kidjo said she has always sung in different languages. She said she chooses which language to sing in based on the music:

> Most of the time, it is the music itself. If I wake up in the morning and the music that I have is still in my head, I have to sing it. When I started singing in Benin, I sang music in the indigenous language, of course. But I also sang in Cameroonian and Zairian languages, and many other languages from Africa but I copy them phonetically. And then you have English too, and Spanish and Portuguese, and many different languages. The thing that matters to me is the beauty of the song, how it makes me feel happy and how I can give it back to people. ("Music Lets Me See beyond Color" 2006; see also Pareles 2014)

She writes much the same thing in her autobiography (Kidjo and Wenrick 2014, 23).

Complaints about Kidjo's and other musicians' use of Western sounds in non-Western recordings frequently stem from a fear of what is usually called cultural "grayout," or a process of "de-differentiation" (Lash 1990). Such arguments seem to me to be too broad and not enough based on what real people are doing in the world, and they are based on the sound of the music rather than its conditions of production. In other words, they are written from the perspective of a consumer of music. There are clear instances of homogenization occurring, just as there are clear occurrences of new musics springing up all over as people come into contact with unfamiliar sounds and bend them to their own uses. Nonetheless, there is a growing global hegemony of financialized neoliberal capitalism, which has resulted, in part, in a globalized music industry, and with it, the standardization of production (see Regev 2013). Up to a point. Grayout is occurring—but so is diversification.

Gender

Kidjo, as a woman in a (Western, white) male-dominated industry, probably faces expectations of forms of authenticity that male musicians do not, or do not face as frequently. These are old problems, however, and nothing much seems to have changed with neoliberal capitalism. As usual, it is an issue of xenophobia and ignorance, combined with sexism. As for the former, Kidjo has said, "I'm not here to fulfill anybody's fantasies. If they [Western critics] want to see exotic African women, they have to fly to Africa. And if they're not careful, when they arrive there, they'll get their faces punched in" (Burr 1994, H28).

Yet some of the problems faced by Kidjo as a woman in the music industry are more general and familiar:

> The music business is macho. When you are a woman, you have to be at a point in life when your mind is at the same place as a man. You have to fight

two times harder because men want the power for themselves and they don't want to share it. The advantage of being a woman is having the pride to do what you do every day. Being there and showing men that because you are a woman you can do it too. That is the only way to gain respect. (Wentz 1993, 43)

In a 1996 interview, she addressed the problem of sexism in the music industry, averring, "Well, I'm tough enough to kick anyone, I have been kicking some arse on my way." When asked who by the interviewer, she replied, "The people who bother me, the people who think I have to have sex with them before I have anything done." Continuing, she said, "I think: 'Okay, it's going to take me more time to get there, but I'm not having sex with you.' That's it, that type of compromise—I never did it and I'm never going to do it." Kidjo believes that sexism is still rampant in the industry:

It still exists, and sometimes it depends on the girls. Some girls are ready to do anything for fame, but I'm not ready to do anything for fame.

No-one ever told me that when you believe in something you want to do you have to sacrifice your body.

And she says she prefers hard work.

You have to give a lot of yourself into it, you have to work hard for it, you have to believe in what you're doing, you have to be able to listen to advice on your way and you have to keep thinking about how you can make it happen. But not by giving your sex. (Chisholm 1996, 49)

Oremi *(1998)*

A particularly illustrative case of the complexity of position-takings by artists and labels in the world music is Kidjo's album *Oremi*, released in 1998. This was her fifth album, and her fourth for Island Records. The label, which had recently dissolved its Mango world music imprint, nonetheless retained Kidjo, and marketed her more as a rhythm and blues (R&B) musician. Alexis Aubrey, product manager for Island Records US, said, "She has demonstrated an enormous potential to touch many different people from children to older people. She crosses all cultural boundaries" (Oumano and Pride 1998, 88). Liz Townsend, international marketing manager for Island UK, said, "We'd like to get her out of the world music ghetto," though she recognized that this wouldn't be easy: "You can't just say Angelique Kidjo is now an R&B artist and expect the dealers to move her records out of that section" (88). As part of this shift, the label shifted away from earthy colors (figures 3.4 and 3.5) to a sepia-toned photograph with Kidjo's name in sky-blue letters (figure 3.6). Kidjo writes in her autobiography that she came to understand the impor-

FIGURE 3.4. Angélique Kidjo: *Ayé* (1994), Cover

tance of visual representations of artists from Island Records label founder
Chris Blackwell: "Music is not just the songs. It's also the way you present it
to the public. A great album cover . . . is like a pair of colored spectacles that
illuminates your music" (Kidjo and Wenrick 2014, 88).

Aubrey also said that the label would concentrate mainly on listening
posts in "appropriate retail locations," and they were trying to push the album
in alternative press in New York, Los Angeles, Chicago, and other key world
music markets in an attempt to cultivate an audience beyond the usual consumer of world music (Oumano and Pride 1998, 88).

The genre-resituating effort worked up to a point. Borders' buyer for
international music bought into Island's marketing plan (using language
celebrating the album's hybridity), saying, "'Oremi' is a cutting-edge fusion
of African, pop, and R&B influences. It's urban music for any city. Borders
will feature 'Oremi' in a front-line listening post, like any major pop release"
(Oumano and Pride 1998, 89). Kidjo appeared at Lilith Fair, the concert tour

FIGURE 3.5. Angélique Kidjo: *Fifa* (1996), Cover

and traveling musical festival that featured women artists, and her album's title track was placed on a Lilith Fair CD entitled *The Lilith Developing Artist Sampler*, created by the tour organizers. According to Aubrey, 2,500 CDs were given away at each Lilith Fair concert (Oumano and Pride 1998, 89). Radio also was part of this campaign. Aubrey said that they wanted to introduce Kidjo to radio listeners on the "hot AC" (Adult Contemporary) and "AC" formats (89). A 12-inch single of the track "Voodoo Child" remixes was released for clubs.

Later Recordings

After her contract with Island expired, Kidjo signed with the jazz department at Columbia Records in 2001, where Columbia Jazz and Legacy Recordings senior vice president Jeff Jones had recently taken over. Jones said that his mandate was to have a diverse group of musicians from traditional and con-

FIGURE 3.6. Angélique Kidjo: *Oremi* (1998), Cover

temporary jazz, world music, blues, and more, and that Kidjo certainly fit (Pesselnick 2002, 86).

Like many popular musicians seeking to find a broader audience, Kidjo collaborated with a producer known for his innovative employment of digital technologies and nonmainstream sounds, Bill Laswell, who is credited as having provided "Reproduction and Mix Translation" for her 2002 recording, *Black Ivory Soul*. Borders' and Tower Records' buyers both remarked on Kidjo's appeal beyond the usual "world music" niche (Pesselnick 2002, 86). At WDET in Detroit, Kidjo had long been popular because she couldn't be confined to the world music category, and the station's music director predicted success for the album. But *Black Ivory Soul* still contained songs not in English. Kidjo said:

> The public has proved to me all these years that it isn't a matter of language— it's what they feel. I think that I achieved that goal and can bring them to

realize that, "Hey, we have one life." After what happened Sept. 11, if a human being does not believe that, then he is in danger. We have to learn to live with each other. We have to learn to heal. (Pesselnick 2002, 86)

Subsequently, Kidjo issued an album, *Djin Djin* (2007), that contains duets, some with well-known Western singers, among them Alicia Keys, Peter Gabriel, and Carlos Santana. This was perhaps her most ambitious recording to date, following the duet albums of famous popular musicians such as Tony Bennett, Johnny Mathis, and many others. This recording, unlike several of the earlier ones, was released not on Columbia but on Razor & Tie, an independent label based in New York City that is distributed by Sony (I have found no explanation anywhere for this shift in labels). Songs were sung in English and French as well as her native languages. *Djin Djin* was coreleased by Starbucks and was sold in Starbucks stores, and it won the Grammy Award for Best Contemporary World Music Album in 2008.

Kidjo's *Õÿö* (2010) musically makes the case for what she had argued from the beginning of her career—that she grew up listening to music from all over, not just Africa, but also the United States and Europe. There are songs originally sung by Miriam Makeba, a hero on whom Kidjo modeled herself, and classic soul songs made famous by James Brown, Curtis Mayfield, and Aretha Franklin, as well as versions of Bollywood songs that were popular when she was growing up. Famous Western stars such as Dianne Reeves and Bono joined her for some tracks. Reviews were mostly excellent, though there were still the predictable gripes about her work with Western musicians and praise for what are viewed as the more "authentic" songs, e.g., "Many of the sets' highlights are entirely African and uncluttered by Western pop stars" (Jenkins 2010, WE06).

Kidjo's most recent recording as of this writing, *Eve* (2013), is perhaps even more eclectic, gesturing this time in more "classical" directions, featuring collaborations with Rostam Batmanglij of the indie rock band Vampire Weekend, a female vocal trio from Benin called Trio Tériba, the legendary singer-songwriter, pianist, and guitarist Dr. John, the Kronos Quartet, and the Orchestre Philharmonique du Luxembourg.

This sketch of Kidjo's career shows that it is, as I have said, only somewhat different from a Western popular musician's over time. Apart from language choice, the position-takings that Kidjo has chosen in her career are not unusual: many a Western popular musician has had to do the same thing. Most Western popular stars find themselves having to reinvent themselves in order to continue to find an audience; in this way they are both reactive and creative. In this respect, world music musicians are much the same. The only real difference is that they face greater xenophobia, if not racism, as well as the barriers of a largely monolingual audience, at least in the United States. But all musicians in whatever field today face an ever more uncertain landscape in which the chances of a contract with a record label are diminishing, opportunities for radio airplay are shrinking (at least in the States), and their income in general is declining.[13]

Ownership

The history of world music, and the history of music more generally with the establishment of copyright in the late eighteenth century, has been a history of someone attempting to profit legally from someone else's music. Increasing access to, and knowledge of, musics of the world and easy ways of capturing them digitally have resulted in frequent appropriations of musics of all kinds, including world music. Probably the most notorious early case is that of the song "The Lion Sleeps Tonight," also known as "Wimba Way" or "Wimoweh," but originally entitled "Mbube" ("Lion") by its author, the South African Solomon Linda, in 1939 (example 3.1). Many groups recorded versions in the 1950s, including some well-known musicians such as the Weavers (example 3.2) and the Kingston Trio (example 3.3); the version by the doo-wop group the Tokens was a number 1 hit in 1961 (example 3.4), and Disney used the song in *The Lion King* (example 3.5). But there were copyright issues almost from the beginning. Solomon Linda was paid 10 shillings (under $1 today) by Gallo Records when he signed over the copyright to that company in 1952.

After living in poverty, Linda died in 1962, and his heirs have struggled as well. An article by the South African writer Rian Malan published in 2000 in *Rolling Stone* documented the success of the song and the paltry sums paid to the Linda estate over the years (Malan 2000). The Linda family sued in 2004, asking $1.5 million in damages. But, since Linda had signed away the rights in 1952, and his widow had done the same in 1982, it was a difficult case. The family claimed that a lawyer had deceived them. Disney, always averse to negative publicity, argued that it had paid the copyright holder without knowing anything more about the history of the song, but nonetheless agreed to pay the family royalties from 1987 to the present (LaFraniere 2006, A6).

This is a tragic but all too common story of exploitation in the music industry by the rich of the poor, white of black, and it has been no less common in the realm of "world music," especially since the rise of digital technologies that have made sampling existing recordings simple and commonplace. Perhaps the most famous example of a sample of "world music" that was exploitative of the original makers was the German band Enigma's use of a folk song by Taiwanese singers of the Amis ethnic group (example 3.6). Enigma's driving force, the Romanian-German Michael Cretu, searched hundreds of recordings of folk and traditional music to sample, and found "Jubilant Drinking Song" on an album called *Polyphonies vocales des aborigènes de Taï-wan*. Cretu legally licensed the song from the French Maison des Cultures du Monde, which owned the copyright to the recording. The resulting song, "Return to Innocence," rose to number 2 on the charts in Europe, number 3 in the United Kingdom, and number 4 in the United States in 1993 (example 3.7). The album that the song was on, *The Cross of Changes*, rose to number 2 in Europe, number 1 in the United Kingdom, and number 9 in the United States.

Two years later, the original singer of the song, Kuo Ying-nan, a seventy-six-year-old betel nut farmer, heard the song on the radio for the first time. Then the song was used as an official song of the 1996 Olympics. The international popularity of the song as measured by sales and its exposure through the Olympics prompted a record label in Taipei, Magic Stone Music, to sue EMI (the parent company of Enigma's label, Virgin). Press reports on compensation to the original musicians are neither clear nor consistent, but it seems that Enigma sent a check to the academic who had made the original recordings in 1978, or perhaps to Kuo himself, or that money was paid by the French Maison des Cultures du Monde, which then paid the Chinese Folk Arts Foundation, which had originally brought the Amis singers from Taiwan to Europe. The lawsuit seemed to stall for a time as Kuo's legal representation changed. Finally, there was an out-of-court settlement in 1999, stipulating that Kuo and his wife, Kuo Shin-chu, another singer on the recording, would receive credit on all future releases of "Return to Innocence" and would receive a platinum copy of the *Cross of Changes* album. And the Kuos would be able to establish a foundation to preserve Amis culture.[14]

While such stories of exploitation have a long history, it is only in the neo-liberal era that cultural industries, including the music industry, have assiduously sought to capitalize on the ownership of copyrights (Frith 1988). The industry is increasingly organized less around the production of "content" than around the creation and protection of copyrighted entities. Just as agri-business seeks to own and copyright/patent local knowledges, as mentioned in chapter 2 (see Harvey 2005), the cultural industries seek to own and maximize the profit of their copyrighted holdings. And as music industry worker Alan Elliott (2013) told me, the biggest growth area in the music industry today is the legal department. Individual musicians' discourses about music as a natural resource, examined earlier, continue in the practices of the music industry.

Questions of ownership and exploitation have been, in part, the impetus behind the growth of protective measures. The Bolivian government in 1968 passed a Supreme Decree that gave its national folklore a "sole copyright approach," in which "ownership and control of certain works became vested in the state" (quoted by Albro 2010, 151). After the 1972 UNESCO Convention concerning the Protection of the World Cultural and Natural Heritage, and Simon and Garfunkel (and others') appropriation of the song "El Condor Pasa" in the early 1970s, the Bolivian government in 1973 asked for an additional protocol to the Universal Copyright Convention to protect popular and national culture of all countries. This request, and actions in other countries such as Japan and South Korea, spurred UNESCO to begin the process of finding a way to protect national cultural heritage (Albro 2010, 151), and it passed several declarations early in the twenty-first century on intangible cultural heritage, including the invention of a new designation of "masterpieces of the intangible heritage of humanity," meant to protect local and traditional forms of knowledge and practice. UNESCO believes that "traditional knowledge and practices lie at the heart of a community's culture and identity but are under serious threat from globalization" (UNESCO n.d.a).[15]

Since the first of these designations, many music, dance, and quasi-musical practices (various forms of chanting) have been named masterpieces of the intangible heritage of humanity, such as the tango of Argentina and Uruguay, the Chinese guqin musical instrument, music of the Aka people of Central Africa, and much more.[16] The naming of a particular genre or practice or instrument as a masterpiece of the intangible heritage of humanity can have the effect of creating or augmenting tourism, or raising the value of musical instruments. For example, the ethnomusicologist Helen Rees (2010) told me that since the guqin was named a masterpiece of the intangible heritage of humanity in 2003, its role in China has changed dramatically. She found it difficult to find a way to learn the instrument when she first went to China in 1987, but now it is easy to find a studio where one can do so. The instrument that Rees paid about $60 for in the 1980s is now worth $30,000–50,000.

UNESCO, and the concept and use of the idea of the masterpiece of the intangible heritage of humanity, might protect local and ancient cultural forms and practices from being appropriated, but, at the same time, it can have the effect of consecrating those very cultural forms and practices, creating a market for them or a touristic culture around them that significantly alters those forms and practices that were intended to be protected. Globalized neoliberal capitalism makes it difficult to isolate local forms and practices from its reach: they become commodified, commercial objects, or, in the case of music, sounds available to be sampled; or, if they are protected, they can become a kind of sanctified commodity with the imprimatur of UNESCO.

The globalization of music under neoliberal capitalism has increasingly meant the acquisition of copyrightable materials and their protection, materials that are sold or licensed to larger and larger audiences around the world. For today's music industry, it has become less important to find good new music to record, market, and distribute than to exploit to the fullest the copyrights that it owns.

4

Digitalization

E. M. Forster's 1909 story "The Machine Stops" tells of Vashti, a woman who lives in a room with the world at her fingertips thanks to The Machine, a device that makes available at a button's push music, communication with friends, food—almost anything one might want. This room "is lighted neither by window nor by lamp, yet it is filled with a soft radiance. There are no apertures for ventilation, yet the air is fresh. There are no musical instruments, and yet, at the moment that my meditation opens, this room is throbbing with melodious sounds" (Forster 1909, 1).

Vashti has a son, Kuno, who has politically radical tendencies. Desiring to live outside the influence of The Machine, on the earth's surface instead of underground where his mother and most people live in their little cells, he tells his shocked mother:

> [The Machine] has robbed us of the sense of space and the sense of touch, it has blurred every human relation and narrowed down love to a carnal act, and it has paralysed our bodies and our wills, and now it compels us to worship it. The Machine develops—but not on our lines. The Machine proceeds—but not to our goal (17).

At one point, Kuno, who has become estranged from his mother, contacts her to tell her, "The Machine stops." This remark is taken to be absurd by Vashti, though she and a friend compare notes on problems that The Machine had lately had in conveying music. Vashti relates to her friend that she had complained to the Committee of the Mending Apparatus of "those curious gasping sighs that disfigured the symphonies of the Brisbane school. They sound like some one in pain" (23). Music becomes the signal defect heralding the end of The Machine. Vashti hounds the Committee to repair the music, but to no avail. The humans soon accustom themselves to the changes in The Machine, which had become the object of religious worship earlier in the story. "The sigh at the crises of the Brisbane symphony no long irritated Vashti; she accepted it as part of the melody" (24), like the scratches and pops on an often-played LP.

The sound emitted by The Machine, which everyone had heard since birth, goes unnoticed until it stops at the story's end, introducing a silence so terrifying that many hope to die.

In some ways, this story is a clear plea for readers to reduce their dependency on technologies and return to an engagement with each other and nature, written in a moment witnessing the rise of the automobile, electricity, telephone, radio, airplane, and other technologies heralding the modern world. Yet it holds other lessons. It could be considered prescient in its treatment of people's replacement of face-to-face encounters with telephonic ones. When Vashti visits Kuno—only acquiescing to do so at his insistence, and his refusal to speak to her again through mediating technologies—Forster writes that this is the first time she has left her cell in years, and she encounters the first person she had seen in months on her voyage.

Forster, to my mind, also skewers the rise of commercial culture and in particular the then-young advertising industry in his treatment of his subject's lives. Forever in search of "ideas," everyone in Forster's story attends lectures or delivers them; Vashti delivers a ten-minute lecture on Australian music early in the story. Yet this portrayal of "ideas" shows them to be vacuous and meaningless, an inflated use of language once employed to describe what a creative idea might actually be, or, might actually have been. "Idea" is a fetishized word and concept in the cultural industries today, along with "creativity" (see Taylor 2012b).

And then, of course, there are the push-buttons, which for decades have been used to tout new technologies, bringing whatever one might want instantaneously, saving both time and effort. Spotify, the music streaming service, is attempting to develop technology that will shave milliseconds from the time between when one pushes the (virtual) "play" button and when the track begins, so users have the sense that the music is on their computer and not being streamed from a server (Rose 2011).

Such critiques (or praises) of technology, new or old, are reasonably familiar to most of us and frequently go hand-in-hand with critiques of the decline of society, or appreciations of the advances it brings. I am old enough to remember when some scholars and others were lamenting the decline of literacy, claiming that we were entering a postliterate age. Then along came the Internet, and more and more people began using e-mail, then, a little later, cellular phones and text messages, written in quite creative shorthands in many languages. We could say that we have entered an era not in which literacy has declined but in which vital and, yes, creative new forms of literacy have emerged.

At the same time, however, it is important to avoid technological determinism, the idea that technology has agency and determines its own usages, and what I would call technological triumphalism, the notion that technology can solve any problem, that technology has changed everything. People are still literate, after all, just literate in new ways. Thus, the problem of studying technology is approaching it with one's historicizing faculties in full swing: Just what is new, and what isn't? All technologies—all—do not create new social relationships, new forms of behavior, or at least not immediately. Instead, they help us do what we have been doing, and only slowly do we find uses for them that could be considered to be new and offering change.

This chapter considers new digital technologies and music, especially how these new technologies have played a powerful role not just in facilitating neoliberal policies and ideologies but in promulgating those policies and ideologies, bringing them into everyday life and the workplace, including places of work that had once been relatively insulated—even isolated—from the workings of the market, such as education or some forms of cultural production. Digital technologies are also an important way that workers, particularly those in offices, have been coerced into laboring harder and harder, though not, in most cases, for greater compensation (see Marvit 2014). Digital technologies are potent new productive powers in neoliberal capitalism as tools but also as Trojan horses that frequently induce users to work longer and harder, as I will discuss below, and displace much clerical work upward to those workers who didn't used to have to do much of it (see Taylor 2012a). It is clear from Marx's writings that new productive powers play an important role in shaping the sort of work that gets done, the nature of the relationship of the worker to her work, the relationship of the worker to those who own the means of production, and social relations in general. In a famous passage, Marx wrote:

> Social relations are closely bound up with productive forces. In acquiring new productive forces men change their mode of production; and in changing their mode of production, in changing the way of earning their living, they change all their social relations. The hand-mill gives you society with the feudal lord; the steam-mill, society with the industrial capitalist. (1977, 103)

And the personal computer gives you society with the neoliberal capitalist. Marx continues:

The same men who establish their social relations in conformity with their material productivity, produce also principles, ideas and categories, in conformity with their social relations.

Thus these ideas, these categories, are as little eternal as the relations they express. They are *historical and transitory products*.

There is a continual movement of growth in productive forces, of destruction in social relations, of formation in ideas; the only immutable thing is the abstraction of movement—*mors immortalis* [immortal death]. (1977, 103; emphases in original)

Noteworthy here is Marx's point on the "continual growth" of productive forces, to which one could add speed of growth as well.

New Sound Technologies: DIY Everything?

There is no need to rehearse the rise and adoption of digital music technologies in the 1980s and after (for that, see Lysloff and Gay 2003; Porcello and Greene 2004; Taylor 2001; and Théberge 1997, among others). Rather, I am interested in historicizing this rise and adoption, showing how these new technologies were products of, and helped produce, neoliberal capitalism.

Much has been written about new digital technologies affording users greater degrees of agency than in the past. One can now make music with a laptop or even a tablet computer or smartphone. The rise of affordable digital technologies has made it possible to make and record one's own music cheaply, and to distribute it online at little or no cost. And one can take preexisting music and manipulate it, extracting samples, adding beats. The possibilities of making music digitally are as ubiquitous as the possibilities of hearing it.

I have discussed the rise of sampling elsewhere (Taylor 2013 and n.d.c), which I believe can be seen as a cultural effect of the growing hegemony of finance capital in the late nineteenth and early twentieth centuries as theorized by theorized by Rudolf Hilferding, discussed in chapter 1 (1981; see also Jameson 1997). Exchange value began to become more important than use value, and one result in terms of cultural production was that composers and other artists began to conceptualize previously excluded sounds as appropriable. That long phase of finance capital, as argued by Giovanni Arrighi (2010), lasted into the rise of the neoliberal moment, when financialization grew enormously, from about 15 percent of all profits in the United States in 1970 to 40 percent by 2005 (Harvey 2010, 51). The growth of financialization, taking root in new metropolitan cultures in which social relationships were increasingly rationalistic and calculating (Simmel 1971), later shaped new conceptions of previously recorded music as sampleable. A new form of abstract, atomized listening emerged as people whose business it was to sample music began to learn how to listen to other music not as other music but as potential material for their own work that employed samples.

Let me examine a scene from the 1990s, when these technologies were becoming affordable and thus widely distributed. It is useful to examine any new technology at such an early juncture for cultural reception of new technologies is clearer at such moments, clearer than when they are later normalized, their effects more difficult to discern. The music is "jungle," (which later became known as drum and bass), an electronic music scene in London in the early to mid-1990s associated mainly with people of color.[1] The first big star of this music, a half-English, half-Jamaican man who went by the name General Levy, described the kind of multicultural mix that led to jungle, a description in which the kinds of affordable technologies are an integral part:

> I was surprised when I went to my first jungle raves—black, white, Indian, and Chinese were all together. It was rare to see so many cultures mixed—and it was a sexy vibe, because the girls all wear sexy clothes, Yard style, the short, skintight ensembles worn by women in Jamaican dancehalls. It was freaky to see the ragga, techno, and hip-hop people all flexing, dancing. That's the genius of jungle. It's a rebel music, made by inner-city, not suburban, people. It's like a cry. The kids who make jungle don't have any luxuries in their life, just a Casio keyboard and a drum machine in their bedroom. If you're suppressed in society, jungle music makes you feel like a warrior. (Goldman 1994, 20)

Jungle music sampled mainly from reggae music, signifying to the ethnic background of many of the people in the scene, as well as films and television shows known to them.

Jungle musicians, whether out of necessity or aesthetics, tended to avoid expensive, hard-to-find technology. So vinyl was in; CDs were not; analog was in, digital out. And much of the point of jungle artistry was the remix; the "original" was often forgotten as it was continually remixed. And junglists produced dubplates—acetates made by DJ's of DATs (digital audio tapes) given them by hopeful jungle musicians. DJs made their reputations and popularity based on exclusive tunes, often spending up to £200 per week on making these acetates.

Junglists ensured that anyone who wanted to make jungle music could make jungle music. And they did. The *Wall Street Journal* wrote in 1990 that sales of electronic keyboards and music software were way up: manufacturers shipped over a hundred thousand electronic keyboards to retailers in 1989, more than double the amount five years previously; music software sales for 1989 were also up 10 percent from the previous year (Tomsho 1990).

This DIY position (about which much has been written; see Luvaas 2012 among many others) was commented upon by people in this and other scenes employing new technologies. Dego, a jungle pioneer, spoke of the kind of production and distribution that hark back to the old days of some African American musicians that Attali puts forward as the precursors to an era of "composition." The interviewer asked him about inspiration of the original techno scene in Detroit.

> It is inspiration. . . . I like the way they went about everything, doin' it themselves. There's a lot of things I can draw the same lines how we started up . . . delivering records around ourselves and all that shit. We didn't have a distribution deal first . . . and that's the same that happened with all them guys out there . . . what they used to do, and how they fought the majors' [record labels] attitudes and all that shit. Innovative . . . a lot of the things they did they done it first. That's why I hold a lot of respect for them (Dego 1994).

Jungle, like many other scenes, was about doing it yourself with equipment you could afford, sampling things that mattered to you and others in your scene, and, though it is not a concern here, speed—the tempos were very fast, and frequently advertised on albums in terms of "beats per minute," or BPM.

Jungle is an early example of how processes of composition or songwriting weren't just the province of those thought to be gifted or with access to expensive gear but could begin to be available to everyone with access to digital technologies. The advent of such technologies has also made it possible for musicians to record themselves at home and distribute their music online. Much has been made of these developments, with many authors assuming that musicians would no longer need record labels. Have all these new technologies made the lives of musicians with dreams of making a living easier? On the one hand, there is the cultural industries' search for the next blockbuster, making it harder for bands to secure a contract with a major label and be played on the radio; on the other, cheap, high-quality technologies of sound recording have made it easier for people to record their own music, which they can distribute online and promote using the seemingly ever-expanding world of social media. So, while the cultural industries are producing less, there is nonetheless more and more available, making it more difficult for musicians to compete. Musicians must work hard to get their work known, and most don't take the time to do it. As one industry veteran observed:

> Musicians are so used to hating major record labels, and it's easy for them to think, "Screw the major labels; I'm going to do the independent thing." But truthfully speaking, most musicians don't really hunker down and do the hard work and the heavy lifting, so they stay right where they are. They might build a page on MySpace, but they'll be one of millions.[2] They'll probably put their money into recording a CD, have it pressed, and make it available for sale online—all of which are good ideas. But then they stop right there, so that in the end, all those independent-music revolutionaries don't end up any better off than before their CD was produced. They are somewhat invisible today, and most of them will be relatively invisible tomorrow. (Levine 2007b, 76)

This "hard work and heavy lifting" is real, and grueling: a story about a musician who markets himself mainly online says that he spends up to six hours per day in e-mail contact with his fans, writing in his blog, viewing fans' videos of his music, and more (Thompson 2007, 42–47).

For musicians who need or want to record in a professional studio, several means have emerged to help them finance the production of their recordings. Perhaps the most well known is Kickstarter, which began in 2009. This is a for-profit company that can be utilized by musicians, filmmakers, and others to solicit funding to get their projects off the ground. Through word of mouth, social media, and other means, contributors are sought. They are not investors in the capitalist sense; they may not receive anything in return for their donation—it is simply a donation. According to one of the cofounders, Perry Chen, "It's not an investment, lending or a charity. It's something else in the middle: a sustainable marketplace where people exchange goods for services or some other benefit and receive some value" (Wortham 2009, B1). If a project is successfully funded, which means that the project has reached the amount desired by its author, Kickstarter charges a 5 percent fee (www.kickstarter.com).

There are problems with this system. Some people promise more rewards than they can deliver, or fulfilling promised obligations can be more time-consuming than imagined by the artist. One musician, for example, in attempting to fund his album, promised personalized songs for pledges of $50 and above and, since he made double his $3,000 Kickstarter goal, has had to write thirty songs for contributors (Gamerman 2013).

Another case points out the more complex issues arising with Kickstarter. Amanda Palmer, former Dresden Dolls singer, famously raised $1 million on Kickstarter in 2012, the most ever raised for a recording at that point.[3] Palmer said:

> This isn't a shtick or a gimmick—the idea of releasing a record on a major label again for me is absurd. The music industry has long needed a new system and crowd-funding is it. The game is reversing—the media and the ma-

chine are following, rather than creating, the content ("Amanda Palmer Raises $1 Million" 2012).

Palmer raised the funds by taking orders for future work and selling events such as backstage doughnut-eating sessions and house parties ("Amanda Palmer on Raising $1,000,000 on Kickstarter" 2012). But her success was not a fluke; the *New York Times* reported that experienced publicists and managers backed Palmer, and that every step of her fund-raising campaign was planned, with new songs, videos, photos, and behind-the-scenes blog posts strategically released (Sisario 2012, C1). In effect, the cost of production and publicity and marketing was not covered by a label but outsourced to fans.

Most of the funds were spent on producing and manufacturing the recording and funding tours; Palmer (2012a) provided a summary on her blog of how the money was spent; no mention was made of all of the supporting musicians. She recruited "professional-ish" musicians to play with her at her tour dates and who were promised to be paid thus: "We will feed you beer, hug/high-five you up and down (pick your poison), give you merch, and thank you mightily for adding to the big noise we are planning to make" (2012b). Musicians complained on her website, and she was denounced by musicians' unions; Raymond M. Hair Jr., president of the American Federation of Musicians, told the *New York Times*, "If there's a need for the musician to be on the stage, then there ought to be compensation for it. Playing is work and there's a value associated with it, and that value ought to be respected" (Wakin 2012b). Palmer defended herself by noting that the musicians had in fact volunteered and were enthusiastic to be onstage, but a few months later she decided to pay the musicians after the backlash from other musicians, the unions, and some fans (Rys 2012; Wakin 2012c).

After Palmer's success and controversy, Kickstarter has come to be regarded by musicians with some skepticism and ambivalence. Is it a way to appear not to be a sellout while actually selling out? ("Kurt Cobain wouldn't have been hawking his Kickstarter campaign," grumbled Greg School, the executive director of Jazz at Lincoln Center [Sisario 2012, C1]). And will those who are successful, such as Palmer, simply adopt the niggardly attitudes of traditional record label executives in their treatment of musicians they employ? There now seems to be some wariness about the entire enterprise (see Trump 2013).

Journalist Rob Trump invokes anthropologist David Graeber's work on debt (Graeber 2011) to discuss Kickstarter in terms of gift exchange practices of the Tiv of West Africa, in which reciprocation is always with a gift of slightly greater or lesser value, thereby keeping the exchange process in motion (2013, 47). But it seems to me that this analogy doesn't work; the major difference between commodities and gifts is that commodities are produced by people unknown to the consumers, a crucial point in Marxian thought. Gift exchange is usually between people who know each other. For local musicians with no fan base other than their friends, this is true enough, but there are plenty of stories of Kickstarter projects failing because the artist's goal wasn't met. With better-known artists such as Palmer, most of the donations come from strangers.

Nevertheless, are we in fact witnessing a new form of exchange with crowdsourcing? It is still a capitalist transaction, even though use value and exchange value are difficult to locate in Kickstarter transactions (and understanding use value for cultural commodities is always a complicated question).[4] Exchange value in this case is also complex, however, for it is not at all clear what users receive for their contributions; there may be a recording (or painting or whatever) if the project is successfully funded and if the artist actually produces what he or she promised. And there are the gifts promised by the artists to reward contributors, reminiscent of what one gets from making a pledge to public radio or television. This does not mean that we are in the realm of gift exchange, however (Mauss 1990; see Graeber 2001 and Myers 2001). Kickstarter seems to me to be a complex process of exchange in which people pledge, then pay money. They are supporting who and what they want in exchange for some sort of gift down the line, plus the satisfaction that they derive from possessing the insider knowledge of something they believe to be cool or important, and the sense that they were there at the beginning before most others. This is no small matter in an era when coolness and hipness matter as much as they do, and when they are thought to wane when whatever they are attached to has become too well known.

No matter how a recording is funded or distributed, there is always the problem of creating a fan base of people willing to purchase the recording. The function of major labels has become, as Scott Lash and John Urry (1994) argued about the culture industry more generally, more and more that of marketers: they produce less and hope to continue to make profits by selling more, and selling more means spending more on advertising. One commentator describes current marketing techniques by noting that the big "corporate acts"—Justin Timberlake, Fergie, Beyoncé—"are still creatures of mass marketing, carpet-bombed into popularity by expensive ad campaigns and radio airplay" (Thompson 2007, 46). Musicians, especially those starting out, need a platform to make their music known. Spotify and other streaming services can help, but since they don't pay well, most musicians still need to find support somewhere so they can build an audience and name recognition.

David Byrne (2013) admits, "I can't deny that label-support gave me a leg up," though, he says, not every successful musician needs it.

Without the backing of a label, musicians can upload their files to sell on iTunes. But the wave of the future seems to be streaming services such as Spotify, Rdio, and Google Play. Users, for a modest monthly fee, can gain access to huge libraries of music licensed from various record labels. But there is a good deal of dissatisfaction among musicians with these services, for they pay very little. According to one musician, it takes 47,680 plays on Spotify to equal the profit of the sale of one LP (Kurkowski 2012). Some prominent musicians such as Thom Yorke from Radiohead and David Byrne have removed their work from Spotify because it pays so poorly ("Paying the Piper" 2013).[5] David Byrne (2013) puts the financials this way: for a band consisting of four people that earns a 15 percent royalty from Spotify, it would require 236,549,020 plays for each band member to earn $15,080 a year. With figures such as these, Byrne says, musicians would be out of work in a year if they relied mainly on such services as their primary income (see also Timberg 2014).

Sean Bohrman of Burger Records in Southern California (about which more in chapter 5) told me in 2012 that he spends a good deal of time each day on social media promoting his label's artists and releases. Even though he and his partner, Lee Rickard, seem to have an ambivalent attitude toward technology, they understand how much new technologies, especially those that host social media, help their business. Rickard (2012) told me, "I'm very grateful for the new media, and the instant gratification. . . . I mean our business wouldn't be what it is if it wasn't for the hype of Facebook or whatever it is—I don't know what it is, I'm not on there." Bohrman told me:

> We do all the media stuff, that's how you stay in the game now. That's why all these huge things are failing, because they have no connection to their audience, and when they use Facebook or something, it's so robotic, and it's not personal or anything. . . . I'm good at being personal when I write, like a conversation. And I'm pretty good at hyping people and getting them excited about things, grabbing them through the Internet. We've done it well, and it's grown and grown. We're learning how to manipulate things like Twitter. This year we had 1,500 people when we started, at the beginning of the year, but Kanye West tweeted 80 times, and we thought we can do better than that, so we tweeted more than 80 times in one day. And we just kept going—every single weird thing that somebody says we tweeted, and people would retweet it, and their followers see that, and now we have 4,000 followers, we've got 3,000 followers this year just by tweeting every stupid thing we think of. Manipulating social media is the way of the future if you're going to be successful, not just in this, but in anything.

Two years after that interview, Bohrman (2014b) told me that they had over 28,000 followers on Twitter; he also uses Facebook, Instagram, and Tumblr. He also uploads some tracks to SoundCloud (a website that allows users to upload music and other audio tracks); he told me, "Blogs pay attention to what we put up [on SoundCloud]. So, the Internet is how you get your music out there and heard." For Bohrman (2012), the main issue is simply

> getting out there, being personal with your fans, and talking to them, and e-mailing you back, and they know I'm the one talking to them, because I'm the only one who does the Internet. When you make a connection with a fan, it's different. I don't think that's what the big labels can do anymore, and that's why we're succeeding. And people are paying attention, and they're telling their friends, "Hey, there's this awesome label, I know them, they're awesome, they're people that I know and can relate to."

Bohrman (2014b) told me that they can reach over 150,000 people through social media and e-mail. In an earlier interview (2012), he said:

> Within 10 minutes I can get a song out to thousands and thousands of people, which is not something we paid for, it's something we earned, and worked hard to do. We started out with nothing. It started from absolutely just this one thing, and now it's this big thing, it's our entire life. It's crazy. (Bohrman 2012)

Bohrman's use of social media was pretty savvy, even at the beginning. He posted at strategic times—lunch, dinner, just before the end of the workday, and late in the evening in California when Europeans were just waking up. Now, he posts even more, "from 8am-9pm every hour, on the hour and at 3am because it's noon in Europe and that's the peak time when people are looking at their social media" (2014b).

Musicians in more marginal genres in terms of sales must also increasingly rely on their own ingenuity and use of social media to promote themselves. A good example from the field of classical music is the Ukrainian-born pianist Valentina Lisitsa (b. 1973) who, after her career went into the doldrums, began posting videos on YouTube in 2007 in order to attempt to cultivate an audience.[6] She had come to realize that "music is a luxury product, and if you see a Mont Blanc pen or Rolex watch in Wal-Mart, people will just pass by. It has to come with a certain package, and you have to have your own audience." (Schweitzer 2013, AR11). After she uploaded videos of herself, Lisitsa's You-Tube audience grew to sixty-two million. Niall O'Rourke, the creative director at Decca Records in London, which signed Lisitsa, said of her strategy that it was more like a pop music approach, and he decided to attempt to tap into her fan base once they saw how many followers she had on YouTube (AR11).

But cases such as this are rare. Most musicians today need to tour and sell merchandise ("merch") or permit their music to be licensed for broadcasting and film if they are going to attempt to make a living at music. And clearly, there is money to be made through touring for most musicians today ("Music's Top 40 Money Makers 2012" 2012). There is also a good deal to be made through sales of merchandise, since, as *Billboard* magazine pointed out, one can't download a T-shirt; according to Dell Furano, CEO of Live Nation Merchandise, "Your concert shirt is your badge and tells everyone a great deal about who you are" (2009, 16). This is part of what has become known as a 360-degree deal in which musicians sign not with a record label but with a touring company such as Live Nation, as Madonna famously did in 2007 ("Madonna Signs Deal with Live Nation" 2007). She said in a statement, "The paradigm in the music business has shifted, and as an artist and a business-woman, I have to move with that shift" (Gallo 2007, 4). Such deals include all an artist's music-making activities—recordings, tours, merchandise, film, and more—and can be the basis for branding a musician or band. Many more artists have signed with Live Nation since Madonna.

But such deals aren't always advantageous to musicians. Dean Spunt (2012), a member of the band No Age and the proprietor of the independent label Post Present Medium, told me:

> When No Age was getting popular, there were labels that really wanted to sign us—I can count ten labels, indie labels and big nonindie labels, major labels, all wanted to sign us and offer us different things. Some of it was very outlandish. Anyway, the big one was the 360 deal, where they would give us a really big advance, but they wanted to control rights to our merchandise, and take money from touring. Play a show, they take part of the money. These 360 deals really try to destroy the livelihood of the artist. I mean, nowadays, you're not making money on record sales, right? It's really hard for an artist to survive on record sales alone. So you're making money touring, and selling objects to fans, right. So if the label gets to take that money, there's a real big problem.

There is also a new and growing class of musicians today who cannot make a living through album sales or (paid) song downloads and for whom touring is a dreary business, and who thus write songs mainly to be placed in commercials. Guides circulate on the Internet offering advice about getting noticed by a music supervisor, such as one entitled "5 Things Music Supervisors Are Looking for in You and Your Music" (Collum 2010). One such musician is Tim Myers, whose song "I Just Want to Thank You" was used in a tribute to mothers for Mother's Day 2013 (example 4.1).[7] Myers has signed with Zync Music Group, a new kind of firm that specializes in placing songs in advertising, film, television, trailers, and video games and promises personal promotion with music supervisors. Myers speaks knowledgeably in interviews about how securing such placements works, demonstrating that film, television, and advertising music no longer follow the trends but attempt to make them. Myers says that bands seeking placements need to know current trends, but also the past, so that they can "grab classic elements" (Laskow 2013).

Songwriters who don't perform publicly are also composing music mainly to be licensed. Perhaps most famous for this is Cathy Heller, who was featured in *Billboard* magazine in an article entitled "Writing Your Own Check" (Gallo 2013). Heller, at least at the time of that article, self-published her own music and employed no manager, agent, or publicist. She made over $100,000 licensing her songs, some for as little as $1,500. Heller's music is generally upbeat and frothy, just the sort of thing that appeals to people in the cultural industries, who are reported as characterizing her music as "accessible" (Bain 2013). Heller appears to be quite strategic, researching particular music supervisors in order to discover things about them, and then writing them personal rather than boilerplate e-mails pitching her music.[8]

Remixing, Co-Creating

New digital technologies have made it possible not only to create one's own music and distribute it but to alter existing music through remixing, that is, manipulating preexisting recordings (this could be done before using analog technologies, as with Jamaican dub). The growth of remixing and remix culture has been explosive with the rise of digital technologies and formats such as the MP3. Remixing software and websites in the late 1990s and early 2000s were full of sales pitches to potential users, telling them that "anyone [can] create, exchange, share and distribute music regardless of experience or ability" (see Taylor 2001, 21). Today's sales pitches are less breathless, but such remix software still exists, making it possible for users—any user—to take an existing recording and do with it what they want.

Later came the "mashup," the simultaneous juxtaposition of recordings thought to be unrelated. Putting them together showed the musical creativity and humor or irony of the masher-upper. This process has a long history since it was technologically possible before the rise of digital technologies, but with digital technologies, there has been something of a rebirth of the practice. Perhaps the most famous mashup project ever was Danger Mouse's (Brian Joseph Burton's) *The Grey Album* from 2004, combining songs from Jay-Z's *The Black Album* (2003) and the Beatles' *The Beatles*, better known as the "White Album" (1968). Danger Mouse's clever juxtapositions garnered a vast amount of attention, including the approval of Jay-Z, Ringo Starr, and Paul McCartney. Danger Mouse did not license the samples but didn't let that stop him from releasing a few thousand copies himself (he wasn't signed to a record label at the time). Commercial projects such as these, however, seem to be endangered, as record companies increasingly insist that artists pay for everything they sample, no matter how small the sample may be, which means that many artists won't bother (see McLeod and DiCola 2011 for a breakdown of the potential cost of licensing the songs on *The Grey Album*).

What has been widely remarked upon with projects such as this is the possibility for taking a mass-produced commodity and personalizing it; remixing has been celebrated as a creative act. Lawrence Lessig, for example, views remixing as a form of creativity, an expression of the freedom (a common yet powerful trope in neoliberal capitalism, as we saw in chapter 2) to take whatever song one might want and create with it (2008, 56). The products of this creativity, according to Lessig, do not compete with those produced in more conventionally creative ways (composing new music, performing music).

Altering existing commodities, at least commodities other than cultural commodities, has been around for decades; this was one of the main arguments put forward by British cultural studies scholars in the 1970s and 1980s (e.g., Hebdige 1988): youth subcultures defined themselves in part by the commodities they purchased and how they altered them. As is always the case, it is thus necessary to historicize the present. Is remixing, altering recorded music, really new? Does it tell us something about today's world—and today's capitalism—that we might not have known otherwise?

Like so much of neoliberal capitalism, it is largely a matter of speed and scale. People who knew how to manipulate tape, or had the ability to record phonograph records, could make remixes before. (One could have accomplished it with cassette technology at home, too, though with results of dubious technical quality.) I have not found sales figures on remix software, though it does seem to be common and popular. Remixing appears to have entered public consciousness in ways that it hadn't in the past, when it was a kind of novelty or clever commentary on an existing song. DJs who can remix on the fly in their live acts have become immensely popular in certain social groups, commanding hundreds of thousands of dollars for a single appearance, at least in Las Vegas, where nightclubs generate as much revenue as gambling (Eells 2013). Nonetheless, these are worshiped practitioners, as are all extravagantly (over)paid musicians, present and past.

What really seems to have shifted is less the fact of remixing than the idea of it—the idea that existing music can be remade, and that one can do it oneself with a computer and affordable software. Even if one never does it oneself, even if one doesn't listen to it, the destabilization of cultural commodities is significant. This could be considered to be liberating (as Lessig and others view it), at least for consumers. But these new technologies are creating more work for professionals in the cultural industries, as I will discuss.

NEW FORMS OF LABOR?

Many scholars have addressed the question of labor in today's capitalism, called "creative" or "immaterial" by most authors—one's choice of term depends on how one views this labor, whether as something to celebrate or at least isolate from other forms of more mundane labor (e.g., Florida 2002), or as a development somewhat less salutary (e.g., Lazzarato 1996; Hardt and Negri 2000 and 2004). It is again a question of historicizing the present: Just as our globalization is simply that—ours—not wholly new, neither are forms of free labor. What, exactly, is new about them, if anything?

For those authors concerned with creative labor such as Richard Florida, the number of people involved in creative work has increased vastly in the last few decades. This is a cause for their optimism, he believes. The new "creative class" that has emerged—thirty-eight million strong, or more than 30 percent of the workforce of the United States according to Florida in 2002 (Florida 2002, ix)—is a positive development, enjoying greater freedom and being more self-reflexive. The marketplace is increasingly welcoming of new creative work. While Florida—a management professor—is quite boosterish, others are nevertheless similar in their tendency to romanticize and fetishize creative labor, relying too often on uninterrogated nineteenth-century notions of artistic creation and creativity. I will thus not rely on them in this study.

Mainly, I would want to rescue "creativity," which is not simply in the (metaphorical) hands of those who work primarily with their brains. A farmer can be more creative in her labor than a poet with his. Creativity, it seems to me, can be found in all people, not in some professions. Almost any form of labor can be creative, and those who work in professions that are thought to be creative must endure plenty of time when their labor is anything but creative, like the independent filmmaker who must spend more time fund-raising than actually making her film. Or perhaps fund-raising is creative labor, too. What is useful in the studies of creative labor is the fact that laborers are being studied at all; studies that shed light on the making of film or advertisements or television programs are useful in and of themselves.[9]

Other authors have concerned themselves with what they call "immaterial labor."[10] In an influential article, Maurizio Lazzarato defines immaterial labor as "the labor that produces the informational and cultural content of the commodity" (1996, 132). The "informational content" of the commodity is a term that is meant to capture the changes taking place in workers' labor in big companies in the industrial and service sectors, in which labor skills are increasingly those involving computers and other high technologies (132). Lazzarato is specifically referring to large companies in the industrial and tertiary sectors, not all forms of labor that could be called immaterial. The other aspect of the commodity is its "cultural content," produced by immaterial labor that is not usually recognized as work, "the kinds of activities involved in defining and fixing cultural and artistic standards, fashions, tastes, consumer norms, and, more strategically, public opinion" (132). This conception thus encompasses workers in advertising, fashion, software production, audiovisual production, etc. (136), but also all the rest of us as we consume, compare notes about products and brands, surf the Web seeking information on products, services, and more.

Lazzarato's ideas were adopted and expanded (and simplified), by Hardt and Negri in *Empire* (2000) and were critiqued by some (see, e.g., Henwood 2003 and Dyer-Witheford 2005). They re-presented their views on the subject more cautiously in their next work, *Multitude* (Hardt and Negri 2004), emphasizing that the labor involved in all immaterial production remains material, since it employs bodies and brains, as does all labor. What is immaterial, they emphasize, is the product of this labor (109). Nonetheless, such claims fail to show how today's labor is somehow different from labor of the past. Workers communicated with each other in the past, just not with computers. Work was generally collective and always social in the past, as it is today (though today's "social" is often less face-to-face than in the past).

Tiziana Terranova's article "Free Labor," first published in 2000, describes the amount of work performed by Internet users early in the days of the World Wide Web such as website design. Now, there are plenty of companies that pay for what was once free, and the free labor that remains is more subtle—relying on consumers' tastes to sell or rent them more of the same, or to sell or rent to others. It is also users who provide data on compact discs to Gracenote, a company that boasts that it "helps music fans identify, discover and connect with more of the music they love" on its website (http://www .gracenote.com/music/). Terranova draws some concepts from Lazzarato (1996), in which his conception of the "cultural content" of commodities was produced by professional workers such as those in advertising and marketing and the media, but also by everyone as we blog, surf the Web, and talk about the films we've seen and the music we've heard, thus making all of us laborers, all of us consumer/producers. She argues that the old model of capital appropriating what it wanted from the culture has been superseded. "Cultural flows" originate in a field that is already capitalist. Incorporation doesn't work by capitalism descending from on high to appropriate what it wants but by channeling collective labor into monetary flows within capitalist business practices (Terranova 2004, 80). I would argue, rather, that both such things happen. Capitalism continues to incorporate what it wants from outside its domain, for it is not, and never will be, total. But within its domain, say, the commercial music industry, what Terranova describes is reasonably accurate.

One problem with much of the writing on new forms of labor is that it is rather lacking in any sort of foundation that one could call empirical: it is both ahistorical and ignorant of what workers today may actually be thinking and doing (Kreiss, Finn, and Turner 2011).[11] Arguments about new forms of labor also tend to rely on what the analyst remembers or believes to have been the case, back in the day, whereas the world of today is thought to be completely different (see also Graeber 2008). But if we are to understand labor, we need to study it in the real world. I would not dispute that free labor is in fact a form of uncompensated labor that produces surplus value for capitalists, but I would argue that this isn't a new phenomenon. In the early days of radio in the 1920s, musicians weren't paid; performing on the radio was a novel adventure that attracted many curious musicians. And in the same period, broadcasters, desperate to learn something about their audiences, routinely gave away free products and held contests as a means of soliciting listener mail in order to ascertain something about the audience. Listener letters were examined for the quality of paper and penmanship, and read for their correctness in grammar and spelling and vocabulary.[12] Listeners in that era were thus not compensated for this labor that provided corporate broadcasters such as the National Broadcasting Company with demographic data, as listeners were not compensated when later and more sophisticated means of audience measurement were adopted (see, famously, Smythe 1977 for an argument about uncompensated labor in that era).[13] More recently, unpaid focus groups have influenced all sorts of cultural production for decades. Broadcast media, whether television programs or advertisements, are routinely tested on audiences.

The distinction between manual and mental labor is, in a sense, academic: If today's worker in a cubicle finds her work mind numbing and soul destroying, is she really different from the assembly line worker in Fordism who found his job to be the same? Can one really separate out so simply "mental" and "manual" labor? Or "material" and "immaterial"? It would seem to be difficult to have the former without the latter: one types or writes poetry by hand, plays a musical instrument in order to compose music, and so forth.

So, again, it is a matter of size and scale. If cultural producers increasingly build in intercourse with users/consumers to their conception, and budgets, of production, we may well be in a new era. The "prosumer" (someone who is part producer, cocreator, and part consumer), may have arrived, the user who is a consultant for a producer. This occurs more in the arenas such as software development, tools for the making of cultural commodities more than cultural commodities themselves, as well as in other arenas such as computer games (see Morris 2003).[14] But all such forms of laboring need to be studied empirically in order to be able to make claims about how new they might be.

At least with the question of labor contributed by prosumers, it is necessary to wonder about the creation of value. If in Marx's thinking the value of a commodity was determined by the amount of socially necessary labor time that went into its production, what if its production is no longer by paid professionals but by knowledgeable but unpaid workers? Technically, value has diminished in the sense that less paid labor time went into the production of that commodity. At the same time, however, users may well come to value (in the everyday sense) the resulting commodity more because of their input into its design. All of this has led some to conclude that the labor theory of value cannot cope with the extreme diffusion in the production of some commodities today, and the myriad forms that labor can take (e.g., Negri 1999; Arvidsson and Colleoni 2011). But I disagree: labor under industrial capitalism was itself enormously complex, and there are forms of value other than economic ones, as I have noted more than once in these pages. Empirical research into labor, its products, and their consumption and the various regimes of value that can arise in the social and cultural life of a good can help us understand how value is constructed by individuals and social groups.[15]

I should also note that if people are laboring in ways that benefit the music or broadcasting or other cultural industries, they do so voluntarily. Does this not matter? Furthermore, if, in industrial and later capitalisms, workers are forced in the wage labor system to sell their labor, thereby becoming alienated from it—one of the most important concepts in Marxist theory—isn't desired, voluntary labor from which one is unalienated (or less alienated), something not to be decried, but to be understood using a more complex and nuanced perspective that takes into account what these prosumers think and feel?

The Changing Nature of Work in the Commercial Music Industry

However one characterizes labor in the cultural industries or understands how to calculate the value of its products today, one thing is clear—labor in and out of the cultural industries has changed with the advent of digital technologies. In this section, I want to speak more generally about the transformations that digital technologies helped to introduce, which, in the lives of working musicians, were massive. Most of the people I interviewed for my book on the history of music in advertising said that the rise of digital technologies was one of the biggest shifts that they witnessed in their years in the industry (Taylor 2012b).

Before digital technologies began to become common in the 1980s, composers for advertising, television, and film usually had some formal training (and sometimes a good deal of it): they knew how to read and write music, arrange music, orchestrate music, and conduct an orchestra playing their scores. They worked at the piano or with a guitar devising melodies and harmonies. They interacted with electronic technology all the time in recording studios, of course, but this was after they had written—*written*—their music.

Digital technologies changed all this. Most of the musicians I have spoken to who were over the age of fifty or so when these technologies emerged left the business rather than learn how to use them. Others had to retrain. Still others, especially younger rock musicians, found that knowing these technologies in another realm of commercial music could give them access to the world of advertising music that might have been denied them before.

The trade press from the music and advertising industries and my oral histories with music industry workers tell a story of the slow acceptance of digital music technologies in the realm of the production of commercial music, beginning as a specialist mode of composition. It is useful to examine just how these new technologies were adopted, and the resistance that they faced, since, as I am arguing, digital technologies of all sorts helped introduce neoliberal ideologies, including those new forms of work, into the culture.

At first, these new technologies were viewed for the new sounds that they could bring to commercial music. People in the industry quickly learned that they could tout these new technologies to drum up business. How-to guides began to treat electronic technologies in greater detail. One exhorts its readers to "learn about synthesizers—their capabilities and sounds. They are being used a lot now to save money on musicians, as well as to complement a 'high-tech' commercial" (Harris and Wolfram 1983, 19–20). These authors also write, "Electronic synthesizers are rapidly becoming a standard part of many music spots, both as sound effects and as an integral part of the basic track" (54–55).

By the mid-1980s, some more mainstream composers were using synthesizers for as much as half of their work. Said one, the head of a commercial music shop in New York City who made a living turning popular songs from the 1960s into jingles, "Anyone who resists the future is going to have a terrible problem. Those comfortable with [electronic] tools have greater potential" (Forkan 1985, 40). In 1984, *Back Stage* magazine, a music industry trade journal, featured a number of stories on the rise of electronic technologies in the production of advertising music. In an interview with the well-known producer Hunter Murtaugh, a question about what has changed the industry more, new music technologies or "creative trends in the visuals," prompted the following reply:

> It's all founded in technology. All the instruments, the synthesizers, the digital recording. Every part of the business is changing. Every six months you find yourself using new techniques, new synthesizers, new players who have got some pieces of equipment you want to try. There's a whole cottage industry of companies that build things that make two synthesizers work together.

The interviewer asked if Murtaugh feels he has to act as a guide to the new technology for the creatives (what creative personnel in the advertising industry are called, as opposed to workers in the business side of the industry) at Young and Rubicam.

> It's not so much of a guide. It's that there's competitive pressure to be on top of what's going on, to know all the new stuff. It's your responsibility to have no one walk in your office and say, "Hey, did you hear about this?" and say, "Gee, I never heard of that." You're supposed to try and keep on *top* of all that stuff (Vagnoni 1984a, 28; emphasis in original).

Nonetheless, *Back Stage* reported that some advertising musicians did not see digital technology as a significant factor in the business (Vagnoni 1984b). Early in 1984, the Society of Professional Audio Recording Studios presented a three-day seminar on digital technologies, the title of which seems to have been "Digital Audio on Trial." A jingle writer in attendance called it a "digital Tower of Babel." The seminar addressed such topics as whether or not digital technology was the wave of the future ("Making Way for Digital Audio" 1984, 1, 52).

Many of the musicians I interviewed who were in the advertising business before the arrival of digital technologies didn't make the leap until the digital era; synthesizers were the province of specialists. Many who were slow to adapt found themselves unemployed. As composer Steve Karmen wrote, one of the signs that convinced him it was time to leave the jingle business in the early 1990s was a client's telling him that his twelve-year-old son used the same synthesizer (2005, 177–78). When the person hailed as "the King of the Jingle" for the better part of two decades decides to quit, it is clear that the business had truly changed.

There were, of course, problems shifting to these new technologies. One was that they were prohibitively expensive, particularly before the introduction of MIDI (Musical Instrument Digital Interface, a standardized interface between computers and other digital technologies including electronic musical instruments). Advertising music composer David Shapiro (2009) told me:

> I took a couple of years off from the business, during which time MIDI and computers came in and I felt like Rip Van Winkle, I just stepped back into a business that I had always known and all of a sudden I just wasn't up to speed. . . . I sold my house in Philadelphia and moved back to Boston. I sold my house and used the profits from that to buy a Synclavier [an early and expensive digital synthesizer].[16]

With the rise of digital technologies and MIDI, the commercial landscape began to change quickly and dramatically. The advent of digital technology, especially the rise of MIDI, created a kind of lingua franca that turned everyone who employed it into a more flexible worker in the world of commercial music of all kinds. MIDI has imposed a degree of standardization on musicians' work across the cultural industries, even as they have had to increasingly adjust to more occasional employment, becoming flexible in another meaning of the term (see Deuze 2007; Menger 1999 and 2002; Stahl 2013). Composer Ann Bryant told me that she was younger than her peers in the business and recognized that she had to learn this new digital technology, as much as she enjoyed writing for orchestras. But MIDI, she says, changed things irrevocably, albeit slowly. The first noticeable indication that things were changing was that people were slowly put out of work. Bryant described this process vividly.

> MIDI first put strings out of business. And then it put the horns out of business, and the sounds got better and better. I think early on you could make pretty good string sounds, not great, but you could work it out, and then the horns got much better. And then when Wham! ["Wake Me Up before You Go-Go"] came out in 1984, I went, "Uh-oh. The horns sound great now." You know, it was all electronic but it sounded really good. It started to sound really good. And then the [live] horns disappeared, and then [recording] sessions became just rhythm, you know, and then a sax solo, guitar overdubs, and everything else was tweaking the synthesizers. And we still brought in synthesizer players; it took a while to have your own studio all set up and wired, which cost a fortune.
>
> Eventually drum programs came in and the drummers started to disappear. I mean, those possibilities came into programming. It started to sound better too; it left the kind of metronomic, artificial feel and got more humanized. So MIDI, I think in a period of eight years, just developed like lightning, you know, and more and more got digitized.

The growing use of electronic technologies had ramifications beyond putting musicians out of work. Bryant also said:

> We started to see real physical changes, like studios shrunk. They used to be these grand rooms, like Media on 57th Street, fabulous, Media A, oof! Huge orchestras recorded in there. We started to work in smaller and smaller studios, and we started to see studios with larger control rooms because the synthesizer players plugged in.

Using synthesizers became cheaper than employing live musicians. Spencer Michlin (2009), a major advertising composer in the 1970s and 1980s, explained it very well:

> Technology had made it possible for individuals to compete by recording music on synthesizers in their homes. This gave these writers a built-in economic advantage. Let's say that a jingle needed a rhythm section and horns (piano, bass, drums, percussion, two guitars, three trumpets, and two trombones). Add in the union-mandated double scale for a leader, plus a contractor and arranger at double scale and a copyist at scale, and that's eighteen units on the AFM [American Federation of Musicians] contract. Unless the composer was a complete pig, he or she could leverage that advantage by charging the equivalent of, say, nine units and cut the musicians' budget in half while keeping more of it.

If studio musicians were put out of work, anybody with a computer and a good microphone could make commercial music: the field became much more crowded almost overnight. Technology has leveled the playing field, according to advertising composer Nick DiMinno (2009): "Thanks to Garage Band [an application for Apple devices that allows users to create music] and thanks to computers and samplers, now anybody that's got a computer is a competitor."

Once these new digital technologies like the Synclavier caught on in the course of the 1980s, clients began to ask for them; new, expensive technologies were a draw, even if, as some composers noted, they imparted a sameness in sound to the music they made. One person in the business in this period said, "It puts a gleam in the eye of clients when they hear someone has one. They like to spend an afternoon among all the technology—it's like being on the bridge of the Enterprise on 'Star Trek' . . . and that's an effective draw for any company" (Morley 1988, 26S). Industry veteran Steve Karmen writes, "Agency clients were fascinated with all the new sounds that could be created by one person at the touch of a button" (1989, 140).

New digital music technologies and the Internet also, as many people told me, made it possible for people outside of the major metropolitan centers to compete, and made it possible for music production companies in New York and elsewhere to hire musicians at a distance. New digital technologies have internationalized the industry; it's no longer just in New York, Chicago, and Los Angeles. As Nick DiMinno (2009) said, "Now you compete with the world." Anthony Vanger (2004), a composer who is creative director and owner of a music production company, Ant Music, in New York City, told me that he was able to hire composers from around the world; his firm could partake of a broader pool of composers. Composer Chris Wong, for example, works in Los Angeles but composes almost exclusively for films produced in Vietnam. Wong told me:

> This kind of working relationship would not have been possible back in the '80s or '90s. If this opportunity had happened to me in the '80s or '90s I think I wouldn't have been able to work with them anymore. But because of the Internet, these days, it's easy to work at home. Basically, they just upload footage to me, and I work on it, and then I upload the music to them. Jimmy Pham, one of the producers in Vietnam who I've done a lot of movies with, I actually don't think I've seen Jimmy for about four years. But in that time we've done about four or five movies together, and we just keep in touch by e-mail. Early on I established my relationship with those people and they liked what I did enough that they've kept working with me, and it's possible to do it online even though we live an ocean away from each other.

Digital technologies have made the sort of group production theorized by Raymond Williams increasingly deterritorialized in neoliberal capitalism.

LONGER, HARDER

The introduction of digital technologies changed producers' expectations of not only what composers and other musicians could do but also how quickly they could do it. Neoliberal capitalism in the cultural industries, as a result of the spread and dominance of digital technologies, has created a work environment in which everything can be done faster, which, instead of shortening the workday, has meant instead that as soon as the task-that-once-took-longer is accomplished, workers move on to the next task. And portable computers and broadband Internet connections have meant that it is much easier to take work home, or to work remotely with someone in a different time zone where the working day has not concluded.

On the subject of the prolongation of the working day, Marx wrote:

> Constant capital, the means of production, considered from the standpoint of the creation of surplus-value, only exist to absorb labour, and with every drop

of labour a proportional quantity of surplus-labour. While they fail to do this, their mere existence causes a relative loss to the capitalist, for they represent during the time they lie fallow, a useless advance of capital. And this loss becomes positive and absolute as soon as the intermission of their employment necessitates additional outlay at the recommencement of work. The prolongation of the working-day beyond the limits of the natural day, into the night, only acts as a palliative. It quenches only in a slight degree the vampire thirst for the living blood of labour. To appropriate labour during all the 24 hours of the day is, therefore, the inherent tendency of capitalist production. (1967, 256)

While this has doubtless been demonstrable throughout the history of capitalism, digital technologies have made it possible to prolong the working day even further, though not always for any good and discernible reason for workers (see Sennett 2006, 65–66).

Most people I spoke to in the commercial music world agreed that digital technologies had resulted in their working harder and longer than ever, in part because of increased competition, a consequence of the leveling of the playing field by digital technologies, but also because clients and bosses know that making changes to music that is stored on the computer isn't difficult, so many demand numerous changes, even at the last possible moment. Many people spoke to me of having to work all night long to make deadlines, essentially working around the clock, the kind of demand increasingly common in neoliberal capitalism (see Crary 2013). Every conceivable measure is taken to shorten the time to produce music, and every step of the production process has been shortened. Andy Bloch (2004), who works in a music production company in New York City, said technology has

radically changed the production process, though the fundamentals of music composition, the creative part, still apply. The new means of production have not made our lives any easier, and it feels like we work longer and harder. People expect more options because they are easily generated, they are coming out of a box rather than a traditional recording studio.

Having to work faster and longer has led Bloch to exploit time differences in the United States.

I just worked with a client uptown who is basically too busy to travel thirteen blocks and sit on the couch because they're spread between so many projects. That's the corporate model these days—less people, more work, work them until they drop, then send them to the glue factory. They're too busy to come to the studio, so they call me at around 6 p.m., and then after my call I call a singer in San Francisco because it's three hours behind there, and I say, "Look, this is the thing, we need this tomorrow." And he'll be working on the track and he'll send me back audio files. You can work with anybody, anytime, anywhere, so that's the good news and the bad news.

Booker White (2012), who works in the music department at Disney Studios, also spoke to me about the time pressures brought by the new technologies, and gave a concrete example, noting that technology has not reduced the number of workers required.

> Schedules can be compressed into a much shorter time frame. However, the same amount of people are needed to accomplish the job because of this. On *Wreck-It Ralph*, we start recording on August 20 [two weeks from the date of the interview]. Years ago, we would have been busily working on it right now, but in this era, I'm not going to see anything at least for another week, which means a week closer to the start of the recording sessions. That's probably the biggest change—it can be done in that amount of time.

Advertising musician David Shapiro (2009) also spoke to me about the expected quick turnaround today, emphasizing the almost impossibly compressed schedules that are the norm:

> There's a joke, you know, somebody calls you at two in the afternoon and, you'll ask them when they need it and they'll say, "five o'clock." They're usually kidding. But we've had just insane deadlines, insane. Not just us of course, every company has that. They know that it can be done. They don't know that it's hard to do. Well, they know. It's very hard to be creative in an hour. But you can certainly write a track in an hour, and certainly within three hours or six hours you can have a more or less finished track, depending on what it is. So overnight is not unusual at all.

To hire musicians on short notice, Shapiro says,

> you shoot out an e-mail to the five guys you work with who you think would be right and each of them is writing a demo, plus you're turning in your five or six library tracks, so by the next day you've got ten things to shoot off to the client—you and the three other companies that you're demo-ing against—so by that next day they have forty or fifty things to listen to. It's that efficient.

Shapiro contrasted this with the way things were before digital technologies resulted in such hectic schedules.

> This is a long way from where a client moves in and talks about what the track should be and you write it together and there's that one track that you like and that goes to air. So that's the difference. Sometimes more is not better, you know. I tend to think that what it's done is gotten rid of using your instincts and going for something. If I were a copywriter or whatever sort of creative

and I had to choose from thirty different tracks which one was the absolute best for my commercial, I might think at two o'clock that it was one thing, at four I might think it's another, and certainly my partner and my client are often going to think differently. It's impossible, compared to the idea that we could just sit down and think this through and ask, "What should happen at this point in the spot, in this scene?," you know, "What were you intending here?" and "Can we do this?"—that sort of pace. Creativity is missing, it's not there anymore. Not always, but to a large extent, I won't say all the time.

Film composer Chris Wong (2012) told me how much had changed, even in the relatively short amount of time he had been in the business. The amount of time he has to write an entire score to a feature film has dropped.

The time frame these days is between four and five weeks. It's pretty fast these days. It's gotten more and more ridiculous. The biggest irony behind everything is that you would think that with all this computer technology, things would get more and more efficient, but I feel like they've gotten less. It's just made it so that people feel like they can change things more often without facing the consequences of it. But I feel like the situation's gotten worse. Because what has happened is, it's made everyone believe that you can change everything at the last minute, because you have a computer now. So, all the higher-ups think, "Oh, we have two days left, we can make it better, tell that guy to change this, and that guy to change this." It's kind of crazy.

As a result, I feel like the schedules have gotten harder and harder. When I was studying with [famed television and film composer] Jerry Goldsmith in the late '90s, what he told us was that six weeks was considered reasonable for a feature. And that's for someone who's pretty experienced and writing very quickly. I remember we asked him how fast he wrote, and he said he averages about three minutes of orchestral score per day to stay on track.

These days, if I can get six weeks, I feel very fortunate. I think the film I did in December was on a four-week schedule. It might have been four weeks and two or three days, but it was pretty much a four-week schedule. The one that I'm starting in August, they sent me the schedule, which says that I have four weeks, though these things always change. They tell you that you have this much time, and then they tell you that the editing's behind schedule. "Oh, so you guys are behind, does that mean that I get more time?" "No." [Laughs] Okay, so now I have less time. The composer is always screwed on the schedule, because music is one of the last things that goes in the picture. And you can't change the release date. People have legal obligations to put the movie in the theater by a certain date.

Music editor Craig Pettigrew (2012) said much the same thing about the seemingly ever-shrinking schedule and increased pressure.

Technology has changed everything except the creative decision. But the conception is that technology has changed literally everything. So the demands are far greater and there's far less time to do the same amount of work, or even more work. But it's a wall that we have to be finished by, and this is our time to compose and orchestrate and record and mix. That time is shrinking all the time; they'll say, "What you did in four days last time, we have to shave a day off the mix schedule." And we talk among ourselves, and we swear that we won't do it, because next time it'll be two days—they'll say, "Well, you did it in three days last time . . ." But we keep on doing it, we keep on meeting their demands. So technology has really changed the perception of what it takes to create recorded mixed music, and you get on a show and there'll be just an unbelievable stress level because of it.

Despite all this hard work, as one person told me, the truth is that most music production companies barely break even. And working musicians are making less, when they can get work.

Things aren't much different for star performers, who are required to labor more and more, often to the detriment of their vocal cords. Dr. Shawn Nasseri, an ear, nose, and throat physician in Beverly Hills who treats many star singers, has noticed an increase in damage to his singer-patients' voices.

Ten years ago, I used to see hemorrhages twice a year; now I see them once a month. When they're successful, there's a lot more of everything—press, promo, they have to tweet, Facebook and chat, they tour and record simultaneously, often late at night. . . . People don't slow down because you've got to strike when the iron is hot. Before, the market would forgive a one- or two-month hiatus [to let the voice recover]; now it's very different. (Halperin 2011; ellipsis in original)

All workers in the cultural industries are working harder and longer, stars included.

But the Internet and other digital technologies have not increased efficiency across the board, as several of my consultants also noted. New York advertising composer Andy Bloch (2004) told me:

Ironically, the Internet has created certain inefficiencies in the way we work with our clients. The ability to make good decisions, to allow the creative process to happen, is being compromised by the rapid tempo of the new technology. It often takes time to recognize a good idea; certainly when you're trying to push the envelope you have to allow time to reflect. That time is becoming harder to find.

I think a big problem in working remotely, communicating by e-mail, listening to music alone, is that you're in some sort of vacuum. It makes it very hard to get to "yes." For example, when somebody comes in here and sits on the couch, we can pretty much go through the range of possibilities in an hour, because you can demonstrate in real time. You narrow it down. It's a personal interaction, and you can read the room.

But when we work with a client virtually, they often give you an assignment and say, "Oh, we have this deadline, here's the brief, we have a client meeting in the morning." You can ask questions in the time allotted but you often get the feeling you're operating on incomplete information. You compose something and they react to it and call you or write you back. What happens on their end is usually fragmented, so the information you get back is not always clear or delivered in a timely fashion. Something that could be resolved in a day can now take a week or longer.

The rise of digital technologies has created certain efficiencies, which are exploited by those employing musicians and music production companies, and these same technologies have created inefficiencies. But both take more workers' time.

Digitized Music as a New Form of Music Objectified

It's hardly necessary at this historical juncture to point out how digital technologies have changed the consumption of music, though I would hasten to clarify that the real revolution in mobile listening began not with the MP3 but with the introduction of the Sony Walkman in 1979. Nonetheless, using computers to acquire and manage one's music collection, which is increasingly digital and decreasingly stored on a compact disc, cassette, or hard drive, or vinyl recording, has become the norm for most listeners.

As I have written elsewhere (Taylor 2007b), one cannot dissociate music as a commodity from the technology that reproduces it. And, perhaps more importantly, one must remember that music is not—and never has been—a commodity in general. It exists in a myriad of practices, some of which could be said to be practices of commodification and some of which are not. And I don't believe that offering a taxonomy of the different forms of the music-commodity is particularly useful.

I do think, however, that the commodification of music as sound that occurred in the late nineteenth and early twentieth centuries with the rise of the player piano, phonograph, radio, and sound film marked a new mode of the commodification of music—commodified music as sound. But since then, music as sound has frequently existed as a commodity, though in different formats (LP, cassette, etc.). It is not my goal here to survey the changing nature of music as a commodity since the rise of the player piano and phonograph (what Taylor 2007b considers); it is clear that major developments

in the reproduction of music technologies since the player piano and phonograph in the late nineteenth century—the long-playing record in the late
1940s, stereo in the late 1950s, the compact cassette in the 1970s, and the Sony
Walkman in the 1980s—all represent different forms of the commodification
of music because of the different social uses of these forms and the different
regimes of value that they could be found in. Yet they all have something in
common in that they are all ways of making music-as-sound tangible, tactile,
as the player piano roll and earlier incarnations of the phonograph did.

TACTILITY

Bicycle or bus or subway or automobile or feet. Feet into shop. Select the
section: rock, classical, jazz, R&B, techno, something else. Thumb through
dozens, hundreds, of recordings in big bins, some new LPs, with cellophane,
some used. Even these could still have the original cellophane. Sometimes the
original price sticker was still there. Were LPs really this cheap in the past?
Did Woolworth's really sell 45s? Thumb, thumb, thumb. Find a potential purchase. Take out the disc, examine for wear. Keep going. Look through every
one—you never know what treasure might be hiding behind the misfiled
Mantovani record or budget Beethoven recording. Flea markets and thrift
stores frequently stored vinyl touching vinyl, no cardboard sleeves or paper
liners. Same for 78 rpm recordings, which made a satisfying though worry-
ing sound clacking against one another. And smells: sometimes dusty, sometimes musty. Carry the prizes to the desk, pay, leave. Wash hands as soon as
possible—secondhand records are usually dirty. It used to be that I would
purchase a backpack for everyday use based on whether or not it would permit me to carry LPs. Those days are gone. Now, when I (very) occasionally
have to carry an LP, I hold it in my hands, a relic from the past; I haven't noticed being stared at on the bus with them.

Jonathan Sterne (2012), in a chapter entitled "Is Music a Thing," usefully
meditates on this question. I would submit, however, that such a question is
an ontological one, whereas I am interested historical and ethnographic ones.
Most people, at least in places where music has been recorded in some fashion, whether as notation or in some other way, have some conception of the
thinginess of music until fairly recently, prompting Sterne's question.

All forms of music recording until digital formats such as the MP3 have
one thing in common (besides the obvious fact that they are music reproduction technologies): they make music a tactile object, as a phonograph record
or cassette tape or something else. The long-playing record, in particular, offered opportunities for compelling cover art that became integral to many

rock recordings from the 1960s and after. There were rituals of removing the cellophane, lifting out the sleeve, which might contain lyrics to songs that could become, or perhaps already were, favorites, carefully treating the disc itself so as not to introduce a scratch, placing it on the turntable platter. Tactility has something to do with immediacy, with liveness and participation. The sensory experiences of handling the recordings, making rituals out of the playing of recordings substitutes for the sensory experience of listening to live music. Many a baby boomer has fond memories of eagerly awaiting the next 45 rpm single or 33 1/3 rpm LP, fetching it from the record store, tearing off the cellophane, removing it from the cardboard sleeve and inner liner, turning it over in one's hands before placing it on the turntable, and lowering the needle. By 1979, a Discwasher might have been employed as part of the ritual, since this LP-cleaning solution was introduced that year.[17] But all of these rituals have largely disappeared. Now one simply downloads (or, less and less frequently, rips) a track or two or three or ten thousand to one's computer or playback device, or streams tracks from a service such as Spotify, Rdio, or Google Play.

Tactility was one of the ways that people once engaged with recorded music. With the introduction of the player piano in the late nineteenth and early twentieth centuries, there was some anxiety over the perceived lack of participation in music-making, to the extent that, through the idea of expression, the player piano's "performer" was integrated at least partially back into the business of producing sound beyond simply powering the machine (since the early models were not electrical but pumped like a pump organ). And, early in the LP era, there were those who argued that 78 rpm recordings—which only contain three to four minutes of music per side—facilitated greater involvement with the music since one had to get up and turn over, or change, records so much more frequently than long-playing recordings, which can hold up to around thirty minutes per side. According to Mark Katz, the great blues singer Son House remembered using a phonograph in the 1920s, which involved "gettin' up, settin' it back, turnin' it around, crankin' the crank, primin' it up, and lettin' the horn down" (2010, 36). In our era, an owner of a vinyl record pressing plant made much the same point, arguing that having to put on a vinyl recording and turn it over engages listeners more, capturing their attention in an era when everyone is accustomed to instant everything (Giffels 2011, 28). Opera lovers who wanted to attempt to bring recorded music to life could create their own miniature stages, as an English music magazine reported in 1929 (Tableau Vivant 1929).[18]

Of course, for most of its previous existence, what was thought of as music wasn't tactile; "music" was what one heard, or could see as a printed score;

tactility was located in playing instruments, feeling one's voice. The objectification of music in the form of recordings is anomalous in the long history of music. But this movement away from tactility does mean something, I think. In the absence of a physical recording, there is no show-and-tell with others. It used to be that when going to the house or apartment or room of a new acquaintance, I would peruse his or her record collection (and books, too) to get a sense of the person's taste. That is much more difficult now. One can share playlists, but reading a list is not the same thing as tilting one's head to read the spines of LPs or CDs, running one's hands along the recordings, occasionally pulling one out for a closer look.

Without cassettes or LPs or CDs, some fans still find clever ways of making their favorite music accessible in/as objects. A colleague told me of a student who was such a Lady Gaga fan that she purchased a second iPod that was dedicated to Gaga's music, so that she could have something tangible to associate with her favorite singer.[19]

A segment on National Public Radio's *All Things Considered* interviewed many musicians, DJs, and other music professionals, many of whom spoke of the loss of tactility with digital music and their preference for vinyl. Andres Santo Domingo, cofounder of a record label, said:

> I think that vinyl in a way represents slow, and I think that's something that's attractive about it also maybe on a subliminal level for consumers that are always on the Internet to get something that's really physical, maybe archaic in a way, but the complete antithesis of what the speed of consuming music on the Internet is. And as much as people might not acknowledge it, I think it does play a little bit into sort of appeal. (Ganz 2011)

Alain Macklovitch, who is a DJ, said, "What I fell in love with was really scratching, physically manipulating these pieces of vinyl, moving the record back and forth and making these crazy sound effects with it. So there's a tactile connection with the record" (Ganz 2011). It also matters that a physical object can become a treasured thing, even an heirloom. Jenn Wasner, a vocalist and guitarist, said, "It looks better. It sounds better. You can hold it in your hand. It's a keepsake. It's something that you can remember and have and treasure for years." She also said that she signed with a particular label that would release her recording as a digital download, a CD, and as a vinyl LP, and, "I always have said that I'll never really feel like a real band until I can hold a record in my hands and look at it and play it. So I'm really happy to say that I'll be able to do that really soon" (Ganz 2011). Others continue to believe that vinyl sounds better than digital recordings (Weber 2014).

There are also the visual aspects of physical recordings, especially in the 78 rpm and LP era. It's not an accident that to this day many still refer to recordings as "albums," for in the 78 rpm era, classical recordings were multidisc affairs housed in albums, sandwiched between heavy cardboard covers with artwork on the front and information on the back. The activity of putting on and taking off many recordings in the course of listening to a long work of music was complemented by the visual display of many recordings in their own sleeves. LPs were much the same, of course, though without the leaves of recordings arrayed album fashion.

As it turns out, the LP is the fastest-growing segment of the music industry; about 2.8 million vinyl records were sold in the United States in 2010, and the figures for 2011 were about 40 percent higher (Giffels 2011, 28; see also Harris 2012); in 2012, the gain was 17.7 percent over the previous year (Christman 2013); and in 2013, sales went up 33 percent more, to 6.1 million albums. Since 2002, vinyl sales have risen 250 percent, while music sales overall have dropped by 50 percent (Weber 2014). (And this doesn't include the many recordings that aren't tracked by Nielsen SoundScan; the president of a small vinyl record company in Cleveland figured that SoundScan captures only about 15 percent of actual sales, adding that most of his company's recordings don't have a bar code, which means they won't be tracked by Sound-Scan [Giffels 2011, 28].) Certain retailers such as Whole Foods and Target that want to appear cool or fun to their customers prominently display LPs for sale (Christman 2013). The executive coordinator for the Southern Pacific Region of Whole Foods says, "Vinyl has created a fun factor in our stores. We have DJs, and shoppers can ask them to play music. We have husbands asking the DJs to play songs for [their] wives . . . customers coming in and dancing down the aisles, having fun" (Christman 2013). Some have compared the continuing viability of vinyl to a kind of audio "slow foods" movement. Vinyl recordings became collector's items, creating hip value for vinyl more generally, so that some bands wanted to release recordings on vinyl. Now they're something of a luxury consumer item (Weber 2014). The success of vinyl recording is such that it is taking longer and longer for recordings to be issued, for the number of new vinyl pressing plants hasn't increased; musicians who once could see their recordings come out in four weeks now must wait three months (Oliphint 2014).

With the advent of the compact disc in the 1980s, reissues of earlier recordings tended to reuse the cover art, but in virtually all cases, what worked well on a 12" × 12" cover seldom scaled down to the 5.5" × 5.76" of a CD cover. Cover art on compact discs, or cassettes, for that matter, always seemed diminished, not an effective presentation of what the recording contained.

Tactility matters on the production side as well. Sean Bohrman (2012), cofounder of Burger Records, told me that anybody can make a CD; it's a simple matter with a personal computer. But

> nobody buys CDs anymore. I can send somebody a link and they can make their own CD, and send them art and they can print out their own art. But if you make a cassette yourself, you got to sit there and make a cassette and it takes time, and people realize that when they're listening to something.

During the course of our first interview at Burger's retail storefront, the day's shipment of cassettes was delivered, and Bohrman explained to me that the cassette factory would assemble the cassettes and inserts for them, "but we tell him, 'No, don't do that.' That way we can put them together ourselves, so we touch and put together every single tape. When you touch something, you're putting some kind of power into it" (2012). They formerly hand-numbered each of the inserts, though they have had to discontinue this because of volume and lack of time; they still hand-number some special issues (Bohrman and Rickard 2014) and still assemble all of the tapes themselves (Bohrman 2014b). Dean Spunt of Post Present Medium, which issues mainly LPs, similarly tries to personalize his releases. At the beginning, PPM releases had silkscreened covers, though he had to stop doing this when the label and his career as a performer didn't allow time for it anymore (Spunt 2012).

And what of conspicuous consumption if one can no longer display row upon row of LPs or cassettes or CDs? How are we to understand each other's tastes and preferences—or even communicate—through our display of goods if those goods exist not physically but as bits on phones or iPods? What does conspicuous consumption look like in the age of digital technologies that facilitate the storage of vast amounts of "information," whether musical, textual, or visual, or something else—amounts so massive that the displays of crudition or acquisitiveness disappear into the iPod or iPad or Kindle or Nook? In some ways, conspicuous consumption is now more about displaying hardware than software, that is, devices that play music rather than the visible collection of music. But it is also about time, or, perhaps better, speed: Who has the latest gadget first? Who has waited in line for hours to acquire the new iPhone or iPad?

Are we on our way to being like Vashti in Forster's story, living an antiseptic existence, with everything, including human contact, available at the touch of a button? It does seem to me that making music together, in Alfred Schütz's (1951) sense, can only attenuate with the decline in familiarity of music concretized in a recording that one can hold in one's hands and display for others. The makers of music become more remote, the workers who brought us their music—not just the musicians, but also the engineers, technicians, factory workers, distributors, truck drivers, and many more—all the more effaced. But the music-commodity is now largely invisible, if not inaudible. All that remains is the b(r)and, today as ephemeral as the technology that plays its music.

Ambivalences and Critiques

As liberating as some may find new digital technologies to be, there are those who have a more ambivalent, even oppositional relationship to them, depending on one's field of production and one's position in it. Amateurs can find that it is easier to make, record, and disseminate their music, while professionals in the cultural industries have found that this very ease is the excuse their bosses use to demand more of them, faster, sooner; technology has increased musicians' workloads, for those who employ them know that with digital technology it is possible to make changes at the last minute.

I want to conclude this chapter with something of a reality check, an antidote to the technological triumphalism that so often accompanies discussions of what new digital technologies are believed to offer, at least in the realm of music. I have already noted the critiques of many workers in the music industry who find themselves working harder and longer, as well as being forced to work less efficiently because they meet face-to-face less frequently with their bosses and clients than in the past. Some also believe that commercial television music has lost some of its subtlety because of the use of the same technologies in many sectors of the industry, the decline of the use of live musicians, and the speed with which music now has to be composed.

Some people I interviewed spoke in more abstract terms about what had changed with the rise of digital technologies. The absence of studio musicians has created a more sterile creative environment, they said. Hunter Murtaugh and many other people I spoke to said that the performance of music is being lost, the synergy of what can happen with great musicians in studios. Murtaugh named a number of great musicians with whom he worked over the years—Keith Jarrett, Herbie Hancock, Ron Carter, Hubert Laws—and said that the music produced by studio musicians in the studio "had a sparkle and a vibrancy" that is now gone.

> Even when somebody writes something interesting, I mean, if you go and create an Earth, Wind & Fire track in your little home studio, I don't care what kind of samples you've got, and what kind of quantizing you're gonna put on your rhythm track, it ain't gonna be the same as having twelve horns in a studio and that rhythm section. (Murtaugh 2009)

Advertising composer Tom McFaul (2009) noted the same thing.

> Using samples and synths also brought about a kind of sameness to the sound
> of ad music as it has done to pop music. With live dates, the exciting thing
> was that the personalities of the great players available always made the work
> distinctive. If our work was not about art, it was at least about craft and mu-
> sicianship.

And Spencer Michlin (2009) told me:

> If you're in the studio, and there's a live band there, those guys are really gifted
> musicians, most of them are good writers, they're certainly good players and
> a lot of them are improvisers. And they add their perspective on whatever
> it is you're doing. You ask them to play ink—in other words, the music in
> front of them—but often you can be a little freer, get a contribution from
> them. Vocal arrangers also have good ideas, and you get all of that and you
> put it together—that's the producer's job, to choose among a lot of wealth, you
> know? But when one guy is doing the whole thing, no matter how talented he
> may or she may be, that part is lost.

Many musicians I spoke to made this point in terms of the sociality of the
recording session experience, often discussing its demise with palpable regret
and nostalgia. Nick DiMinno (2009) said:

> You know, a couple of years ago, Michael Brecker [a well-known saxophonist]
> passed. And I went to his memorial service; there were people there I used
> to see every day, every week, that I haven't seen in years, you know? Because
> those days are gone. Those days are gone. And I don't think the business is
> better for it. I don't mean to sound like a dinosaur—I just don't think it is.

Another composer, David Horowitz (2009), told me, "I'm sitting in front of
my digital performer rig, I'm working on a spot right now, sitting alone in a
room with a computer and all this incredible software, just me. And the only
thing I have to relate to is software."

Music production today is greatly depersonalized compared to in the past,
as are the relations between clients and employees. Digital technologies have
permitted workers not only to labor faster but to collaborate with strangers
across thousands of miles. Social relationships in some corners of contemporary American culture have been commercialized and commodified because
they have been technologized (as discussed in chapter 2), but digital technologies have also introduced new forms of alienated labor, and alienation from
one's fellow laborers.

But in the day-to-day crush of work, what digital technologies have
mainly wrought in the realm of music production has meant working lon-

ger and harder, and increased standardization. These are not new features in neoliberal capitalism, for both are familiar from Marx and Weber and many later writings. Yet these changes are real, and keenly felt by workers, many of whom in our interviews said that working in film or television or advertising music today "is not a young man's game." Neoliberalism has taken advantage of new technologies to speed up the assembly line for many workers, even if those same technologies offer some others an illusion of freedom and creativity.

Singing in the Shadows of Neoliberal Capitalism

In chapter 2, I discussed the changes introduced by neoliberal capitalism to the music industry, a term I employ to cover the various industries of recording, concert presentation, publishing, and more. But this industry has its fringes, its marginal players to which it has had variable relationships over the years. In this chapter, I want to examine some small, independent record labels (independent means that the labels do not control the means of the distribution of their physical recordings, unlike the major labels) to see how they negotiate the ever-shifting landscape of today's capitalism. What can they tell us about the workings of neoliberal capitalism and other modes of production, other ways of creating, and protecting, value?

Motivated by Music

Small, independent record labels such as Burger Records in Orange County, California (discussed in the previous chapter), while attempting to turn a profit and earn an income for their artists in a capitalist marketplace, nonetheless try to eschew the worst tendencies of today's capitalism, even if they participate in other aspects of it. And Anthony Seeger (2012), director emeritus of Smithsonian Folkways Recordings, told me that that label had no qualms about using the capitalist infrastructure of distribution networks to disseminate its music: "At Folkways I always thought I was taking advantage of the capitalist system to distribute a kind of music that was unpopular, by definition, and strategically unpopular, it was trying to do something that wasn't to create the brand of an artist." He continued:

It seemed to me that capitalism and the market system actually was a really efficient way, if it worked, for anybody anywhere in the world being able to get what they cared about. It seemed to me in principle you could in fact take advantage, sort of ride on the back of the capitalist system to do something it wasn't made for . . . and I think a number of independent record labels do that. A number of people who use it to distribute in various ways and look commercial, are in fact taking advantage of something that was built for something else. And that means that we did that [at Smithsonian Folkways].

A system designed to extract surplus value could be employed to distribute commodities produced not simply for the purpose of exchange, representing other sorts of values.

Bill Nowlin and Ken Irwin, two of the three cofounders (with Marian Leighton Levy) of Rounder Records, talked of the idealism with which they started that label in 1970 while still in college, at first simply by trying to distribute, and record, music that they liked.[1] They only cared if they broke even in the early years of the company. Nowlin (2012) told me that they looked at how the record industry worked, and decided to double the usual royalty rate, from twenty-five to fifty cents. They didn't begin paying themselves until they had run the business for four years. And, Nowlin said,

we all lived in the same place . . . the same apartment, and we kept expenses down; we just didn't have elaborate tastes. It was the tail end of the hippie era, and we weren't into consumerism and so forth. This became our mission, and so all of our resources were focused on what we were doing. We were only in it for the sense that we were doing something useful, maybe even important, and that was good payment.

But as the label grew, it became increasingly difficult to sustain this level of idealism. Musicians wanted more than just to be signed to a label; they wanted their records promoted. Nowlin (2012) said, "So basically we became like other record companies in the sense of thinking a little bit more about whether this record's going to sell or not, and having the kind of pricing structure and royalty structure and business sensibility [of other labels]." Nonetheless, even as the company grew, the founders tried to keep the profit motive at bay as much as possible.

We would always consider, "Is this a record we are going to break even on? Can we make some money? Is there a strategic value to putting this record out? Maybe this artist is a friend of somebody else that we'd really like to work with and maybe if we do a good job with this one we can also start working with this other artist?" Those concerns always crossed our minds. And so I could never say that we were totally innocent about that all, and looking back there's some albums that we look at now, and we think, "Why did we ever put that out?" And then we remember, somebody talked us into it for one reason or another. But by and large, we can still look back after forty-some years and say that most of the time, if there wasn't something in the music that really gripped one of us musically, we wouldn't have done the record. At least 95 percent of the recordings we issued, one or more of us really believed passionately in it and it wasn't done without a sense of how it was going to go over business-wise—and it was often done without the profit motive being the primary thing.

But as the music industry began to experience trouble in the early twenty-first century with the dominance of digital means of distribution of music, the rise of digital piracy, and, as Ken Irwin (2012) put it, the "the demise of retail," economic considerations forced their way to the forefront of Nowlin's concerns and those of his colleagues.[2]

It's gotten harder and harder, especially in the past ten years, when the whole record business began to collapse; now every decision has to be made with a very, very careful eye towards how well we can do. It used to be that hoping we could break even was a good enough reason to put out a record, if we really liked it; about twenty years ago, it started to be that we absolutely had to break even on it. (Nowlin 2012)

Irwin seconded his colleague's comments on the difficulties faced by record labels in the twenty-first century.

We've turned down lots of artists that we wouldn't have, that we would have signed and whose music we would have released, but we didn't see a way to make it work. Our last question in our A&R meetings at this point is "How can we win with this artist?" Or "How can we win with this project?" And that wasn't really discussed early on. If the three of us liked it, and it seemed like we could sell enough to break even then we would do it.

However, Rounder, like independent labels generally, is able to be more nimble and can work with artists longer to help sales than a major label. And they are still able to sign a band they want to sign and take a risk. Irwin said:

We're about to be signing a group called the Time Jumpers, who are a bunch of the best studio musicians and singers in Nashville who have been playing for about a decade at one club every Monday night when they're in town, and I think they probably made the rounds of the country labels in Nashville, and everybody passed because—and this is my guess—because they didn't feel that they had a hit and they didn't think they would be doing regular touring. And we just think it's great music, and that people will respond and we'll be able to sell enough to make a profit. I think that the overall decision-making is easier; I think overall longevity, in terms of staff, tends to be greater with the independent labels.

Jeff Castelaz (2012), cofounder of Dangerbird Records in Los Angeles (who is now the president of Elektra Records), shares much the same pessimism as Nowlin and Irwin even though his label releases very different music. Nonetheless, he said that even as a small indie label, he was in the same situation as the major labels, for they still have to try to place their recordings in the same few major retailers. He was thus less invested on the major-label-vs.-indie-label distinction that many make. "I'm much less bullish on the us-against-them thing, because I really do think that when you look at how Best Buy and Walmart and Target are treating all of us, we're all in the same boat. We just are."

But he was less troubled by piracy than by new business models that don't take the desires and needs of musicians into consideration. Workers in the music industry, he says, are victims of neoliberal capitalism, and

> have become clowns, or jesters who are performing in the courts of people who have created economic paradigms that have nothing to do with returning money to the content creators, the artists, and the IP investors, the labels—they are simply building their own paradigms, which they will run off and sell, or go public with, or whatever, but it will be of no benefit to the people who actually attracted humans to go to their sites in the first place. And I'm talking about Spotify, Facebook, Twitter, and the like.

Castelaz was basically pessimistic about the industry, which he viewed as being squeezed from a number of directions. But he tries to continue to work in a regime of value in which the music he and others are moved by can still succeed in economic regimes of value. He told me:

> The beauty is, when you're breaking an artist, when you find someone that just makes you feel some incredible way—the singer's got a great voice, the conceit of the entire band is just mind-blowing to you, they have at least one great, great song and a bunch of really good songs—that's what you kind of need, 'cause let's face it, one great song is really all you need, you can't have four great songs on the radio at once—but if you have these basic building blocks and you have a fire for an artist, you can change the world. And that's been our story with the Silversun Pickups and Fitz and the Tantrums, and we have another band, Royal Teeth, that we just signed out of New Orleans, and they just got that first commercial radio ad on Monday, and total passion from the program director at Norfolk, Virginia. And you sit there and go, "This is that feeling all over again." You never know, one radio ad does not mean you're

a chart-topper, it all starts somewhere, and there's nothing like that feeling, 'cause at the end of the day you're changing people's lives on both sides of the speakers, if it goes well. And I know that music had saved my life more than a hundred times, more than that, I've lost count, so if we could have a small hand in that, on our label side, it's beautiful.

Bruce Iglauer (2012), founder of Alligator Records in Chicago, tells a story similar to Nowlin's and Irwin's of an early love for music underrepresented on recordings—blues in his case—and his haphazard entry into the business. In the forty-plus years that Iglauer has been in the business, he has witnessed a number of changes, from the consolidation of distribution networks to the demise of the record store. He has been able to adapt to the changing industry by emphasizing sales at shows, employing local media to promote his music, which the major labels don't do, and he started selling recordings and other goods online in 1995, earlier than most labels. He views selling at shows and attempting to create grassroots enthusiasm for their artists to be crucial.

> So the more successful the gig, the more sales by the artist, thus giving us big incentive to publicize the gig. Until around 2000, we hardly thought about artist sales. Now they are essential to our marketing plans (whereas the majors spend very little energy on them).

Iglauer sounds less negative about the state of the industry than the other independent label founder/operators I spoke to. Utilizing some of the same marketing venues the major labels exploit, and many they don't, is key to his success; he points out that "the artists who left us for bigger labels (Albert Collins, The Kinsey Report and Johnny Winter come to mind) didn't do as well with their sales as they did on little ol' Alligator."

But just because a record label is independent doesn't mean that its owners aren't attempting to turn a profit, and just because someone works for a major label doesn't mean that he or she is only interested in profit; there are those who, even in a capitalist industry, struggle to maintain noneconomic sorts of values.[3] Billy Mann (www.billymann.com), who is in the mainstream, profit-oriented music industry, attempts to make decisions based on his perception of the quality of music and performance.[4] Mann is a songwriter, record producer, and music executive; he was formerly chief creative officer and later president of EMI Music International A&R, then president of Creative at BMG, and currently (while continuing to actively write and produce for artists such as P!nk, John Legend, Cher, and others) is the founder/CEO of what his website describes as "a new hybrid label/publishing company for songwriters," Green & Bloom Entertainment (www.greenandbloom.net). Mann (2012) expressed a fair amount of self-described idealism in our interview but admitted it was difficult to maintain it while being at board level at a multinational music corporation. He described the dynamic in the industry as a seesaw process:

> I think on the one hand you are at the axis between two extremes. So one extreme, which is music, your passion, your drive—especially for me. I'm not someone who's a lawyer by background who all of a sudden realized he had magical musical powers; I grew up as a musician. So I have one side of the seesaw, the creative side, and then there's the business side, and there are days that you have to make painfully difficult decisions that the music side is saying "yes," and the business side is clearly saying "no way." And I think the part of the music industry that is the most mystical part, the part that is the mystical dark art part, is knowing when to pay closer attention to one side than the other. There are far too many successful artists whose music and career narrative lacks logic or couldn't have been predicted by trends, and that's the beauty of art. So this is where instincts and belief falls into play in terms of everything. Of course it's judgment, people, songs, producers, songwriters, managers, but overall for me I would say, leadership means maintaining a balance between the music and then business without losing your nerve to risk failure for something you believe in.

Mann spoke in vivid and metaphorical terms about the power of the business side of the industry:

> Today if you look at the music industry, you have an army of middle-upper executives that all claim to carry guns, but they lack any true delegated authority so, guns aside, they don't have bullets. And unless they lobby internally and politick, they struggle to shoot even once. So, to an artist they claim they can effectively sign or work, the best they can do is point and threaten, but they don't have any bullets that allow them to pull the trigger on signing, developing, and breaking a new act without a chain of approvals. That said, they do have pretty intimidating uniforms; they have a pretty awesome army base with those fancy offices.

Mann related an incident in which he prevailed in a debate with an executive over an artist he wanted to promote, the French DJ David Guetta.[5]

> When I was in EMI I was president of International New Music, and there were thirty-four territories and thirty-two countries, etc.—everything but the US and the UK. At the time, David Guetta was already a successful DJ who had pretty much sold primarily singles, with one in particular called "Love Is Gone" that had a great run, but he hadn't really sold nearly enough albums to rationalize as a global priority. At the time, I believe the aggregate sales was under 140,000 units; not global priority level. I had traveled to EMI France to do a business review, and David and I met in the back of a taxi going to a Cold-

play concert. He's truly one of the most magical people you will ever meet. For the people who wonder how a guy can stand up on stage as a DJ and raise both his hands up and make hundreds of thousands of people go mad-crazy, part of it is just he has this fun, unspeakable kind of energy about him—he's just an incredible guy. And the two of us are sitting in the back of this taxi, heading to see Coldplay, and he wants to play me some music he was just working on, and we immediately have a good rapport. I put the headphones on, and I'm listening, and I'm listening to the voice of Kelly Rowland, who happens to be an artist who I worked with over the years, writing and producing for, and is one of my closest friends. Meanwhile David has no idea I'm listening to one of my dearest friends, someone who literally comes and stays at my house and plays with my kids, and he's playing me this song called, "When Love Takes Over" in the back of this taxi. And I'm looking at him, and I'm hearing Kelly's voice, and the song is just an absolute smash. And I'm thinking, "I must go to war for this." Now at that moment, there was no scale. There is the listening, as someone who's been in the music industry for over twenty years and is meant to have some kind of more refined judgment, I suppose, on a good day, but in that moment I'm thinking about David and I'm thinking about Kelly. I'm thinking this is a very mystical moment, because I'm just getting my feet under the desk at EMI, where, really, for me, meeting each artist was important—I wanted to connect with people—but here I'm listening to one of my closest friends sing this song that's a total smash, and I'm really excited. Then immediately after that I turn to David and I go, "Kelly is one of my dearest friends and this song is a smash and I love it and it's going to be huge, but we're going to have to fight for it."

I immediately went back to London, and the way that the company was run during that time was under an odd "matrix" structure, which at times made it virtually impossible to execute decisions, and there was a fierce debate on whether or not David Guetta should receive the kind of marketing push that I was suggesting. And one of the more finance-oriented marketing people said in a meeting, which was attended by the board—in a really pretty awesome British accent [adopts accent]—"So what you're suggesting is that we should invest millions of pounds in a DJ, who neither sings nor dances, who stands behind a table, because you heard this song and are convinced that it will be globally successful based on your experience." It was just, like, a cartoon version of an old British banker yelling "Turn that noise down" at a teenager listening to Queen. It was just so awful. Anyway, the debate followed, and fortunately, I won, and in the end the artist and the company won the debate, and the song went on to be a global smash, win the Grammy, and David has of course since gone on to massive, massive global success. While he had started already successful in his world, for me, calling *Billboard* and lobbying the then-EIC [editor in chief] to put him on the cover was just a wonderful moment, because it all went back to the taxi, which then had to go to the board discussion and the date.

One of the reasons why I was so passionately committed to David was because the economy was starting to sour. And I had randomly read an article about the rise of dance music during tough economic times. So I don't think I ever told anyone that, but there was a part of me that remembered reading that article and thinking, "These are tough economic times, and he's such a positive upbeat guy, and I think his brand of dance music and electronica are going to work."

This story demonstrates just how personal and subjective individual taste can be, how much success can depend on pure happenstance, how important a factoid about sales of a certain kind of music is in difficult economic times, and just how powerful the business side of the industry is. Mann's experience also is a vivid example of the work of translation that is required to move from one regime of value—musical, emotional—to the capitalist economic regime, and the uncertainty of that work's success.

Burger Records: "Keeping the Teenage Spirit Alive"

In the independent-label world of garage punk and almost everything else in Southern California, there is a remarkably different set of practices occurring. Sean Bohrman, one of the founders of Burger Records, codirects what I suppose one could call the quintessential DIY independent label. There is a retail storefront (an innovation of Brian Flores, a later partner), but the real work seems to occur in the back room, where Bohrman also lives, one wall nearly covered with VHS tapes (until they gave way to a station where Burger produces podcasts), other walls with posters of *Star Trek: The Next Generation* characters, Elvis, and more. This is the epicenter (or one of them) of independent record labels in Southern California. It has yet to turn a profit (Sisario 2014), since Bohrman and Lee Rickard use all income to expand the business.

Until the mid-2010s, Burger's system was simple. Artists came to them (or were solicited by them) with .wav (i.e., CD-quality) audio files and, sometimes, artwork in hand. If Burger thought the music was worthy of release, it ordered 250 cassettes to be manufactured. The artist received 50 tapes; Burger kept the rest to sell in its shop and at shows. If the band should run out of its tapes, which it mainly sells at its shows, it could go back to Burger and ask for more. If the music was really good, Bohrman told me, Burger might release it on an LP, which requires more money up front. Now, Burger may advance a band some funds in order to make a recording, which could possibly be done

FIGURE 5.1. Brian Flores, Sean Bohrman, and Lee Rickard of Burger Records (photo by Peter Tran)

in Burger's new studio, Studio B, in Los Angeles. Artists that Burger wants to release don't necessarily need to come to the label with recordings in hand anymore. Burger will also engage studio musicians for its artists.

At the beginning and for the first few years, no contracts were involved: "I don't need to own someone else's song," Bohrman told me. But Burger's rapid growth (they released 310 recordings in five years, 800 by mid-2014) meant that they had to begin to consider contracts in 2012. Lee Rickard, Burger's other cofounder, told me then that they wanted their contracts to be "the best in the business." Since that 2012 interview, Bohrman and Rickard have indeed begun to start using contracts, because the success of the label has necessitated signing their artists to contracts so that they can't be poached by another label. Rickard says they try to make their contracts as artist-friendly as possible (Bohrman and Rickard 2014). They maintain two-year control of artists' masters in order to try to make the most of placement and other opportunities.

After its founding, Burger started a subsidiary called Wiener Records, in which musicians pay for the production of the tape plus a little extra for Burger's expenses. Bands can supply the artwork themselves or Bohrman can provide it, and

> you can get it mastered by our guy, or you can not get it mastered, and we will put it out and release it through Wiener Records, hype it through Wiener, and

we'll keep 10 percent, sell it off the Wiener website and send it to you, and we make a little money, and they get their tapes made, and everybody wins.

"Everyone's a Wiener!" says the website (www.wienerrecords.org). Bohrman told me in 2012:

> The first person we put out was this band, Wax Witches . . . and it was just this one kid from the Gold Coast of Australia who had no chance of getting his music heard in America, or getting any kind of physical thing out in America 'cause he's from some small town. And it was actually really good. So that was the first release through Wiener, and it got written up in a bunch of blogs, and he was totally stoked. And that was the reason why we started Wiener, for people like him to get their music heard. He paid the money, got his tapes, and we sold out of ours instantly. That was our idea for our subsidiary.

Part of the reason that Burger's preferred format is cassettes is that they're cheap to produce, just $1 per tape, Bohrman told me. But another reason was that cassettes had all but disappeared; no one was producing them anymore. To make a cassette is retro, cool. Bohrman told me, gesturing with some disdain at his notebook computer:

> Anybody can make a CD. I can make you a CD of anything in ten seconds on my computer, and the fact that you can do that totally eliminates any kind of cool factor, collectability, or anything from a CD. . . . We sell 100 tapes to every CD that we sell. Probably more than that. We barely sell any CDs.

And Cathy Illman (2012a) told me, "I've been with cassette tapes all my life, and that's what I use."

The Burger artists I interviewed, and those whose releases I have seen, do not seem to have much of a sense of ownership of their music. For them, it's more about making the music and participating in a community. All of the Burger Records releases I have seen (which is by no means a majority, since there are hundreds now) did not include copyright information. I asked Lee Rickard (2012) about this, and he said that when they started the label, they were like chickens with their heads cut off, not really knowing what they were doing. But as some of their music is licensed for film and television use, and as some of their bands sign contracts, copyright will become more of an issue.

I also asked Cathy Illman (2012b) about whether or not she copyrighted her music.

> I suppose I haven't done it because of a few things—number one being lazy, procrastinating, that kind of thing. Number two, I don't know anyone who copyrights their songs so I never think of it. Number three, I assume that no one is ever going to steal my music, and if they do, I feel like I have enough

FIGURE 5.2. Cathy Illman (Veloura Caywood) (photo courtesy of Cathy Illman)

evidence to support that I wrote the song. . . . But maybe I'm just naïve about that; I honestly don't know how that whole thing works. It doesn't really cross my mind. Oh, and number four—Don't you have to pay to do that? I don't want to pay any money for stuff if I don't think I absolutely need it.

In a similar vein, none of the Burger artists seemed to care if I recorded an interview, and all waved away my patient and careful explanation that the interview recordings would not be broadcast or podcast.

None of the Burger musicians I spoke to seemed to have aspirations to being a professional musician or winning a contract with a major label. Most said that a contract with a major label would limit their freedom to make the songs they want to make and perform the songs they want to perform. One, however, has signed to an important label, Sub Pop, yet remains part of the Burger community. Kyle Thomas (2012) of the band King Tuff told me:

I first started working with Burger maybe four years ago, and they just kind of came at me out of nowhere. I had no idea who they were, and they just called me up one day and asked if they could put out the tape of this record I'd made, so I was like, "Okay, no one really puts out cassette tapes," but I like them, and, so, why not? And they put out the tape, and over the years, they kept reprinting it and reprinting it, and they really developed a large part of my fan base

FIGURE 5.3. Kyle Thomas (King Tuff) (photo by Dan Monick)

for me, just by getting those tapes around. And the thing about Burger is, it's a very community kind of feeling—all the bands know each other. It's just been this thing that's growing over the years, and everyone feels like they're a part of it, and it's all happening organically, and it's just a really cool thing to be a part of, and feel like eventually they could be a label like Sub Pop, or they could go to that next level. It's been a really interesting journey, and it's a crazy cast of characters; everyone involved is kind of cartoonish and full of energy. I feel blessed to be a part of it.

The amount of things they've done for me is incredible. Like when I moved out here [from Vermont], they really helped me. They were one reason I moved out here, so I could be closer to that whole scene; it just helped me so much with going on tour and everything, so I'm really grateful for them.

These indie rock musicians I interviewed had varying degrees of interest in the products of the mainstream music industry; not all of them viewed themselves as in an oppositional relationship to it. Bohrman and Rickard will purchase its recordings—on LP. But Cathy Illman (2012a) told me she didn't like what the mainstream music industry produced:

The new stuff that's out is horrible. I don't like it at all, it's really bad. You can't help but hear it when you're out, to the stores and stuff, people are playing it in the restaurants, and it sounds awful. It makes me angry, it makes me want to be violent. I hate Auto-Tune [a device that automatically corrects singers' faulty intonation], I think that's horrible, and I don't like the slick sound—it has no soul to it. But as far as new stuff that I do like, I could probably count it on both hands. But I don't actively seek out new bands to listen to, I seek out stuff from like the '60s and '50s and '70s to listen to, that's more the stuff I actually like to listen to.

Illman, who was discovered by Bohrman, writes and records her own songs in her rented house in Haslett, Michigan. They can be unforgettably melodic but are clearly "lo-fi," a moniker she likes (example 5.1).[6] Illman, like several other Burger artists, told me that if she were offered a major label contract, she would turn it down, fearing it would interfere with her freedom to make the music she wants on her own terms. Illman (2012a) told me:

> People were trying to get me to [sign a record contract], but I don't know that I would have the ambition or the drive to keep churning out songs that they want. You know, if I had a contract that said I had to turn out an album in six months I would feel too much pressure, I think, to come up with all this stuff, and also raise my kid. I like to do things at my own pace. Even if they had a good deal that I could do things at my own pace, I wouldn't really want to be well known, either. I like to stay in the shadows, like this.

And Fletcher Shears (2012), who plays in a band with his twin brother, Wyatt, told me that they'd be happy to sign to a label on their own terms. "But you know, if it was some stupid thing where we had to sign some contract, or play certain specific songs every show for two years, something stupid like that, I'm not into that. I like to express myself, and make new songs, I don't like to be chained down."[7] I suspect that some of these musicians would in fact sign with a bigger label if they could, but they are articulating the sort of independent discourse that is common in indie music scenes.

I've listened to a fair number of Burger's releases. The songs and performances are well done, and the recording quality is generally high (unless they are trying not to be, like Veloura Caywood's "lo-fi" recordings). Stylistically, the music ranges quite a bit from cassette to cassette, and even on a single cassette, though much of it seems retro in various ways, which might signify "unoriginal" or "unmarketable" in the mainstream commercial music world. Summer Twins, for example, make music that is strongly reminiscent of 1960s girl groups, described on their website as "dreampop" and "rock 'n roll songs with a touch of California sun" (www.summertwinsmusic.com/about), which strikes me as quite accurate (example 5.2). The Resonars' MySpace page classifies their music as Pop/Psychedelic/Rock (www.myspace.com/theresonars); it sounds to me as if Matt Rendon, who is the Resonars, wants to be the neo-

FIGURE 5.4. The Summer Twins (photo by Joy Newell)

Beatles (example 5.3). This is not to criticize these musicians at all: they are clearly making the music they want to make, and doing so at a high level, and if the commercial music industry might find their styles to be unmarketable or unprofitable, the musicians don't seem to care.

Bohrman and his colleagues and friends and artists in the Burger Records scene are not simply releasing recordings. They are also encouraging their followers to have a different relationship to recorded music, and thus the music industry more generally. In 2012, they had only one album on iTunes, though now they have over a hundred recordings on Spotify, aided by the distributor they have recently engaged (Bohrman 2014a). They also use Bandcamp (about which more below), and they release some recordings on CD in order to receive college radio airplay. They want to encourage listeners to seek out what they want to hear. Bohrman (2012) told me:

FIGURE 5.5. Matt Rendon (the Resonars) (photo by Winston Henning)

So, if you want to find something that is personal, you have to search for it. Most people are content with the radio giving them what they want to hear, and that's their extent of music research. . . . It's laziness that stops people from finding new music or from listening to things. If you want to hear something, Google it, it'll come up. Getting started is the hardest part for people, and getting someone to hear something for the first time is the hardest thing. . . .

People say, "Oh, there's no good music anymore, there was no good music in the '80s," or whatever; they're absolutely, positively wrong, there's always good music, somewhere, forever. Somewhere in the world, someone is making good music, you just have to find it, and find them, as hard as it may be. Some of the people we find are just totally off the grid, living in the woods somewhere, but they have a friend of a friend who got a tape from a friend, and we heard it, and we put it out.

Bohrman mentioned Veloura Caywood in this context.

Burger and many of its musicians also make use of a website called Bandcamp. Since the rise of the popularity of the Internet and World Wide Web in the early to mid-1990s, much has been made of the potential for musicians to sell their music directly to their fans. But this model hasn't really taken off: unknown musicians need to become known in order to be able to make a living from their music. It has been mainly famous artists who have been able to sell their music online, but they became famous by signing with a major label that spent a good deal of money promoting them. Now, however, there is

Bandcamp (www.bandcamp.com).[8] Artists can sell their music and merchandise directly to fans, who can search Bandcamp to find music they might like. On its homepage, Bandcamp tells users how many millions fans have given artists to date, and in the last thirty days (the former figure is approaching $100 million as of this writing). Things move so quickly in the online world that it is difficult to say if this model will be around long, though it certainly seems to be growing quickly.

Bohrman possesses a kind of incrementalist view of how to build a fan base for his bands and Burger Records, attempting to create a network, connecting with existing ones.

> The tapes are so easy to distribute, so easy to make, and so cheap to make in quantity, that we're able to put out tons of different bands from all over the world. I wanted to put out the best band in every city across the world, 'cause if you do that, you're dropping fifty tapes in that city, and they go to fifty people in that city, and it keeps growing, we sell them. And that's what we did to begin with, we just put out different bands from different parts of the world, and started spreading and spreading and growing and growing. It's like dropping bombs or planting seeds, it just grows and grows, and that was a conscious decision on our part. (Bohrman 2012)

Later in that interview, Bohrman discussed the interconnected nature of the music world as he sees it.

> Music is a web. Before I started the label or the band or anything, every time I bought a record I'd look it up online and see who the producer was, the story behind the band and the album, to connect the dots between producers and band players and engineers and record labels. There's just this whole web where everybody is interconnected somehow: Nick Lowe was Johnny Cash's son-in-law—that's a weird rock and roll connection that I love. And we're making such a huge net, throwing out all these webs between all these bands.

Burger Records and Dean Spunt's label, Post Present Medium, at least for now, are clearly operating in a field of restricted production (Bourdieu 1993) in which the musicians make music mainly for each other and a small but dedicated fan base, but it is a field that is not defined generically: unlike many independent labels, which frequently specialize in a particular (sub)genre of music, Burger is quite eclectic. Bohrman (2012) told me:

> I grew up around music, my dad has been in rock and roll bands since I was born, so I just grew up around it, and I know what I like. It's not just rock music; I love rap music. We put out the Pharcyde, the rap album from 1992 on cassette, and put out some other rap stuff and electronic music and ambient music. We're into all sorts of stuff, not just rock. It just turns out most of our

friends make rock music, so that's what we do. . . . I love all music, and I'm excited about people being excited about music, even if it's not specifically music I listen to.

Similarly, Lee Rickard (2012) told me:

Well, that's the beauty of Burger, you know what I mean? There are gourmet burgers, there are fast food burgers, there are all kinds of burgers. We're equal Burger opportunists, you know? We like all kinds of music. We're music lovers, we can't just like pop and nothing else. We love pop, we love classical, we love rock, we love funk, we love soul, we love garage, we love dirty stuff and weird stuff, anything in between.

Since I first encountered Burger Records, and Bohrman and Rickard, in 2012, the label has quickly grown. Bohrman and Rickard haven't hired anyone new to help run the label, but it has expanded to include a publishing company (Burger Music Publishing, for licensing music), a placement company (Burger Placements, for placing Burger recordings in film, television, and commercials, which is a partnership with an existing company, Natural Energy Lab), and a concert booking company; they have engaged a distributor, Redeye Distribution, that handles the production of their cassettes, a promotion company that promotes them, and another company that gives them access to college radio. And the label now produces video, released on YouTube (BRGRTV), and podcasts (BRGR Radio) (Bohrman and Rickard 2014). Bohrman and Rickard are working eighteen-hour days, they told me.

Bohrman summed up the change the label had undergone this way: "Before, there were no hoops to jump through. We got a record and we put it out, and it was out. As soon as we got the record, the record was out. Now we get the record and we sit on it for three months and then it's out." Rickard interjected that they had to link everyone up together to launch the recording, calling this work "synergy." Bohrman continued, "Before it was making sure all the manufacturers were in place, like jackets and labels and the actual manufacturing, and now it's making sure that our team is in place for the release because Redeye's handling the manufacturing, so I need to make sure that the radio's ready to go and the PR's all ready. It's a whole different thing now" (Bohrman and Rickard 2014).

Burger's field of cultural production cannot be characterized by genre. It is more like a scene in Will Straw's (1991) now-classic formulation, even though some of its participants—musicians, fans, and collectors—are delocalized, far from Southern California, and increasingly global, as Bohrman and Rickard pointed out (2014). The local manifestation of this scene is based partly on punk notions of irreverence and community, partly on a do-it-yourself ethic, partly on a rejection (to varying degrees) of not just the mainstream music industry and its products but also its technologies—digital means of distributing, storing, and listening to music. The cassettes are not commodity-fetishes but more like audio snapshots of friends.

Let me explore the question of restricted production, for it seems to me that the creation of a scene, a little culture (McCracken 1997), is one way to attempt to escape the ever-expanding net of today's capitalism. For Bourdieu, the field of restricted production is largely synonymous with artistic production, which is opposed to the field of large-scale cultural production—mass culture. But this distinction between the restricted and large-scale fields monolithizes the field of large-scale cultural production, failing to allow for restricted fields that might not be high art but nonetheless have some qualities in common with an artistic restricted field. And when one factors in questions of genre and/or style, matters become more complex, for Burger musicians mostly produce music in recognizable genres, that is to say, genres that occur in large-scale fields.

According to Bourdieu, the restricted and large-scale fields are in an oppositional relationship to each other. Fields of restricted production produce cultural goods mainly for other producers of cultural goods, whereas in the field of large-scale cultural production, cultural goods are produced for non-producers of cultural goods (1993, 115). Yet this isn't really the case for the Burger musicians, or at least, not all of them. Most do listen to what the mainstream music industry produces, and their musical styles and genres all emanate from what the industry has released. The Burger musicians don't view themselves as locked in this kind of relationship at all, but are rather aloof from it. Even when a Burger artist such as Kyle Thomas (King Tuff) signs with a commercial label (Sub Pop in his case), he doesn't terminate his relationship with Burger but instead continues to appear at shows with other Burger bands. Sub Pop permits him to record on Burger if he wishes, though Sub Pop does seem to have first refusal on any song he might want to take there. He told me, "I can't just put something out on Burger without telling them about it. They definitely want to know everything that's going on" (Thomas 2012). Dean Spunt (2012) of the band No Age, proprietor of the label Post Present Medium (PPM), made a similar deal.

> We signed a deal with Sub Pop that basically said that our full-length records come out on Sub Pop. We had to go back and forth with the contract, with the lawyer on their side, because if they had it their way, we would have signed a contract for three records plus anything we made from the time we signed it—which is from 2007 till it ends, which would be sometime next year when we

hope to turn in our next record for Sub Pop—they would own everything that we had recorded during that time. We had to change the contact to say that it was important for us to be able to put records out on smaller labels—singles, other things—because that's really the world we operate in, and was important for us to still be able to do that. So they agreed to let us do that. They wanted to own the master rights to our nonalbum songs, too, but we didn't want that, because it's most important for us to maintain a relationship with small labels that we want to work with. So we're allowed to record a record for PPM, for instance, as long as it's not a full-length, there's a certain amount of songs we're allowed to make, not really a time limit, but I think it can't be more than four songs or something, so we could technically put out a record every month on another label, if we wanted to. So that's how it works.[9]

These sorts of arrangements strike me as unusual in the sense that, not too long ago, large labels would absorb smaller labels, or their artists, in order to own them wholly. Today, labels such as Sub Pop seem to be willing to let small indie labels remain small and independent, and they can derive credibility among indie music fans from their artists' appearances on these small labels. It is more of a symbiotic relationship than a predatory one as was the case in the past. Cultural production companies in neoliberal capitalism seem to be less voracious about acquiring the means of the production of hip and cool than in the past, preferring instead to manage their relationship to the producers of the hip and the cool.

Another feature of the field of restricted production according to Bourdieu is that it usually develops its own criteria for evaluating its products, to the extent that a restricted field's autonomy can be measured by its power to delineate its own criteria for the production and evaluation of its products (1993, 115). This is demonstrably true of many artistic fields, though not true of the Burger crowd. The main criterion seems to be that they must like what they hear before agreeing to release it, which largely explains the great eclecticism of the label's roster and recordings. On one of my visits to the Burger Records shop, Claude Debussy's *La Mer* was playing on the store's stereo.

Burger, however, has achieved some autonomy in Bourdieu's conception of this idea. Bohrman told me that there are some collectors who purchase all of Burger's releases. They have successfully cultivated a dedicated fan base that values all the label's products. Bourdieu writes that another way that the autonomy of a restricted field can be measured is by the degree to which it is capable of functioning as a specific market, creating value that is incommensurable with economic value (1993, 117). Burger is quite successful at exemplifying the hip and the cool, an unlabel run by real people who love music, not run by suits.

It is also worth noting the complex ways that Burger recordings move in and out of commodity and gift status, different sorts of values. Most musicians pay to record their music before they bring it to Burger, but once Burger decides to release it, no money changes hands. Musicians' recordings of their songs are essentially gifts made to the label, which then turns them into cassettes, some of which it gives back to the musicians. Burger can sell the cassettes in its shop or online, and the musicians can sell cassettes at gigs, or digital versions of songs or albums to download, but since the Burger Records community is a fairly restricted field, musicians also purchase recordings from each other in what I would consider a form of generalized reciprocity (Sahlins 1974) even though these recordings are not technically gifts; the money that changes hands, however, is canceled out since everyone is paying much the same price for each other's cassettes. Musicians' recordings therefore move in and out of commodity and gift statuses. Thus, as mentioned in chapter 2, to conceptualize neoliberal capitalism as a capitalism that gobbles up everything in its path isn't accurate (though it is useful, as Tsing [2013] points out, for arguing against it). Goods move in and out of various statuses, regimes, but in different ways in different contexts.

This is perhaps the right point to examine these musicians sociologically. All of the Burger Records people I spoke to came from working-class or lower-middle-class backgrounds; most did not have a college education, and most of those who did attended regional public colleges or universities. All are WASPs, to use a now-quaint term (though the label's roster includes musicians of color), and many are in their early thirties and younger. In refusing to become mere consumers of what the dominant culture offers and making their own music (or their own record label), the Burger folks are participating not just in a scene but, to revisit a useful concept, in a "little culture" (McCracken 1997), one that is largely autonomous from the dominant culture(s). The Burger folks do not seem to view themselves as being oppressed by a dominant culture, victims of symbolic violence. This doesn't mean that they aren't, but I do think that their overall indifference to the dominant culture—both as represented by high art and by the mainstream music industry—needs to be examined.

With the waning of the prestige of the fine arts and the shift toward eclecticism in the taste of elite groups (see chapter 2), the kind of hierarchical structure that Bourdieu identified has been destabilized to the degree that I would say there are no longer two sorts of fields that exist in a dominant/subordinate relationship. This structure, in fact, was shifting even while Bourdieu was studying it as a result of the "conquest of cool" (Frank 1997) and the "artistic critique" of capitalism (Boltanski and Chiapello 2005; see also

McGuigan 2009). With the strength of this hierarchy diminishing, the "dual-
istic structure of the field of cultural production" (Bourdieu 1993, 53) is giving
way to a more amorphous structure—if it can be called that at all—in which
the field of large-scale cultural production becomes increasingly monolithic,
driven by the search for the next blockbuster, whether in publishing, film,
broadcasting, or music. This structure is part of a larger dynamic in which
restricted fields, little cultures, proliferate, occasionally aided by new digital
technologies or, in the case of Burger Records, the rediscovery and reuse of
obsolete ones such as the cassette, promoted heavily by Bohrman on social
media, without which, Rickard told me, "our business wouldn't be what it is"
(2012).

The Burger Records is becoming increasingly influential in the world of inde-
pendently produced and distributed music, so much so that the label is being
looked to as an arbiter of what is hip and cool. This seems to me to be an unusual phenomenon, since Bohrman and Rickard are not "youth"—normally
the originators of the hip and the cool—and they do not occupy the class
positionality of, say, the new petite bourgeoisie, which is the social group that
is most occupied with the promulgation of taste. We may be witnessing the
rise of a new social formation that is finding ways to create forms of capital
for itself that are gaining traction outside of that social group. That is, rather
than some members of the new petite bourgeoisie, who are themselves pos-
sessors of fairly high amounts of educational and financial capital, shaping
mainstream tastes, it may be the case that more marginal groups, in terms of
their possession of volume of educational, financial, and cultural capital, are
slowly finding ways of becoming tastemakers as well.[10]

The Burger Records proprietors' attitudes toward technology warrant further discussion in this regard. Sean Bohrman seems to use his personal computer mainly for e-mail, access to social media to promote Burger Records
releases, and the design of cover art for Burger recordings. His daily work
plan is kept in a small notebook with extremely neat handwriting. Rickard
does not own some technologies that many today deem to be essential: "I
don't have a cell phone," he told me (2012). "I mean I just got one for the last
tour, but it was annoying, and I let it die. I didn't have one for eight years, and
I barely had it, and I got a $1,500 phone bill, so I don't need it; less is more to
me." And he doesn't have a computer: "My whole life I could never keep up
with technology . . . get a Nintendo, Super Nintendo, Genesis, and I didn't
care, there's too many buttons, not my thing." Bohrman and Rickard's other
partner, with whom they started the Burger Records retail store, doesn't have
a computer either.

Part of the Burger musicians' refusal to fully embrace new technologies can be attributed to their class positionality. Nobody associated with Burger Records that I interviewed (an admittedly small sample size) comes from a wealthy background, and nobody possesses particularly high amounts of cultural, educational, or financial capital. Partly, Burger Records issues cassettes because they're cheap to manufacture and thus to sell, which means almost anyone can afford their music. But partly, also, I think, Burger releases cassettes as a way of resisting the hype of the latest music technology and digital format. Bohrman (2012) showed what I took to be uncharacteristic impatience with those who don't have a way of playing a cassette: "People who complain, like, 'A tape? Where am I going to play that?' 'Well, go to a thrift store and buy a tape player!'" I also think that the recourse to old technologies such as cassettes (and video cassettes—Bohrman had a wall of them in his home/office at the back of the Burger Records store, but they gave way to a station where they could create podcasts) is a way of not being pulled into today's neoliberalized, informationalized universe in which the personal computer has turned us all into clerks, administrators, and technocrats (see Graeber 2012 and Taylor 2012a).

Bohrman and Rickard's attitudes toward technology is not a middle-class, high-educational-capital resistance to consumption (though perhaps some of their resistance just described could be attributed to those in that social group); it's mainly a working- or lower-middle-class resistance, opting out of a world in which coolness is defined in part by the gadgets one owns, and hipness is partly defined by one's knowledge of obscure music. Bohrman told me, "That was our whole thing—we don't want to be selective, like, 'This is for these people only, and squares get out,' or 'Adults get out,' or all that kind of stuff. We want to have everybody in one happy family, everybody enjoying it" (2012).

Cassettes aren't cool because they're retro—Bohrman and Rickard seemed to have no interest in that (Bohrman told me he's glad that Walmart is now selling LPs, for example). Cassettes are cool because you can make them yourself, they can be personalized as Burger does, they are as mass-produced as CDs, and you can manufacture and sell them at prices affordable to any fan. Bohrman (2012) told me that while it was blogs that paid attention to their music in digital form on SoundCloud,

> the physical stuff is for fans and collectors and people who have tape players in their car who just want to hear music. And the beauty of cassettes is that they're so cheap to buy, they're like $5–$6. They are $6 online and $5 in our store. And sometimes, there are two or three albums on a cassette, and you can't beat twenty-five to thirty songs for $5.

This is not the claim of somebody who is (merely) in the record business or someone attempting to promote the hip and the cool, but of someone who uses sophisticated digital technologies to disseminate word about his label's releases in an effort to expand the Burger Records community in Southern California and beyond, one cassette at a time. With small labels like Burger Records, the medium isn't the (only) message. The mode of cultural production is one message, and the noneconomic regime of value that Burger operates in is another, a regime in which Bohrman and Rickard's taste, and the recording of bands that keep the teenage spirit alive, matter most of all.

Conclusions: Capitalism Is People, Too

Capitalism as an economic system and social form has been with us for centuries, making it difficult to discern what might be new about it with any definitiveness. Everything corrosive and destabilizing and unfair and rapacious and voracious that we have long known about capitalism seems to be true, and ever truer: it is making some things happen more quickly than ever before; it is spreading over the globe, farther and more quickly than ever before; social relations continue to attenuate because of it; the rich continue to get richer, the poor poorer. I have had to go through this book and make sure that I have not overused the adverb "increasingly," apt though it is much of the time in describing today's culture in a comparison to what has gone before. Marx and Engels's famous characterization of capitalism, made, now, over 150 years ago, seems ever more accurate:

> Constant revolutionising of production, uninterrupted disturbance of all social conditions, everlasting uncertainty and agitation distinguish the bourgeois epoch from all earlier ones. All fixed, fast-frozen relations, with their train of ancient and venerable prejudices and opinions, are swept away, all new-formed ones become antiquated before they can ossify. All that is solid melts into air, all that is holy is profaned, and man is at last compelled to face with sober senses his real conditions of life, and his relations with his kind. (1964, 7)

Nonetheless, I have endeavored in the course of this book to historicize the present by wondering in what ways today's capitalism in the West is different from earlier capitalisms. It is partly a matter, as I have said, of speed and scale. Digital technologies make it easy to communicate, trade stocks, and send documents, photographs, or audio around the world, one reason

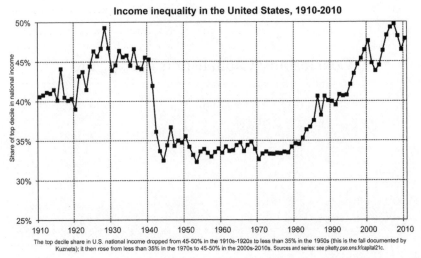

FIGURE 6.1. Income Inequality in the United States, 1910–2010 (from Piketty 2014, 24)

that today's music production can be increasingly fragmented. For the US entertainment industry, audio production of various kinds remains mainly in Santa Monica, California (greater Los Angeles), but increasingly for reasons of hipness and the desire to be near one's tribe and less for reasons of convenience, since audio or video tapes or film no longer need to be physically transported as they were in the past.

Neoliberal policies and ideologies have succeeded miraculously—from the perspective of their adherents—at moving wealth upward while depriving the poor and shrinking the middle class. According to the Congressional Budget Office in 2011, in the last thirty years, the top 1 percent of earners in the United States more than doubled their share of income, in part because the federal government since the late 1970s has done less to reduce the concentration of income in the wealthiest groups. From 1979 to 2007, income grew by 275 percent for the wealthiest 1 percent of the population; for others in the top 20 percent, income grew by 65 percent. For the 60 percent of people in the middle, the growth of income was just under 40 percent. And for the poorest 20 percent of the population, income grew by only 18 percent (Pear 2011, A20). In 2012, the top 10 percent of the US population garnered more than 50 percent of the country's total income, the highest level recorded since the government began collecting such data a century ago (Lowrey 2013, B1). Figure 6.1 shows income equality in the United States from 1910 to 2010; table 6.1 shows income inequality across time and space.

Advertising Age, the main weekly chronicle of the advertising industry in the United States, writes in sober and matter-of-fact tones about the shrink-

TABLE 6.1. Inequality of Total Income (Labor and Capital) across Time and Space (adapted from Piketty 2014, 249)

Share of different groups in total income (labor + capital)	Low inequality (≈ Scandinavia, 1970s–1980s)	Medium inequality (≈ Europe 2010)	High inequality (≈ US 2010, Europe 1910)	Very high inequality (≈ US 2030?)
The top 10% ("upper class")	24%	35%	50%	60%
Including the top 1% ("dominant class")	7%	10%	20%	25%
Including the next 9% ("well-to-do class")	18%	25%	30%	35%
The middle 40% ("middle class")	45%	40%	30%	25%
The bottom 50% ("lower class")	30%	25%	20%	15%

ing middle class. The magazine, a champion of not only advertising but of consumption more generally, seeks to tell the truth to its subscribers in the industry, who need to know how to continue to advertise and market goods to the largely unsuspecting market, two-thirds of which is considered to be overweight or obese thanks to the advertising industry's success at marketing of foodstuffs, oversweet drinks, and restaurants (see Morrison 2011, 40). An *Advertising Age* article on the middle class notes how brands are selling more downscale goods, because "America's backbone is bending toward the breaking point," and points out that in the last decade, all consumers curtailed spending by 4.2 percent in 2010 dollars. The middle class cut spending by 10 percent to 13 percent, and the upper 20 percent of earners cut spending by 6 percent (Carmichael 2011, 4). A study conducted by Stanford University shows that the number of Americans living in middle-class neighborhoods has diminished significantly since 1970; in that year, 65 percent of families lived in middle-income areas; by 2007, the last year for which the study has data, the figure was 44 percent. This shift is a result of the upward movement of wealth, impoverishing people at the bottom of the system and forcing some in the middle class into the ranks of the working poor (Tavernise 2011, A15).

Rich richer, poor poorer. Clearly, the mission of elite groups to raise their incomes has been a great success. The signs are everywhere. And not just signs of declining neighborhoods and increased struggle. Food marketers are packaging goods in smaller containers in order to display lower prices for the increased number of consumers who subsist paycheck to paycheck (Carmichael 2011, 4; see also Schultz 2011).

As I hope is clear in these pages, neoliberal capitalism isn't just an economic system but a social form, one with profound ramifications for culture, one of my other main concerns in this book. Our culture—American culture, at least—has become one of almost unremitting consumption, fueled by equally omnipresent advertising. The abundance of consumable goods Americans believe themselves to enjoy is, as I said in the introduction, one of the main signs of our capitalism as a cultural system. Perhaps music is one of the most potent signs of this plenitude, since one can access virtually anything one wants online; there is more music available than one could ever listen to. One can put more music than one could ever listen to on a single device, whether iPhone or computer. Yet many people acquire more and more music. We have become a culture choked with goods, believing ourselves to have myriad choices, though the "differences" between most commodities is largely concocted by advertising agencies. Commodities take up more and more of our time in our contemplation of them and in their use, and in earning wages in order to purchase them. The "moods and motivations" discussed by Geertz in "Religion as a Cultural System" (1973) can be found in attitudes toward consumption since the rise of neoliberal capitalism, when people routinely speak of activities such as "retail therapy" and employ slogans such as "When the going gets tough, the tough go shopping!"

There are plenty of critics of neoliberal capitalist consumer cultures, of course (see N. Klein 2000 for just one prominent example). My strategy in these pages has mainly been to offer implicit, not explicit, critiques, and to offer positive, even hopeful, examples, as in the previous chapter. And it must be remembered that there are plenty of musicians who are working hard just to make a living at music, musicians who would be very happy to have their work commodified so they can make a living from doing what they love and are good at. But this has gotten harder and harder, as record labels wait for bands to make their own success before signing them, instead of nurturing bands as they did in the past. One person I interviewed spoke of this with a good deal of bitterness. Michael Fiore (2014) of the Echo Park, Los Angeles, band Criminal Hygiene told me that a lot of the bigger labels

> now want a band that's pretty much on their own, to do everything themselves to the point where they can't anymore. Labels want to take over when a band is ready to make them money already, instead of developing an artist like they did years ago—there used to be artist development teams as part of a label, and they'd essentially pick a band that they thought was great, or had a great live show, and they'd go, "This is the band," and they'd help develop a career. Now, the band does everything, goes broke until they're fucking eating ramen every day, Top Ramen, fifty cents, every day on the road, and the label says, "We'll sign them now, 'cause they'll make us money." Then if you don't sell records for them in a year or two, you're done.

All Fiore and most people in this scene aspire to is to make a living at music.

Value in the Informal Logic of Actual Life

Clifford Geertz once argued that the "informal logic of actual life" should be the focus of cultural analysis (1973, 17), and that is what I have attempted to chronicle in many of these pages. How do real people—composers, performers, producers, other music industry laborers—work with, work against, and work in, today's capitalism? Capitalism is not a gigantic, logy, devouring machine but a structure, a social form, one that shapes thoughts and practices as it is shaped by them. It is in people's heads as a cultural system, a set of ideologies, an ensemble of practices. People live the informal logic of their lives in and against the structure of capitalism.

But this structure is massive, making possible the creation of not just economic regimes of value but, as we have seen, other regimes of value (Appadurai 1986; Myers 2001), existing alongside different modes of production (Tsing 2013), and in other sorts of histories (Chakrabarty 2000), all of which capitalism depends on and can draw from. The history of popular music in the United States is a history that is littered with forms of music that were produced in other regimes, modes, histories, that were unknown to capitalists or ignored by them, musics produced by and for people who possessed their own regimes of value for them. That many of these musics became part of the capitalist music industry is not a simple story of commodification but rather a series of different and complex histories of how music produced in one regime of value was brought—by real social actors in real times and places— into a capitalist economic regime, sometimes slowly, sometimes tumultuously. Chakrabarty (2000) has called such activities "translation." It took a long time, a lot of advertising time and expenses, as well as trial and error, to convince people that purchasing recordings in the form of player piano rolls was superior to making music oneself (as discussed in Taylor 2007b). The segregation of musics by southern African Americans and European Americans into commercial genres in the first half of the twentieth century was another long and complex process (see Miller 2010). Rock and roll had to be deracinated sufficiently to appeal to white America, requiring a good deal of time and effort.

In these pages, I have discussed how workers at the fringes of the mainstream music industry attempt to negotiate the values they have for their music at small, independent labels while at the same time interacting with the capitalist music industry, as well as one person, Billy Mann, an industry insider, who negotiates similar issues. And we have seen how Angélique Kidjo has maneuvered in the mainstream music industry, attempting to be an agent of this translation process, making music under the commercial "genre" of "world music." Burger Records' label principals and musicians, and other indie musicians in Southern California, make and release the music they like, which sometimes catches the attention of the music industry and sometimes does not; some want to be noticed by the mainstream music industry, and some, like Cathy Illman, prefer to remain in the shadows. But most are making music for the extended community of Southern California indie rock with its own conceptions of value, and its own modes of production and exchange, closer to gift exchange than capitalist forms of exchange, as I argued in chapter 5.

In this book, I have attempted to move beyond earlier studies of the cultural industries, particularly Horkheimer and Adorno (1990) in their monolithic treatment of the cultural industries and pessimism about them and their products. But the cultural industries are not monoliths with undifferentiated workers simply producing sterile commodities. And consumers do not conform to lofty theories about them, just as, despite the best market research money can buy, they do not obediently populate neatly demarcated homogeneous groups. People have actual lives. While it is imperative to know what the mainstream music cultural industries are doing in order to view capitalist ideologies and practices in action (though these industries are inhabited in part by figures such as Billy Mann who possess deep understandings of more than one regime of value), it is just as important to attend to workers on the fringes of the mainstream cultural industries such as those discussed in chapter 5. And while it is crucial to "study up" (Nader [1969] 1974), to study the strategies of those in power, studying "down," studying tactics in de Certeau's (1984) sense is just important, perhaps more necessary now. As neoliberal capitalism becomes increasingly pervasive and pernicious across the globe, if we are to find ways of making it more just and humane, our best guides will be the tacticians.

Notes

Introduction

1. There is a very useful overview in chapter 2 of Jarvis 1998 on Adorno's thinking about capitalist society, however.

2. See Taylor n.d.a for a consideration of cultural goods and value. For useful writings on the conception of value of goods, see Appadurai 1986, Graeber 2001 and 2005, and Myers 2001. Thanks are due to Steven Feld for recommending the last book.

3. See the introduction to Taylor 2007a and, for a now-classic articulation, McClary 1987.

4. I would be remiss, however, not to mention Maróthy 1974, a product of high Soviet-style Marxism.

Chapter One

1. For discussions of the ups and downs of the music publishing industry in its first couple of centuries, see Bianconi 1987 and Chanan 1994.

2. Miège posits three types: unique products (such as a painting), reproducible products (reproductions of paintings, recordings of music, etc.), and "non-material performances" that are the objects of a "direct relation between producer and consumer of a material object" (1989, 24). For other taxonomies, see Lawrence and Phillips 2002; Lacher and Mizerski 1994; and Scott 2004.

3. For more on the music publishing industry in this era, see Suisman 2009.

4. I explore the question of finance capital and musical production in greater detail in Taylor 2013.

5. See Bourdieu 1993 and 1996 for a discussion of the rise of the autonomous literary field of cultural production in France.

6. And the origins of capitalism in England are bound up with English colonialism—in Ireland before the New World—and changing conceptions of the uses of land and the amount of labor required to produce commodities (Wood 2005). See Wood 2002 and Perelman 2000 for more on the origins of capitalism.

7. For a collection of some specific cases, see Salmen 1983 and Weber 2004.

8. For reports on this event, see Wakin 2012a. For a study of a symphony concert as ritual, see Small 1987.

9. See Taylor, Katz, and Grajeda 2012 for a reprint of Edison's article, as well as a collection of other early writings.

10. Thanks are due to David Suisman for this.

11. For other writings on the importance of consumption and music, see Taylor 2007a and 2012b. For an influential historical study, see Campbell 1989.

Chapter Two

1. Thanks are due to Anne Phillips for providing me a copy of this unpublished article.

2. The company has a website at http://www.hitsongscience.com.

3. This history of the 1980–81 AFM strike and the rise of the package deal are from Elliott 2013, with thanks.

4. Thanks are due to Breena Loraine, who had the idea of perusing the first of these books, as well as other how-to guidebooks.

5. This seems to be from Gobé 2001; a newer edition is Gobé 2009.

6. For more on cobranding and music, see Love-Tulloch 2012.

7. Will.I.Am seems to be taking his new role seriously, having contributed an article on selling to *Advertising Age* (Will.I.Am. 2011).

8. Thanks are due to Joanna Love for telling me of this commercial.

9. For a critique of these sales and representation tactics by a young female classical musician, see Furness 2014.

10. Intangible value is increasingly accepted as monetary value, however; see Foster 2013. I will discuss this further below.

11. Steve Karmen, lauded as the "King of the Jingle" in the 1970s and 1980s before the jingle became thought of as uncool, wrote a book on the form's demise. In his interviews with advertising agency personnel, Karmen found that "the phrase 'cutting-edge' (or 'edgy') came up again and again in every interview. . . . It's the industry buzz word, the ongoing metaphor for that elusive quality that every sponsor wants—"hip music with a smile in it," one composer delicately called it—something that is totally replaceable on a moments [*sic*] notice as soon as someone anoints a newer, though not necessarily more memorable, version of cutting-edge" (2005, 20).

12. See Cross 2000; Cohen 2003; Lee 1993; McGovern 2006; Slater 1997; and Taylor 2012b.

13. Fans of old films may have noticed that a music supervisor is occasionally credited, but this was an entirely different profession and included some duties normally performed by music editors. For more on music supervisors, see Anderson 2014.

14. Douridas was invited by Logan Clark, a teaching assistant in one of my classes at UCLA, and I would like to think her for this, and Chris for coming.

15. For more on music supervisors, see Lewandowski 2010.

16. This quotation from Jobs was from a press conference on 1 September 2010, available at http://www.apple.com/apple-events/september-2010/; last accessed 21 September 2010.

17. For more on music supervisors and recommendation systems, see Taylor 2014c.

18. Thanks are due to Dave Wilson and Mike D'Errico for telling me about this phenomenon.

19. I examine sociality as a value of the Irish traditional music scene in southern California in Taylor n.d.d.

20. See also Kaplan 1988.

21. See also Suzanne Ciani's opinion in Doerschuk 1989.

22. For more by Bourdieu on the threats to the autonomy of the artistic fields, see Bourdieu 1998 and Bourdieu and Haacke 1995.

Chapter Three

1. Such as Castells 1996; Comaroff and Comaroff 2001; and Tsing 2005.

2. This was the album *Agwaya*, released in 1982. I have found no evidence of CBS following suit.

3. I treat this issue more extensively in Taylor 2012c.

4. I have considered all of these developments in greater detail in Taylor 1997a, 2012c, and 2014b.

5. In her 2014 autobiography, Kidjo takes a more sober tone: "In some ways, what is considered traditional music is actually quite modern, for over the course of the years it has adapted and has been enriched. If it hadn't modernized in this way, it would have disappeared. I always have a problem with people who see themselves as purists of African music, ones who talk to me of traditional music without having a clue about its evolution. They have a vision of some original, fossilized thing that needs to be preserved like a museum piece. It's a rather sectarian, rigid bias, as if Africa is some exotic thing that can't, or shouldn't, evolve. It's a Western fantasy—a belief in an imaginary primitive land that hasn't changed since Homo sapiens left Africa" (Kidjo and Wenrick 2014, 128). At the same time, as Louise Meintjes (2003) has shown, some non-Western musicians such as those South Africans she studied increasingly make music aimed at an international audience.

6. Ray Phiri, a musician on the *Graceland* album, says that Simon's copy was a bootleg version from London and that Simon had no idea what the music was or where it was from, and solicited the aid of his record company, Warner Bros., to track down the source (Mgxashe 1987, 31).

7. I treat this case at greater length in Taylor n.d.b.

8. For more on this recording, see Feld and Kirkegaard n.d. and Feld 2012.

9. For more on this album, see Feld 1996.

10. For a few examples, see Sony's library entitled Continental Drift: World Music Loops & Samples, with sample audio available at http://www.sonycreativesoftware.com /continentaldrift; and the Garritan World Instruments library, http://www.garritan.com/index .php?option=com_content&view=article&id=151&Itemid=169.

11. I consider world music as a field of cultural production at greater length in Taylor 2014a.

12. See, for just one example, Elder 1992.

13. David Byrne usefully outlines the landscape for musicians today in Byrne 2012.

14. See Taylor 2001 for a more in-depth treatment of this case.

15. For more on UNESCO and intangible cultural heritage, see Di Giovine 2009; Seeger 2009; and Taylor 2014d.

16. For the complete list, see UNESCO n.d.a.

Chapter Four

1. This is a very brief description, so, for more on jungle, see Reynolds 1994a, 1994b, 1995a, and 1995b; Shapiro 1999; Strauss 1994; and Toop 1994.

2. At the same time, MySpace was spending millions on increasing the availability of music on its site. See "MySpace COO Explains Massive Music Marketing Expansion Plans" (2008).

3. I am indebted to M.A. students at the Irish World Academy of Music and Dance, University of Limerick, for telling me of the Amanda Palmer case.

4. I consider the value of cultural commodities at length in Taylor n.d.a.

5. Thanks are due to Logan Clark for the Yorke story. See also Sisario 2013.

6. See also Knopper 2013.

7. Thanks are due to Matt Mugford for informing me of Tim Myers, and to Dave Wilson for introducing me to Matt.

8. Thanks are due to Breena Loraine, who first told me of Cathy Heller.

9. See, for one, Hesmondhalgh and Baker 2011.

10. For a useful comparison of creative labor writings and those on immaterial labor, see Brouillette 2009.

11. Thanks go to Adam Fish for recommending this article.

12. I discuss this at greater length in Taylor 2012b.

13. I am indebted to Charles McGovern for pushing me on the question of labor in the early days of radio.

14. Thanks are due to Mike D'Errico for this reference.

15. See Taylor n.d.a for one such consideration.

16. The cost of a New England Digital Synclavier, introduced in 1977, would be nearly $300,000 in today's dollars. By 1988, the Synclavier was still hugely expensive, $75,000–$250,000 for the "basic system" plus another $65,000–$240,000 for the "direct-to-disc computer storage units." (This is a range of roughly $136,750–$456,000 and $118,500–$438,000 in today's dollars.)

17. I am indebted to Emily Thompson for reminding me of the importance of the Discwasher in the listening ritual.

18. Thanks are due to Mark Katz for telling me of this article.

19. Thanks are due to Jeremy Grimshaw for this anecdote.

Chapter Five

1. Thanks are due to Anthony Seeger for helping me get in touch with Nowlin and Irwin.

2. Piracy predates digital technologies, of course; see Cummings 2013.

3. Thanks are due to Anthony Seeger for stressing this point.

4. Thanks are due to Charles B. Ortner for helping me reach Billy Mann.

5. For a report on Guetta's success for EMI, see Pichevin 2009.

6. See Tupica 2008.

7. The Shears brothers have recently become models for Yves Saint Laurent; see Cunningham 2013. Thanks are due to Shelina Brown for telling me of this article.

8. Thanks go to Kimberly Fox for pointing out to me the significance of Bandcamp.

9. Music lawyer Charles B. Ortner informs me that this is a provision in contracts called an override, which permits artists to record on other labels occasionally, normally for some of the profits.

10. I am grateful to Ben Court for helping me think about this point.

References

Unpublished Materials

INTERVIEWS

Backer, Bill. 2004. Telephone interview by author. 4 May.

Bissen, Georg, and Victoria Gross. 2004. Interview by author. 7 April, New York City.

Bloch, Andy. 2004. Interview by author. 20 April, New York City.

Bohrman, Sean. 2012. Interview by author. 23 July, Fullerton, CA.

Bohrman, Sean, and Lee Rickard. 2014. Interview by author. 18 July, Fullerton, CA.

Bryant, Anne. 2009. Telephone interview by author. 6 August.

Castelaz, Jeff. 2012. Interview by author. 26 July, Los Angeles.

Crenshaw, Randy. 2009. Telephone interview by author. 10 October.

DiMinno, Nick. 2009. Telephone interview by author. 10 September.

Doddy, Fritz. 2004. Interview by author. 14 April, New York City.

Drayton, Bernie. 2009. Telephone interview by author. 14 August.

Elliott, Alan. 2013. Interview by author. 3 May, Los Angeles.

Farber, Sharon. 2012. Interview by author. 30 July, Granada Hills, CA.

Fiore, Michael. 2014. Interview by author. 5 September, Los Angeles.

Horowitz, David. 2009. Telephone interview by author. 11 September.

Illman, Cathy. 2012a. Telephone interview by author. 31 July.

Irwin, Ken. 2012. Telephone interview by author. 18 June.

Kazerouni, Nima. 2014. Interview by author. 20 November, Santa Monica, CA.

Mann, Billy. 2012. Telephone interview by author. 21 June.

Michlin, Spencer. 2009. Telephone interview by author. 29 July.

Murtaugh, Hunter. 2009. Telephone interview by author. 16 October.

Nowlin, Bill. 2012. Telephone interview by author. 17 June.

Pettigrew, Craig. 2012. Interview by author. 27 August, Studio City, CA.

Rabinowitz, Josh. 2004. Interview by author. 21 April, New York City.

Rees, Helen. 2010. Interview by author. 30 April, Los Angeles.

Rickard, Lee. 2012. Interview by author. 1 August, Fullerton, CA.

Shapiro, David. 2009. Telephone interview by author. 7 August.

Seeger, Anthony. 2012. Interview by author. 15 June, Los Angeles.

Shears, Fletcher. 2012. Telephone interview by author. 7 August.

Spunt, Dean. 2012. Interview by author. 11 November, Los Angeles.

Steingold, Marissa. 2009. Interview by author. 15 October, Los Angeles.
Stern, Michael. 2012. Interview by author. 24 August, Calabasas, CA.
Thomas, Kyle. 2012. Interview by author. 9 August, Los Angeles.
Vanger, Anthony. 2004. Interview by author. 15 April, New York City.
White, Booker. 2012. Interview by author. 6 August, Burbank, CA.
Wong, Chris. 2012. Interview by author. 20 July, Los Angeles.

OTHER UNPUBLISHED MATERIALS

Appert, Catherine. 2012. "Modernity, Remixed: Music as Memory in Rap Galsen." Ph.D. diss., Department of Ethnomusicology, University of California, Los Angeles.
Bohrman, Sean. 2014a. Personal communication (email). 18 July.
———. 2014b. Personal communication (email). 3 November.
Coventry, Chloe. 2013. "Rock Bands/Rock Brands: Mediation and Musical Performance in Post-liberalization Bangalore." Ph.D. diss., Department of Ethnomusicology, University of California, Los Angeles.
Douridas, Chris. 2013. Lecture at the University of California, Los Angeles, 3 June.
Gubner, Jennie Meris. 2014. "Tango, Not-for-Export: Participatory Music-Making, Musical Activism, and Visual Ethnomusicology in the Neighborhood Tango Scenes of Buenos Aires." Ph.D. diss., Department of Ethnomusicology, University of California, Los Angeles.
Iglauer, Bruce. 2012. Personal communication. 22 August.
Illman, Cathy. 2012b. Personal communication. 31 July.
Love-Tulloch, Joanna. 2012. "'The Choice of a New Generation': 'Pop' Music, Advertising, and Meaning in the MTV Era and Beyond." Ph.D. diss., Department of Musicology, University of California, Los Angeles.
McFaul, Tom. 2009. Personal communication, 3 September.
Morris, Sue. 2003. "WADs, Bots and Mods: Multiplayer FPS Games as Co-Creative Media." Paper delivered at Level up: Digital Games Research Conference, Utrecht, Holland, November.
"Paying the Piper: Music Streaming Services in Perspective." 2013. National Public Radio, *All Things Considered*, 28 July.
Phillips, Anne. n.d. "Why Isn't My Business Fun Anymore?" Photocopy.
Rose, Joel. 2011. "How Spotify Works: Pay the Majors, Use P2P Technology." National Public Radio, *All Things Considered*, 9 November.
St. John, Lara. 1996. Interview by Robert Siegel. National Public Radio, *All Things Considered*, 11 November.
Samples, Mark Christopher. 2011. "A Package Deal: Branding, Technology, and Advertising in Music of the 20th and 21st Centuries." Ph.D. diss., University of Oregon.
Starch, Daniel. 1928. "A Study of Radio Broadcasting Based Exclusively on Personal Interviews with Families in the United States East of the Rocky Mountains." Photocopy.

Discography

The Best of Celtic Music. 2006. Music Brokers MBB 9101.
Buena Vista Social Club. 1997. *Buena Vista Social Club*. Nonesuch RTH 79478.
Byrne, David. 1989. *Rei Momo*. Luaka Bop/Sire 9 25990-2, 1989.

Cooder, Ry, and Ali Farka Touré. 1994. *Talking Timbuktu*. Hannibal Records HNCD 1381.

Copeland, Stewart. 1985. *The Rhythmatist*. A&M CD 5084.

Deep Forest. 1992. 550 Music/Epic BK-57840.

Eno, Brian, and David Byrne. 1981. *My Life in the Bush of Ghosts*. Sire/Warner Bros. 9 45374-2.

Kidjo, Angélique. 1994. *Ayé*. Mango/Antilles 1625 9934 4.

———. 1996. *Fifa*. Mango 162-531 039-2.

———. 1998. *Oremi*. Island 314-524-521-2.

———. 2002. *Black Ivory Soul*. Columbia CK 85799.

———. 2004. *Oyaya!* Columbia CK 89053.

———. 2007. *Djin Djin*. Razor & Tie 793018296-2.

———. 2010. *Ôÿö*. Razor & Tie 7930183062-2.

———. 2013. *Eve*. 429 Records FTN 17968.

Lawton, Liam. 1997. *The Clouds' Veil*. GIA Publications CD-415.

Polyphonies vocales des aborigènes de Taïwan. [1989]. Inédit, Maison des cultures du monde, W 2609 011.

Simon, Paul. 1986. *Graceland*. Warner Bros. W2-25447.

St. John, Lara. 1996. *Works for Violin Solo*. Well-Tempered Productions, WTP 5180.

Vanessa-Mae. 1995. *Toccata & Fugue: The Mixes*. Angel 7243 8 58508 2 0.

Wes. 1997. *Welenga*. Sony Music 48146-2.

World Hits. 2007. Putumayo PUT 267-2.

Filmography

Paul Simon: Born at the Right Time. 1992. Burbank, CA: Warner Reprise Video.

Books and Articles

Aaker, David A. 1996. *Building Strong Brands*. New York: Free Press.

Aaker, Jennifer. 1997. "Dimensions of Brand Personality." *Journal of Marketing Research* 34 (August): 347–56.

Aaker, Jennifer, and Susan Fournier. 1995. "A Brand as a Character, a Partner and a Person: Three Perspectives on the Question of Brand Personality." *Advances in Consumer Research* 22. http://www.acrwebsite.org/search/view-conference-proceedings.aspx?Id=7775. Last accessed 1 July 2014.

Adorno, Theodor. 1973. *Philosophy of Modern Music*. Translated by Anne G. Mitchell and Wesley V. Blomster. London: Sheed and Ward.

———. 1976. *Introduction to the Sociology of Music*. Translated by E. B. Ashton. New York: Continuum.

———. 1984. *Aesthetic Theory*. Translated by C. Lenhardt. Edited by Gretel Adorno and Rolf Tiedemann. London: Routledge and Kegan Paul.

———. 1987. "Late Capitalism or Industrial Society?" Translated by Fred Van Gelder. In *Modern German Sociology*, edited by Volker Meja, Dieter Misgeld, and Nico Stehr. New York: Columbia University Press.

———. 2001. *The Culture Industry*. Edited by J. M. Bernstein. New York: Routledge.

———. 2002. *Essays on Music*. Edited by Richard Leppert. Translated by Susan H. Gillespie. Berkeley and Los Angeles: University of California Press.

———. 2009a. "Analytical Study of the NBC *Music Appreciation Hour*." In *Current of Music: Elements of a Radio Theory*, edited by Robert Hullot-Kentor. Malden, MA: Polity.

———. 2009b. "The Radio Symphony: An Experiment in Theory." In *Current of Music: Elements of a Radio Theory*, edited by Robert Hullot-Kentor. Malden, MA: Polity.

Adorno, Theodor, and Walter Benjamin. 1999. *The Complete Correspondence, 1928–1940*. Edited by Henri Lonitz. Translated by Nicholas Walker. Cambridge, MA: Polity.

Albro, Robert. 2010. "Neoliberal Cultural Heritage and Bolivia's New Indigenous Public." In *Ethnographies of Neoliberalism*, edited by Carol J. Greenhouse. Philadelphia: University of Pennsylvania Press.

"Amanda Palmer on Raising \$1,000,000 on Kickstarter." *New Musical Express*, 4 June. http://www.nme.com/news/amanda-palmer/64138. Last accessed 1 July 2014.

"Amanda Palmer Raises \$1 Million from Fans to Fund New Album." 2012. *New Musical Express*, 31 May. http://www.nme.com/news/amanda-palmer/64069. Last accessed 1 July 2014.

Anderson, Tim J. 2014. *Popular Music in a Digital Music Economy: Problems and Practices for an Emerging Service Industry*. New York: Routledge.

"Angélique Kidjo 'Oyaya!'" 2004. *Washington Post*, 18 June, T07.

Appadurai, Arjun. 1996. *Modernity at Large: Cultural Dimensions of Globalization*. Minneapolis: University of Minnesota Press.

———, ed. 1986. *The Social Life of Things: Commodities in Cultural Perspective*. New York: Cambridge University Press.

Appleby, Joyce. 2010. *The Relentless Revolution: A History of Capitalism*. New York: W. W. Norton.

Aronczyk, Melissa, and Devon Powers, eds. 2010. *Blowing Up the Brand: Critical Perspectives on Promotional Culture*. New York: Peter Lang.

Arrighi, Giovanni. 2010. *The Long Twentieth Century: Money, Power and the Origins of Our Times*. Rev. ed. New York: Verso.

Arvidsson, Adam. 2006. *Brands: Meaning and Value in Media Culture*. London: Routledge.

Arvidsson, Adam, and Elanor Colleoni. 2012. "Value in Informational Capitalism and on the Internet." *Information Society* 28: 135–150.

Attali, Jacques. 1985. *Noise: The Political Economy of Music*. Translated by B. Massumi. Minneapolis: University of Minnesota Press.

Aubert, Laurent. 1992. "The World Dances to a New Beat." *World Press Review*, January, 24–25.

Azerrad, Michael. 1992. "Angélique Kidjo: Politics with a Beat." *Rolling Stone*, 14 May, 32.

Bain, Katie. 2013. "Here's the Secret to Making Money Licensing Your Songs." *LA Weekly*, 1 March. http://www.laweekly.com/westcoastsound/2013/03/01/heres-the-secret-to-making-money-licensing-your-songs. Last accessed 1 July 2014.

Bakhtin, M. M. 1981. *The Dialogic Imagination*. Edited by Michael Holquist. Translated by Caryl Emerson and Michael Holquist. Austin: University of Texas Press.

Banet-Weiser, Sarah. 2012. *Authentic™: The Politics of Ambivalence in a Brand Culture*. New York: New York University Press.

Battersby, Christine. 1989. *Gender and Genius: Towards a Feminist Aesthetics*. Bloomington: Indiana University Press.

Baudrillard, Jean. 1981. *For a Critique of the Political Economy of the Sign*. Translated by Charles Levin. St. Louis: Telos.

———. 1988a. "Simulacra and Simulations." In *Selected Writings*. Edited by Mark Poster. Stanford: Stanford University Press.

———. 1988b. "The System of Objects." In *Selected Writings*. Edited by Mark Poster. Stanford: Stanford University Press.

Benjamin, Walter. 1969. "The Work of Art in the Age of Mechanical Reproduction." In *Illuminations*. Translated by Harry Zohn. Edited by Hanna Arendt. New York: Schocken Books.

Beville, H. M., Jr. 1939. *Social Stratification of the Radio Audience*. Princeton, NJ: Princeton Office of Radio Research.

———. 1940. "The ABCD's of Radio Audiences." *Public Opinion Quarterly*, June, 195–206.

Bianconi, Lorenzo. 1987. *Music in the Seventeenth Century*. Translated by David Bryant. New York: Cambridge University Press.

Blank-Edelman, David N. 1994. "Stewart Copeland: The Rhythmatist Returns." *RMM*, February, 38–39.

Boltanski, Luc, and Eve Chiapello. 2005. *The New Spirit of Capitalism*. Translated by David Elliott. New York: Verso.

Borzillo, Carrie. 1994. "U.S. Ad Uses Adds to Commercial Success of Deep Forest." *Billboard*, 11 June, 44.

"Boston Survey Shows It's the Program Not the Station That Gets the Listeners." 1930. *Broadcast Advertising*, June, 9.

Bourdieu, Pierre. 1984. *Distinction: A Social Critique of the Judgement of Taste*. Translated by Richard Nice. Cambridge: Harvard University Press.

———. 1990. *The Logic of Practice*. Translated by Richard Nice. Stanford: Stanford University Press.

———. 1993. *The Field of Cultural Production*. Edited by Randal Johnson. New York: Columbia University Press.

———. 1996. *The Rules of Art: Genesis and Structure of the Literary Field*. Translated by Susan Emanuel. Stanford: Stanford University Press.

———. 1998. *Acts of Resistance: Against the Tyranny of the Market*. Translated by Richard Nice. New York: Free Press.

———. 2003. *Firing Back: Against the Tyranny of the Market 2*. Translated by Loïc Wacquant. New York: New Press.

Bourdieu, Pierre, and Luc Boltanski. 1976. "La Production d'idéologie dominante." *Actes de la recherché en sciences sociales* (June): 3–73.

Bourdieu, Pierre, and Hans Haacke. 1995. *Free Exchange*. Cambridge, MA: Polity.

Brand, Ira. 1996. "Kidjo's Seducing Voodoo Beat." *Toronto Star*, 1 August, G10.

Brouillette, Sarah. 2009. "Creative Labor." *Mediations* 24: 140–49. http://www.mediationsjournal .org/articles/creative-labor. Last accessed 1 July 2014.

Brown, Wendy. 2005. *Edgework: Critical Essays on Knowledge and Politics*. Princeton: Princeton University Press.

Bruno, Anthony. 2008. "In with the New." *Billboard*, 12 April, 10.

Bull, Michael. 2005. "No Dead Air! The iPod and the Culture of Mobile Listening." *Leisure Studies* 24: 343–55.

Burnett, Robert. 1996. *The Global Jukebox: The International Music Industry*. London: Routledge.

Burr, Ty. 1994. "From Africa, Three Female Rebels with a Cause." *New York Times*, 10 July, H26.

Byrne, David. 2012. *How Music Works*. San Francisco: McSweeney's.

———. 2013. "The Internet Will Suck all Creative Content out of the World." *Guardian*, 11 October. www.theguardian.com/music/2013/oct/11/david-byrne-internet-content-world.

Caldwell, John. 2008. *Production Culture: Industrial Reflexivity and Critical Practice in Film/ Television*. Durham: Duke University Press.

Campbell, Colin. 1989. *The Romantic Ethic and the Spirit of Modern Consumerism*. Cambridge, MA: Basil Blackwell.

Carah, Nicholas. 2010. *Pop Brands: Branding, Popular Music, and Young People*. New York: Peter Lang.

Carmichael, Matt. 2011. "What's Left of the Middle Class Is More Diverse, Harder Working—and Still Shrinking." *Advertising Age*, 17 October, 4–5.

Castells, Manuel. 1996. *The Rise of Network Society*. 1996. Vol. 1 of *The Information Age: Economy, Society and Culture*. Cambridge, MA: Basil Blackwell.

———. 1997. *The Power of Identity*. Vol. 2 of *The Information Age: Economy, Society and Culture*. Cambridge, MA: Basil Blackwell.

Caves, Richard E. 2000. *Creative Industries: Contracts between Art and Commerce*. Cambridge: Harvard University Press.

Centeno, Miguel A., and Joseph N. Cohen. 2010. *Global Capitalism: A Sociological Perspective*. Malden, MA: Polity.

Chakrabarty, Dipesh. 2000. *Provincializing Europe: Postcolonial Thought and Historical Difference*. Princeton: Princeton University Press.

Chanan, Michael. 1994. *Musica Practica: The Social Practice of Western Music from Gregorian Chant to Postmodernism*. New York: Verso.

Chen, Adrian. 2013. "Jay-Z's New Album is Basically a Massive Data-Mining Operation." *gawker*, 3 July. http://gawker.com/jay-zs-new-album-is-basically-a-massive-data-mining -op-661499440. Last accessed 1 July 2014.

Chisholm, Caroline. 1996. "Kidjo Takes off the Kid Gloves." *The (Sydney) Daily Telegraph*, 12 September, 49.

Christman, Ed. 2013. "Why Target, Whole Foods Are Making a Play for Vinyl." *Billboard*, 17 September. http://www.billboard.com/biz/articles/news/branding/5695504/from-this-weeks -billboard-why-target-whole-foods-are-making-a. Last accessed 1 July 2014.

Chritton, Susan. 2012. *Personal Branding for Dummies*. Hoboken: John Wiley and Sons.

"Challenging the Giants." 1957. *Newsweek*, 23 December, 70.

Cohen, Lizabeth. 2003. *A Consumer's Republic: The Politics of Mass Consumption in Postwar America*. New York: Alfred A. Knopf.

Collum, Josh. 2010. "5 Things Music Supervisors Are Looking for in You and Your Music." *music think tank*, 23 March. http://www.musicthinktank.com/mtt-open/5-things-music -supervisors-are-looking-for-in-you-and-your-m.html. Last accessed 1 July 2014.

Columbia Broadcasting System. 1934. *Ears and Incomes*. New York: Columbia Broadcasting System.

Comaroff, Jean, and John L. Comaroff. 2001. "Millennial Capitalism: First Thoughts on a Second Coming." In *Millennial Capitalism and the Cultural of Neoliberalism*, edited by Jean Comaroff and John L. Comaroff. Durham: Duke University Press.

Copeland, Stewart. 1985. Liner notes to *The Rhythmatist*. A&M CD 5084, 1985.

Coulangeon, Philippe. 2003. "La Stratification sociale des gouts musicaux. Le modèle de la légitimité culturelle en question." *Revue française de sociologie* 44: 3–33.

———. 2004. "Classes sociales, pratiques culturelles et styles de vie: Le modèle de la distinction est-il (vraiment) obsolete?" *Sociologie et société* 36 (Spring): 59–85.

Crary, Jonathan. 2013. *24/7: Late Capitalism and the Ends of Sleep*. New York: Verso.

Cross, Gary. 2000. *An All-Consuming Century: Why Commercialism Won in Modern America.* New York: Columbia University Press.

Crouch, Colin. 2011. *The Strange Non-Death of Neoliberalism.* Malden, MA: Polity.

Cummings, Alex Sayf. 2013. *Democracy of Sound: Music Piracy and the Remaking of American Copyright in the Twentieth Century.* New York: Oxford University Press.

Cunningham, Erin. 2013. "Meet Saint Laurent's New Muses, Wyatt and Fletcher Shears." *Daily Beast*, 20 August. http://www.thedailybeast.com/articles/2013/08/20/meet-saint-laurent-muses-wyatt-and-fletcher-shears.html. Last accessed 1 July 2014.

de Certeau, Michel. 1984. *The Practice of Everyday Life.* Translated by Steven Rendall. Berkeley and Los Angeles: University of California Press.

Dego. 1994. Interview by Edward Luna, 18 August. http://www.ele-mental.org/ele_ment/con.versations/dego.conversation-ptl.html. Last accessed 1 July 2014.

DeNora, Tia. 1995. *Beethoven and the Construction of Genius.* Berkeley and Los Angeles: University of California Press.

Denselow, Robin 2004. "We Created World Music." *Guardian*, 29 June, 10.

Dent, Alexander. 2009. *River of Tears: Country Music, Memory, and Modernity in Brazil.* Durham: Duke University Press.

Deuze, Mark. 2007. *Media Work.* Malden, MA: Polity.

DiCola, Peter. 2006. "False Premises, False Promises: A Quantitative History of Ownership Consolidation in the Radio Industry." Future of Music Coalition. https://www.futureofmusic.org/article/research/false-premises-false-promises. Last accessed 1 July 2014.

Di Giovine, Michael A. 2009. *The Heritage-Scape: UNESCO, World Heritage, and Tourism.* Lanham, MD: Lexington.

DiMaggio, Paul. 1986. "Cultural Entrepreneurship in Nineteenth Century Boston: The Creation of an Organisational Base for High Culture in America." *Media, Culture and Society* 4 (January): 33–50.

Doerschuk, Bob. 1985. "Suzanne Ciani & Her Ace Apprentices Set the Pace of Commercial Synthesis." *Keyboard*, April, 16.

Donaton, Scott. 2004. *Madison & Vine: Why the Entertainment & Advertising Industries Must Converge to Survive.* New York: McGraw-Hill.

Donnat, Olivier. 2004. "Les Univers culturels des français." *Sociologie et sociétés* 36: 87–103.

Doogan, Kevin. 2009. *New Capitalism? The Transformation of Work.* Malden, MA: Polity.

Dorothy Decides: A Story of Human Interest. 1918. Chicago: John H. Steinmetz.

Duménil, Gérard, and Dominique Lévy. 2004. *Capital Resurgent: Roots of the Neoliberal Revolution.* Translated by Derek Jeffers. Cambridge: Harvard University Press.

———. 2011. *The Crisis of Neoliberalism.* Cambridge: Harvard University Press.

Dunlevy, T'cha. 2007. "True Queen of Afro-pop." *Montreal Gazette*, 29 June 2007, D5.

Dyer-Witheford, Nick. 2005. "Cyber-Negri: General Intellect and Immaterial Labor." In *Resistance in Practice: The Philosophy of Antonio Negri*, edited by Timothy S. Murphy and Abdul Karim Mustapha. London: Pluto.

Eells, Josh. 2013. "Night Club Royale." *New Yorker*, 30 September, 36–41.

Ehrenreich, John, and Barbara Ehrenreich. 1979. "The Professional-Managerial Class." In *Between Labor and Capital*, edited by Pat Walker. Boston: South End.

Elder, Bruce. 1992. "Spellbinding New Sounds of Africa." *Sydney Morning Herald*, 17 March, 14.

Elliott, Stuart. 2005. "Burger King Moves Quickly to Take a Product from TV to the Table." *New York Times*, 21 January, C4.

Erikson, Erik. 1950. *Childhood and Society*. New York: W. W. Norton.

"Facebook Unveils New Breed of Media Apps at F8." 2011. *Advertising Age*, 22 September. http://adage.com/article/digital/facebook-unveils-breed-media-apps-f8/229992/. Last accessed 1 July 2014.

Feist, Daniel. 1992. "Angelique Kidjo Gives FrancoFolies an African Beat." *Montreal Gazette*, 2 October, C5.

Feld, Steven. 1996. "Pygmy Pop: A Genealogy of Schizophonic Mimesis." *Yearbook for Traditional Music* 28: 1–35.

———. 2002. "A Sweet Lullaby for World Music." *Public Culture* 12: 145–71.

———. 2012. "*My Life in the Bush of Ghosts*: 'World Music' and the Commodification of Religious Experience." In *Music and Globalization: Critical Encounters*, edited by Bob W. White. Bloomington: University of Indiana Press.

Feld, Steven, and Annemette Kirkegaard. n.d. "Entangled Complicities in the Prehistory of 'World Music': Poul Rovsing Olsen and Jean Jenkins Encounter Brian Eno and David Byrne in the Bush of Ghosts." *Popular Musicology Online* 4. http://www.popular-musicology-online.com/issues/04/feld.html. Last accessed 1 July 2014.

Finnegan, Ruth. 2007 [1989]. *The Hidden Musicians: Music-Making in an English Town*. Middletown, CT: Wesleyan University Press.

Fisher, Melissa, and Greg Downey, eds. 2006. *Frontiers of Capital: Ethnographic Reflections on the New Economy*. Durham: Duke University Press.

Florida, Richard. 2002. *The Rise of the Creative Class*. New York: Basic.

Ford, Phil. 2013. *Dig: Sound and Music in Hip Culture*. New York: Oxford University Press.

Forkan, James P. 1985. "Turning '60s Music in '80s Ads." *Advertising Age*, 25 April, 40.

Forster, E. M. 1909. "The Machine Stops." Nook edition.

Foster, Robert J. 2013. "Things to Do with Brands: Creating and Calculating Value." *HAU: Journal of Ethnographic Theory* 3:44–63.

Foucault, Michel. 2008. *The Birth of Biopolitics: Lectures at the Collège de France, 1978–1979*, edited by Michel Sennelart. Translated by Graham Burchell. Basingstoke, Hampshire, UK: Palgrave Macmillan.

Fox, Aaron. 2004. *Real Country: Music and Language in Working-Class Culture*. Durham: Duke University Press.

Frangos, Alex. 2002. "Here's My Advice . . . If Amazon Has a Suggestion for You, Be Prepared for Some Good Ideas—and a Lot of Confusion." *Wall Street Journal*, 14 January, R15.

Frank, Thomas. 1997. *The Conquest of Cool: Business Culture, Counterculture, and the Rise of Hip Consumerism*. Chicago: University of Chicago Press.

———. 2002. "Shocked, Shocked! Enronian Myths Exposed." *Nation*, 21 March, 17–21.

Friedman, Milton. [1962] 1982. *Capitalism and Freedom*. Chicago: University of Chicago Press.

Frith, Simon. 1983. *Sound Effects: Youth, Leisure, and the Politics of Rock 'n' Roll*. London: Constable.

———. 1988. "Copyright and the Music Business." *Popular Music* 7 (January): 57–76.

Fulcher, James. 2004. *Capitalism: A Very Short Introduction*. New York: Oxford University Press.

Furano, Dell. 2009. "How to Make a T-shirt that Really Sells." *Billboard*, 24 April, 16.

Furness, Hannah. 2014. "Sex Isn't What Sells Classical Music, Nicola Benedetti Says." *Telegraph*, 1 April. http://www.telegraph.co.uk/culture/music/classicalmusic/10734630/Sex-isnt-what-sells-classical-music-Nicola-Benedetti-says.html. Last accessed 1 July 2014.

Gallo, Phil. 2007. "Live Nation's New Citizen Is Madonna." *Variety*, 17 October, 7.

———. 2013. "Writing Your Own Check." *Billboard*, 25 May, 27.

Gamerman, Ellen. 2013. "The Trouble with Kickstarter." *Wall Street Journal*, 21 June. http://online.wsj.com/article/SB10001424127887324021104578551313657138252.html. Last accessed 1 July 2014.

Gans, Herbert J. 1985. "American Popular Culture and High Culture in a Changing Class Structure." In *Prospects: An Annual of American Culture Studies* 10, edited by Jack Salzman. New York: Cambridge University Press.

Ganz, Jacob. 2011. "Slow and Steady, Vinyl Survives." National Public Radio, *All Things Considered*, 2 March. http://www.npr.org/templates/transcript/transcript.php?storyId=134204727. Last accessed 1 July 2014.

Geitner, Paul. n.d. "African Pygmy Chants Go Europop in 'Deep Forest.'" Associated Press. http://www.deepforest.co/dfpress_94-03-23PygmyChantsEuropop.htm. Last accessed 1 July 2014.

Geertz, Clifford. 1973. *The Interpretation of Cultures.* New York: Basic.

Giddens, Anthony. 1971. *Capitalism and Modern Social Theory: An Analysis of the Writings of Marx, Durkheim and Max Weber.* Cambridge: Cambridge University Press.

———. 1979. *Central Problems in Social Theory: Action, Structure, and Contradiction in Social Analysis.* Berkeley and Los Angeles: University of California Press.

Giffels, David. 2011. "Building a House of Wax." *New York Times Magazine*, 23 October, 28.

Gilbert, Eugene. 1957. *Advertising and Marketing to Young People.* Pleasantville, NY: Printers' Ink.

Gladwell, Malcolm. 1997. "The Coolhunt." *New Yorker*, 17 March, 78–88.

Gobé, Marc. 2001. *Emotional Branding: The New Paradigm for Connecting Brands to People.* New York: Allworth Press.

———. 2009. *Emotional Branding: The New Paradigm for Connecting Brands to People.* Rev. ed. New York: Allworth Press.

Goldman, Vivien. 1994. "General Levy Takes Command of Jungle Scene." *Billboard,* 29 October, 20.

Gooley, Dana. 2004. "Franz Liszt: The Virtuoso as Strategist." In *The Musician as Entrepreneur, 1700–1914,* edited by William Weber. Bloomington: Indiana University Press.

Gordon, Steve. 2011. *The Future of the Music Business.* 3rd ed. Milwaukee, WI: Hal Leonard Books.

Graeber, David. 2001. *Toward an Anthropological Theory of Value: The False Coin of Our Own Dreams.* New York: Palgrave.

———. 2005. "Value: Anthropological Theories of Value." In *A Handbook of Economic Anthropology,* edited by James G. Carrier. Northampton, MA: Edward Elgar.

———. 2008. "The Sadness of Post-Workerism, or, 'Art and Immaterial Labour' Conference: A Sort of Review." http://www.tenstakonsthall.se/uploads/38-graebersadness.pdf.

———. 2011. *Debt: The First 5,000 Years.* New York: Melville House.

———. 2012. "Of Flying Cars and the Declining Rate of Profit." *Baffler* 19. http://thebaffler.com/past/of_flying_cars. Last accessed 1 July 2014.

Gramit, David. 2004. "Selling the Serious: The Commodification of Music and Resistance to It in Germany, circa 1800." In *The Musician as Entrepreneur, 1700–1914,* edited by William Weber. Bloomington: Indiana University Press.

Gramsci, Antonio. 1971. *Selections from the Prison Notebooks of Antonio Gramsci.* New York: International Publishers.

Grunwald, Edgar A. 1937. "Program-Production History, 1929–1937." In *Variety Radio Directory, 1937–1938.* N.p.: Variety.

Guilbault, Jocelyne. 2007. *Governing Sound: The Cultural Politics of Trinidad's Carnival Music.* Chicago: University of Chicago Press.

Halperin, Shirley. 2011. "Adele, Keith Urban, John Mayer: Why Are So Many Singers Having Surgery?" *Hollywood Reporter*, 9 November. http://www.hollywoodreporter.com/news/adele-keith-urban-john-mayer-259505.

Hampp, Andrew. 2010. "Why Disney Pictures Could Soon Look a Lot like Procter & Gamble." *Advertising Age*, 20 December, 1.

———. 2011. "Will.I.Am Is with the Brands—and Damn Proud of It." *Advertising Age*, 28 February, 10.

Harris, Marilyn and Mark Wolfram. 1983. *Getting into the Jingle Business (a Source Book)*. New York: Sound Studio Publications.

Hardt, Michael, and Antonio Negri. 2000. *Empire*. Cambridge: Harvard University Press.

———. 2004. *Multitude: War and Democracy in the Age of Empire*. New York: Penguin.

Harris, John. 2012. "The Antidote to Rampant Capitalism? 33 1/3 Revolutions per Minute." *Guardian*, 25 December. http://www.theguardian.com/commentisfree/2012/dec/25/antidote-to-capitalism-33-revolutions-minute. Last accessed 1 July 2014.

Hartley, John, ed. 2005. *Creative Industries*. Malden, MA: Blackwell.

Harvey, David. 1989. *The Condition of Postmodernity: An Enquiry into the Origins of Cultural Change*. Cambridge, MA: Basil Blackwell.

———. 2005. *A Brief History of Neoliberalism*. New York: Oxford University Press.

———. 2010. *The Enigma of Capital and the Crises of Capitalism*. New York: Oxford.

Hayek, F. A. [1944] 1994. *The Road to Serfdom*. Chicago: University of Chicago Press.

Hearn, Alison. 2008. "Variations on the Branded Self: Theme, Invention, Improvisation and Inventory." In *The Media and Social Theory*, edited by David Hesmondhalgh and Jason Toynbee. New York: Routledge.

Hebdige, Dick. 1988. *Subculture: The Meaning of Style*. New York: Routledge.

Henwood, Doug. 2003. *After the New Economy*. New York: New Press.

Herbstein, Dennis. 1987. "The Hazards of Cultural Deprivation." *Africa Report*, July–August, 33–35.

Hesmondhalgh, David. 2013. *The Cultural Industries*. 3rd ed. Thousand Oaks, CA: Sage.

Hesmondhalgh, David, and Sarah Baker. 2011. *Creative Labour: Media Work in Three Cultural Industries*. London: Routledge.

Hilferding, Rudolf. 1981. *Finance Capital: A Study of the Latest Phase of Capitalist Development*. Edited by Tom Bottomore. Translated by Morris Watnick and Sam Gordon. London: Routledge.

Hirschkind, Charles. 2009. *The Ethical Soundscape: Cassette Sermons and Islamic Counterpublics*. New York: Columbia University Press.

Holt, Douglas. 2000. "Postmodern Markets." In *Do Americans Shop Too Much?* Edited by Juliet Schor. Boston: Beacon.

———. 2004. *How Brands Become Icons: The Principles of Cultural Branding*. Boston: Harvard Business School Press.

Horkheimer, Max, and Theodor Adorno. 1990. *Dialectic of Enlightenment*. Translated by John Cumming. New York: Continuum.

Hosokawa, Shuhei. 1984. "The Walkman Effect." *Popular Music* 4: 165–80.

IFPI (International Federation of the Phonographic Industry). 2012. "Investing in Music: How Music Companies Discover, Nurture and Promote Talent." http://www.ifpi.org/content/library/investing_in_music.pdf.

Ingham, Geoffrey. 2008. *Capitalism*. Malden, MA: Polity.

Jaggi, Maya. 2007. "Rhythms without Frontiers." *Sunday Times* (London), 23 September, 37.

Jameson, Fredric. 1984. "Postmodernism, or, the Cultural Logic of Late Capitalism." *New Left Review* 146 (July–August): 53–92.

———. 1997. "Culture and Finance Capital." *Critical Inquiry* 24: 246–65.

Jarvis, Simon. 1998. *Adorno: A Critical Introduction*. Malden, MA: Polity.

Jenkins, Mark. 2010. "In a League of Her Own." *Washington Post*, 26 March, Weekend section, WE06.

Kaplan, Mary Jo. 1988. "Sing along with Pitch; HEA." *Advertising Age*, 1 August, 18S.

Karmen, Steve. 1989. *Through the Jingle Jungle: The Art and Business of Making Music for Commercials*. New York: Billboard Books.

———. 2005. *Who Killed the Jingle? How a Unique American Art Form Disappeared*. Milwaukee: Hal Leonard.

Kassabian, Anahid. 2013. *Ubiquitous Listening: Affect, Attention, and Distributed Subjectivity*. Berkeley and Los Angeles: University of California Press.

Katz, Mark. 2010. *Capturing Sound: How Technology Has Changed Music*. 2nd ed. Berkeley and Los Angeles: University of California Press.

Kidjo, Angélique, and Rachel Wenrick. 2014. *Spirit Rising: My Life, My Music*. New York: Harper Design.

Klein, Bethany. 2009. *As Heard on TV: Popular Music in Advertising*. Burlington, VT: Ashgate.

Klein, Naomi. 2000. *No Logo: Taking Aim at the Brand Bullies*. New York: Picador.

———. 2008. *The Shock Doctrine: The Rise of Disaster Capitalism*. New York: Picador.

Knopper, Steve. 2013. "Seven Ways Musicians Make Money off YouTube." *Rolling Stone*, 19 September. http://www.rollingstone.com/music/news/seven-ways-musicians-make-money-off -youtube-20130919. Last accessed 1 July 2014.

Kopytoff, Igor. 1986. "The Cultural Biography of Things." In *The Social Life of Things: Commodities in Cultural Perspective*, edited by Arjun Appadurai. New York: Cambridge University Press.

Kraar, Louis. 1956. "Teenage Customers: Merchants Seek Teens' Dollars, Influence Now, Brand Loyalty Later." *Wall Street Journal*, 6 December, 1.

Kreiss, Daniel, Megan Finn, and Fred Turner. 2011. "The Limits of Peer Production: Some Reminders form Max Weber for the Network Society." *New Media and Society* 13: 243–59.

Kurkowski, Damon. 2012. "Making Cents." *Pitchfork*, 14 November. http://pitchfork.com/features /articles/8993-the-cloud/. Last accessed, 15 December 2014.

Kukral, Jim, and Murray Newlands. 2011. *What Is Personal Branding? How to Create a Memorable & Powerful Brand that Sells YOU!* N.p.: Amazon Digital Services.

Lacher, Kathleen T., and Richard Mizerski. 1994. "An Exploratory Study of the Responses and Relationships Involved in the Evaluation of, and in the Intention to Purchase New Rock Music." *Journal of Consumer Research* 21 (September): 366–80.

LaFraniere, Sharon. 2006. "In the Jungle, the Unjust Jungle, a Small Victory." *New York Times*, 22 March, A1.

Lash, Scott, and Celia Lury. 2007. *Global Culture Industry: The Mediation of Things*. Malden, MA: Polity.

Lash, Scott, and John Urry. 1987. *The End of Organized Capitalism*. Madison: University of Wisconsin Press.

———. 1994. *Economies of Signs and Space*. Newbury Park, CA: Sage.

Laskow, Michael. 2013. "Tim Myers Interview; TAXI Road Rally 2012." *TAXI Transmitter*. http://www.taxi.com/transmitter/1305/tim-myers-interview.html. Last accessed 1 July 2014.

Lawrence, Thomas B., and Nelson Phillips. 2002. "Understanding Cultural Industries." *Journal of Management Inquiry* 11 (December): 430–41.

Lazzarato, Maurizio. 1996. "Immaterial Labor." In *Radical Thought in Italy: A Potential Politics*, edited by Paolo Virno and Michael Hardt. Minneapolis: University of Minnesota Press.

Lee, Martyn J. 1993. *Consumer Culture Reborn: The Cultural Politics of Consumption*. New York: Routledge.

Lee, Nick, and Rolland Munro, eds. 2001. *The Consumption of Mass*. Malden, MA: Blackwell.

Leonard, Andrew. 2014. "Big Brother Is in Your Spotify: How Music Became the Surveillance State's Trojan Horse." *Salon*, 28 March. http://www.salon.com/2014/03/28/big_brother_is_in _your_spotify_how_music_became_the_surveillance_states_trojan_horse/. Last accessed 1 July 2014.

Lessig, Lawrence. 2008. *Remix: Making Art and Culture Thrive in the Hybrid Economy*. New York: Penguin.

Levin, Rachel B. 2011. "Boogie Nights: 'Silent Disco' Is Making Itself Heard." *Los Angeles Times*, 19 August, D16.

Levine, Mike. 2007a. "Q&A: Jack Rudy." *Electronic Musician*, 1 February, 80.

————. 2007b. "Q&A: Michael Laskow." *Electronic Musician*, 1 March, 76.

Lewandowski, Natalie. 2010. "Understanding Creative Roles in Entertainment: The Music Supervisor as Case Study." *Continuum: Journal of Media and Cultural Studies* 246 (December): 865–75.

Liner notes to *Deep Forest*. 1992. 550 Music/Epic BK-57840.

Liner notes to *Welenga*. 1997. Sony Music 48146-2.

Lipsitz, George. 1998. "Consumer Spending as State Project: Yesterday's Solutions and Today's Problems." In *Getting and Spending: European and American Consumer Societies in the Twentieth Century*, edited by Susan Strasser, Charles McGovern, and Matthias Judt. Cambridge: Cambridge University Press.

Lowrey, Annie. 2013. "Top 10% Took Home Half of U.S. Income in 2012." *New York Times*, 11 September, B1.

Lowry, Tom. 2006. "Finding Nirvana in a Music Catalog." *Business Week*, 2 October, 80.

Lukács, György. 1971. *History and Class Consciousness: Studies in Marxist Dialectics*. Translated by Rodney Livingstone. Cambridge: MIT Press.

Lury, Celia. 2004. *Brands: The Logos of the Global Economy*. Abingdon, UK: Routledge.

Lury, Celia, and Liz Moor. 2010."Brand Valuation and Topological Culture." In *Blowing up the Brand: Critical Perspectives on Promotional Culture*, edited by Melissa Aronczyk and Devon Powers. New York Peter Lang.

Luvaas, Brent. 2012. *DIY Style: Fashion, Music and Global Digital Cultures*. New York: Berg.

Lysloff, René T. A., and Leslie Gay, Jr., eds. 2003. *Technoculture and Music*. Middletown, CT: Wesleyan University Press.

"Madonna Signs Deal with Live Nation." 2007. *New Musical Express*, 16 October. http://www .nme.com/news/madonna/31846. Last accessed 1 July 2014.

"Making Way for Digital Audio." 1984. *Back Stage*, 20 April, 1, 52.

Malan, Rian. 2004. "Where Does the Lion Sleep Tonight?" *Rolling Stone*, 25 May, 54–66, 84–85.

Malnic, Eric. 1981. "Studio Musicians Returning to Work: Union Members Admit They Were Beaten on Key Strike Issue." *Los Angeles Times*, 16 January, C8.

Marks, John. 1996. "Selling 'Jailbait' Bach: Dressing up Classical CD Sales—by Undressing." *U.S. News and World Report*, 11 November, 58.

Maróthy, János. 1974. *Music and the Bourgeois, Music and the Proletarian*. Budapest: Akadémiai Kiadó.

Marvit, Moishe Z. 2014. "The Wages of Crowdwork." *Nation*, 24 February, 18–25.

Marx, Karl. 1967. *Capital: A Critique of Political Economy*. Vol. 1, *A Critical Analysis of Capitalist Production*. Translated by Samuel Moore and Edward Aveling. Edited by Frederick Engels. New York: International.

———. 1973. *Grundrisse: Foundations of the Critique of Political Economy*. Translated by Martin Nicolaus. New York: Vintage.

———. 1977. *The Poverty of Philosophy*. 3rd ed. Peking: Foreign Languages Press.

———. 1990. *Capital: A Critique of Political Economy*. Vol. 1. Translated by Ben Fowkes. London: Penguin.

———. n.d. *Theories of Surplus Value*. Translated by Emile Burns. Edited by S. Ryazanskaya. Moscow: Foreign Languages Publishing House.

Marx, Karl, and Friedrich Engels. 1964. *The Communist Manifesto*. Translated by Paul M. Sweezy. New York: Monthly Review.

———. 1970. *The German Ideology*. Edited by C. J. Arthur. New York: International.

Masterson, Andrew. 1994. "Exile within Finds Expression in Song." *The Age* (Melbourne, Australia), 16 September, Entertainment Guide, 3.

Mauss, Marcel. 1990. *The Gift: The Form and Reason for Exchange in Archaic Societies*. Translated by W. D. Halls. New York: W. W. Norton.

Max, D. T. 2011. "Her Way." *New Yorker*, 7 November, 58–65.

McClary, Susan. 1987. "The Blasphemy of Talking Politics During Bach Year." In *Music and Society: The Politics of Composition, Performance and Reception*, edited by Richard Leppert and Susan McClary. Cambridge: Cambridge University Press.

McCracken, Grant. 1988. *Culture and Consumption: New Approaches to the Symbolic Character of Consumer Goods and Activities*. Bloomington: Indiana University Press.

———. 1997. *Plenitude*. Toronto: Periph.: Fluide.

———. 2008. *Transformations: Identity Construction in Contemporary Culture*. Bloomington: Indiana University Press.

McDonald, Patrick. 2009. "The Beautiful Kidjo." *Advertiser* (Adelaide, Australia), 26 March, supplement, p. 7.

McGovern, Charles F. 2006. *Sold American: Consumption and Citizenship, 1890-1945*. Chapel Hill: University of North Carolina Press.

McGuigan, Jim. 2009. *Cool Capitalism*. New York: Pluto.

McKinley, James C., Jr. 2013. "Who Needs the Critics? Go Cryptic Instead." *New York Times*, 21 June, C1.

McLeod, Kembrew, and Peter DiCola. 2011. *Creative License: The Law and Culture of Digital Sampling*. Durham: Duke University Press.

McNally, David, and Karl D. Speak. 2011. *Be Your Own Brand: Achieve More of What You Want by Being More of Who You Are*. 2nd ed. San Francisco: Berrett-Koehler.

Meintjes, Louise. 1990. "Paul Simon's *Graceland*, South Africa, and the Mediation of Musical Meaning." *Ethnomusicology* 34 (Winter): 37–73.

———. 2003. *Sound of Africa! Making Music Zulu in a South African Studio*. Durham: Duke University Press.

Mendieta, Eduardo. 2005. *The Frankfurt School on Religion: Key Writings by the Major Thinkers*. New York: Routledge.

Mengel, Noel. 1997. "Exotic Blend of Cooder and Cuba." *Courier Mail* (Queensland, Australia), 16 August, Weekend section, 13.

Menger, Pierre-Michel. 1999. "Artistic Labor Markets and Careers." *Annual Review of Sociology* 25:541–74.

———. 2002. *Portrait de l'artiste en travailleur: Metamorphoses du capitalisme.* Paris: Seuil.

Metzer, Paul. 1998. *The Crescendo of the Virtuoso: Spectacle, Skill, and Self-Promotion in Paris during the Age of Revolution.* Berkeley and Los Angeles: University of California Press.

Mgxashe, Mxolisi. 1987. "A Conversation with Ray Phiri." *Africa Report*, July/August, 31–32.

Miège, Bernard. 1989. *The Capitalization of Cultural Production.* New York: International General.

Miller, Karl Hagstrom. 2010. *Segregating Sound: Inventing Folk and Pop Music in the Age of Jim Crow.* Durham: Duke University Press.

Moor, Liz. 2007. *The Rise of Brands.* New York: Berg.

Moran, Charlie. 2008. "Rapper Common Learns to Make Music with Microsoft." *Advertising Age*, 13 October, 22.

Morley, Hugh. 1988. "The Wages of Syn." *Advertising Age*, 1 August, 26S.

Morrison, Maureen. 2011. "Why Some Say Marketers Deserve Bulk of Blame for a Fat America." *Advertising Age*, 17 October, 40.

"Music Lets Me See beyond Color, Beyond Language." 2006. *Africa News*, 7 April.

"Music's Top 40 Money Makers 2012." 2012. *Billboard.com*, 9 March. http://www.billboard.com /articles/list/502623/musics-top-40-money-makers-2012. Last accessed 1 July 2014.

Myers, Fred R., ed. 2001. *The Empire of Things: Regimes of Value and Material Culture.* Santa Fe: School of American Research Press.

———. 2002. *Painting Culture: The Making of an Aboriginal High Art.* Durham: Duke University Press.

"MySpace COO Explains Massive Music Marketing Expansion Plans." 2008. *Advertising Age*, 28 July.

Nader, Laura. [1969] 1974. "Up the Anthropologist—Perspectives Gained from Studying Up." In *Reinventing Anthropology*, edited by Dell Hymes. New York: Vintage.

Negri, Antonio. 1999. "Value and Affect." Translated by Michal Hardt. *boundary 2* 26 (Summer): 77-88.

Negus, Keith. 1999. *Music Genres and Corporate Cultures.* London: Routledge.

"New $10 Billion Power: The U.S. Teen-age Consumer." 1959. *Life*, 13 August, 78–84.

"New Pepsi Television Ad Features Music Superstars Michael Jackson, Britney Spears, Kanye West, Ray Charles and Mariah Carey." 2011. http://www.prnewswire.com/news-releases/new -pepsi-television-ad-features-music-superstars-michael-jackson-britney-spears-kanye-west -ray-charles-and-mariah-carey-130254388.html. Last accessed 1 July 2014.

Ntone, Jean-Noel. 1999. "The World Is a Ghetto for African Musicians." *Africa News*, 29 April.

Nuttall, Pete. 2009. "Insiders, Regulars and Tourists: Exploring Selves and Music Consumption in Adolescence." *Journal of Consumer Behavior* 8: 211–24.

Oliphint, Joel. 2014. "Wax and Wane: The Tough Realities behind Vinyl's Comeback." *Pitchfork*, 28 July. http://pitchfork.com/features/articles/9467-wax-and-wane-the-tough-realities -behind-vinyls-comeback/. Last accessed 5 August 2014.

Oppelt, Phylicia. 1998. "Angelique Kidjo's Song of Herself." *Washington Post*, 23 September, D1.

O'Malley, Frank Ward. 1920. "Irving Berlin Gives Nine Rules for Writing Popular Songs." *American Magazine*, October, 37, 239–46.

O'Reilly, Daragh, Gretchen Larsen, and Krzysztof Kubacki. 2013. *Music, Markets and Consumption*. Woodeaton, Oxford, UK: Goodfellow.

Ortner, Sherry B. 1996. *Making Gender: The Politics and Erotics of Culture*. Boston: Beacon.

———, ed. 1999. *The Fate of "Culture": Geertz and Beyond*. Berkeley and Los Angeles: University of California Press.

———. 2006. *Anthropology and Social Theory: Culture, Power, and the Acting Subject*. Durham: Duke University Press.

———. 2013. *Not Hollywood: Independent Film at the Twilight of the American Dream*. Durham: Duke University Press.

Oumano, Elena, and Dominic Pride. 1998. "Island Targets R&B Market with New Album from Kidjo." *Billboard*, 23 May, 1.

Packer, George. 2013. *The Unwinding: An Inner History of the New America*. New York: Farrar, Straus and Giroux.

Palladino, Grace. 1996. *Teenagers: An American History*. New York: Basic.

Palmer, Amanda. 2012a. "Where All This Kickstarter Money Is Going." 22 May. http://amandapalmer.net/blog/20120522/. Last accessed 1 July 2014.

———. 2012b. "Wanted: Horn-Y and String-Y Volunteers for the Grand Theft Orchestra Tour!!!!" http://blog.amandapalmer.net/20120821/. Last accessed 1 July 2014.

Pareles, Jon. 2014. "A Continent on Her Musical Map." *New York Times*, 19 January, AR19.

Pear, Robert. 2011. "It's Official: The Rich Get Richer." *New York Times*, 25 October, A20.

Pels, Peter. 1998. "The Spirit of Matter: on Fetish, Rarity, Fact and Fancy. In *Border Fetishisms: Material Objects in Unstable Places*, edited by Patricia Spyder. New York: Routledge.

Perelman, Michael. 2000. *The Invention of Capitalism: Classical Political Economy and the Secret History of Primitive Accumulation*. Durham: Duke University Press.

Pesselnick, Jill. 2002. "Columbia's Kidjo Bares Her 'Black Ivory Soul.'" *Billboard*, 9 March, 1.

Peterson, Richard A. 1990. "Audience and Industry Origins of the Crisis in Classical Music Programming: Towards World Music." In *The Future of the Arts: Public Policy and Arts Research*, edited by David B. Pankratz and Valerie B. Morris. New York: Praeger.

———. 1992. "Understanding Audience Segmentation: From Elite and Mass to Omnivore and Univore." *Poetics* 21 (August): 243–58.

———. 1997. "The Rise and Fall of Highbrow Snobbery as a Status Marker." *Poetics* 25 (November): 75–92.

Peterson, Richard A., and Roger M. Kern. 1996. "Changing Highbrow Taste: From Snob to Omnivore." *American Sociological Review* 61 (October): 900–907.

Peterson, Richard A., and Albert Simkus. 1992. "How Musical Tastes Mark Occupational Status Groups." In *Cultivating Differences: Symbolic Boundaries and the Making of Inequality*, edited by Michèle Lamont and Marcel Fournier. Chicago: University of Chicago Press.

Pham, Alex. 2011. "Live Nation Swings to a Profit as Concert Attendance Grows." *Los Angeles Times*, 11 August. http://latimesblogs.latimes.com/entertainmentnewsbuzz/2011/08/live-nation-profit.html. Last accessed 1 July 2014.

Pichevin, Aymeric. 2009. "The Billboard Q&A: Billy Mann." *Billboard*, 24 October, 18.

Piketty, Thomas. 2014. *Capital in the Twenty-first Century*. Translated by Arthur Goldhammer. Cambridge: Belknap Press of Harvard University Press.

Porcello, Thomas, and Paul Greene, eds. 2004. *Wired for Sound: Engineering and Technology in Sonic Cultures*. Middletown, CT: Wesleyan University Press.

Regev, Motti. 2013. *Pop-Rock Music: Aesthetic Cosmopolitanism in Late Modernity*. Malden, MA: Polity.

Reynolds, Simon. 1994a. "Above the Treeline." *Wire*, September, 36.

———. 1994b. "Generation E: British Rave." *Artforum*, February, 54–57.

———. 1995a. "Will Jungle Be the Next Craze from Britain?" *New York Times*, 6 August, H28.

———. 1995b. "Jungle Boogie." *Rolling Stone*, 23 March, 38.

Robicheau, Paul. 1998. "Listening to History." *Boston Globe*, 25 September, D15.

Roehl, Harvey N. 1973. *Player Piano Treasury: The Scrapbook History of the Mechanical Piano in America*. 2nd ed. Vestal, NY: Vestal Press.

Romney, Jonathan. 1991. "African Queen." *Guardian*, 8 October, retrieved from LexisNexis.

Rys, Dan. 2012. "Amanda Palmer Agrees to Pay Guest Musicians." Billboard.com, 20 September. http://www.billboard.com/articles/news/475007/amanda-palmer-agrees-to-pay-guest-musicians. Last accessed 1 July 2014.

Sahlins, Marshall. 1974. *Stone Age Economics*. Chicago: Aldine-Atherton.

———. 1981. *Historical Metaphors and Mythical Realities: Structure in the Early History of the Sandwich Islands Kingdom*. Ann Arbor: University of Michigan Press.

Salmen, Walter, ed. 1983. *The Social Status of the Professional Musician from the Middle Ages to the 19th Century*. Translated by Herbert Kaufman and Barbara Reisner. New York: Pendragon Press.

Savà, Peppe. 2012. "'God Didn't Die, He was Transformed into Money'; an Interview with Giorgio Agamben." http://libcom.org/library/god-didnt-die-he-was-transformed-money-interview-giorgio-agamben-peppe-savà. Last accessed 1 July 2014.

Schuessler, Jennifer. 2013. "In History Departments, It's Up with Capitalism." *New York Times*, 6 April, A1.

Schultz, E. J. 2011. "Packages Shrink to Fit Spending-Power Decline." *Advertising Age*, 17 October, 40.

Schütz, Alfred. 1951. "Making Music Together: A Study in Social Relationships." *Social Research* 18: 76–97.

Schweitzer, Vivian. 2013. "Concerto for Piano and YouTube." *New York Times*, 13 October, AR11.

Scott, Alan J. 2004. "Cultural-Products Industries and Urban Economic Development: Prospects for Growth and Market Contestation in Global Context." *Urban Affairs Review*, 39 (March): 461–90.

Seeger, Anthony. 2009. "Lessons Learned from the ICTM (NGO) Evaluation of Nominations for the UNESCO Masterpieces of the Oral and Intangible Heritage of Humanity, 2001–2005." In *Intangible Heritage*, edited by Laurajane Smith and Natsuko Akagawa. New York: Routledge.

Sennett, Richard. 2006. *The Culture of the New Capitalism*. New Haven: Yale University Press.

Seno, Alexandra. 2007. "The Sounds of Success." *Newsweek* (Europe), 30 July, 32.

Sewell, William H. 2005. *Logics of History: Social Theory and Social Transformation*. Chicago: University of Chicago Press.

Shankar, Avi, Richard Elliott, and James A. Fitchett. 2009. "Identity, Consumption and Narratives of Socialization." *Marketing Theory* 9 (2009): 75–94.

Shapiro, Peter. 1999. *Drum 'n' Bass: The Rough Guide*. London: Rough Guides.

Sherwin, Adam. 2006. "Pop Picker Takes the Hit and Miss out of Music Making." *Times* (London), 1 April, 9.

Silverman, Carol. 2012. *Romani Routes: Cultural Politics and Balkan Music in Diaspora*. New York: Oxford University Press.

Simmel, Georg. 1971. "The Metropolis and Mental Life." In *Georg Simmel: On Individuality and Social Forms: Selected Writings*, edited by Donald N. Levine. Chicago: University of Chicago Press.

Simmons, Lee. 2012. "Musical Instrument Sales Improve." *Bizmology*, 15 May. http://bizmology.hoovers.com/2012/05/15/musical-instrument-sales-improve/. Last accessed 1 July 2014.

Simon, Paul. 1986. Liner notes to *Graceland*. Warner Bros. W2-25447.

Sinnreich, Aram. 2010. *Mashed Up: Music, Technology, and the Rise of Configurable Culture*. Amherst: University of Massachusetts Press.

Sisario, Ben. 2010. "Looking to a Sneaker for a Band's Big Break." *New York Times*, 10 October, AR1.

———. 2012. "Giving Love, Lots of It, to Her Fans." *New York Times*, 6 June, C1.

———. 2013. "As Music Streaming Grows, Artists' Royalties Slow to a Trickle." *New York Times*, 29 January, A1.

———. 2014. "Garage Rock's Latest Nerve Center." *New York Times*, 18 May, AR22.

Slater, Don. 1997. *Consumer Culture and Modernity*. Malden, MA: Polity.

Sly, David. 1992. "Kidjo's Soul Reason." *Advertiser* (Adelaide, Australia), 9 April.

Small, Christopher. 1987. "Performance as Ritual: Sketch for an Enquiry into the True Nature of a Symphony Concert." In *Lost in Music: Culture, Style and the Musical Event*, edited by Avron Levine White. Sociological Review Monograph 34. London: Routledge and Kegan Paul.

Smith, Adam. 1980. *Essays on Philosophical Subjects*, edited by W. P. D. Wightman and J. C. Bryce. Oxford: Clarendon Press.

Smythe, Dallas W. 1977. "Communications: Blindspot of Western Marxism." *Canadian Journal of Political and Social Theory* 1 (Fall): 1–27.

Stahl, Matt. 2013. *Unfree Masters: Recording Artists and the Politics of Work*. Durham: Duke University Press.

Stapleton, Chris, and Chris May. 1989. *African All★Stars*. London: Paladin.

Stedman Jones, Daniel. 2012. *Masters of the Universe: Hayek, Friedman, and the Birth of Neoliberal Politics*. Princeton: Princeton University Press.

Steger, Manfred B., and Ravi K. Roy. 2010. *Neoliberalism: A Very Short Introduction*. New York: Oxford University Press.

Sterne, Jonathan. 2012. *MP3: The Meaning of a Format*. Durham: Duke University Press.

Stewart, Andrew. 1995. "Image Questioned for Violinist, 16." *Billboard*, 4 March, 1.

Stokes, Martin. 2010. *The Republic of Love: Cultural Intimacy in Turkish Popular Music*. Chicago: University of Chicago Press.

Strauss, Neil. 1994. "The Pop Life." *New York Times*, 22 September, C18.

Straw, Will. 1991. "Systems of Articulation, Logics of Change: Communities and Scenes in Popular Music." *Cultural Studies* 5 (October): 368–88.

Suisman, David. 2009. *Selling Sounds: The Commercial Revolution in American Music*. Cambridge: Harvard University Press.

Sullivan, Laurie. 2014. "U.S. Marketers to Spend $103 Billion on Interactive Media by 2019." *MediaPost*, 10 November. http://www.mediapost.com/publications/article/237944/us -marketers-to-spend-103-billion-on-interactiv.html. Last accessed 10 December 2014.

Susman, Warren I. 1984. *Culture as History: The Transformation of American Society in the Twentieth Century*. New York: Pantheon.

Sutton, Shane. 1994. "Out of Africa." *Advertiser* (Adelaide, Australia), 8 September.

Sydell, Laura. 2009. "New Music Software Predicts the Hits." National Public Radio, *Morning Edition*, 12 October.

———. 2013. "New Jay-Z Album Tests the Musician and Samsung." National Public Radio, *Morning Edition*, 3 July.

Tableau Vivant. 1929. "Gramophone-Opera with a Model Stage." *Gramophone Critic and Society News*, August 1929, 402–3.

Tamm, Eric. 1989. *Brian Eno: His Music and the Vertical Color of Sound*. Boston: Faber and Faber.

Taruskin, Richard. 2010a. *Music from the Earliest Notations to the Sixteenth Century.* Vol. 1 of *The Oxford History of Western Music.* New York: Oxford University Press.

———. 2010b. *Music in the Seventeenth and Eighteenth Centuries.* Vol. 2 of *The Oxford History of Western Music.* New York: Oxford University Press.

Tavernise, Sabrina. 2011. "Middle-class Areas Shrink as Income Gap Grows, New Report Finds." *New York Times,* 15 November, A15.

Taylor, Deems. 1922. "The Wonder of the Duo-Art." *Harper's New Monthly.* Reprint, n.p.: International Association of Player-Piano, Roll-Playing and Automatic Instrument Enthusiasts, 2003.

Taylor, Timothy D. 1997a. *Global Pop: World Music, World Markets.* New York: Routledge.

———. 1997b. "Ry Cooder's Next Grammy." *Village Voice,* 9 December, 88.

———. 1998. "Fair Use Isn't Fair: A Response to Sheila Whiteley." *Popular Music* 17 (January): 129–32.

———. 2001. *Strange Sounds: Music, Technology and Culture.* New York: Routledge.

———. 2002. "Music and Musical Practices in Postmodernity." In *Postmodern Music/Postmodern Thought,* edited by Judith Lochhead and Joseph Auner. New York: Routledge.

———. 2007a. *Beyond Exoticism: Western Music and the World.* Durham: Duke University Press.

———. 2007b. "The Commodification of Music at the Dawn of the Era of '"Mechanical Music."'" *Ethnomusicology* 51 (spring/summer 2007): 281–30.

———. 2009. "Advertising and the Conquest of Culture." *Social Semiotics* 4 (December): 405–25.

———. 2012a. "The Seductions of Technology." *Journal of Music, Technology & Education* 4 (February): 227–32.

———. 2012b. *The Sounds of Capitalism: A History of Music in Advertising.* Chicago: University of Chicago Press.

———. 2012c. "World Music Today." In *Music and Globalization: Critical Encounters,* edited by Bob W. White. Bloomington: Indiana University Press.

———. 2013. "Stravinsky and Others." *Avant: The Journal of the Philosophical-Interdisciplinary Vanguard* 4. http://avant.edu.pl/wp-content/uploads/Timothy-D-Taylor-Stravinsky-and -Othersl.pdf. Last accessed 1 July 2014.

———. 2014a. "Fields, Genres, Brands." *Culture, Theory and Critique* 55: 159–74.

———. 2014b. "Les Festivals de musiques du monde: La diversité comme genre." *Cahiers d'ethnomusicologie* 27: 49–63.

———. 2014c. "The New Capitalism, Globalisation, and the Commodification of Taste." In *The Cambridge History of World Music,* edited by Philip V. Bohlman. New York: Cambridge University Press.

———. 2014d. "The New Capitalism, UNESCO, and the Reenchantment of Culture." In *Networking the International System: Global Histories of International Organizations,* edited by Madeleine Herren. Berlin: Springer.

———. n.d.a. *Music and Social Theory: Culture and Capitalism in a Globalizing World.* In preparation.

———. n.d.b. "Music on the Move." In *The Cambridge History of the World,* edited by J. R. McNeill and Kenneth Pomeranz. New York: Cambridge University Press, forthcoming.

———. n.d.c. "Neoliberal Capitalism and the Rise of Sampling." In *The Auditory Culture Reader,* edited by Michael Bull and Les Back. 2nd ed. New York: Berg, forthcoming.

———. n.d.d. "World Music, Value, and Memory." *Beiträge zur Popularmusikforschung* 42, forthcoming.

Taylor, Timothy D., Mark Katz, and Tony Grajeda, eds. 2012. *Music, Sound, and Technology in America: A Documentary History of Early Phonograph, Cinema, and Radio*. Durham: Duke University Press.

Teixeira, Antonio, Jr. 1974. *Music to Sell By: The Craft of Jingle Writing*. N.p.: Berklee Press.

"Tentative Pact Reached in Musician Strike." 1981. *Los Angeles Times*, 15 January, 1.

Terranova, Tiziana. 2004. *Network Culture: Politics for the Information Age*. New York: Pluto.

Thayer, Alexander Wheelock. 1921. *The Life of Beethoven*. Vol. 3. Edited by Henry Edward Krehbiel. New York: Beethoven Association.

Théberge, Paul. 1997. *Any Sound You Can Imagine: Making Music/Consuming Technology*. Middletown, CT: Wesleyan University Press.

Thompson, Clive. 2007. "Sex, Drugs, and Updating Your Blog." *New York Times Magazine*, 13 May, 42–47.

Thompson, Robert Farris. 1988. "David Byrne: The Rolling Stone Interview." *Rolling Stone*, 21 April, 42.

Thrift, Nigel. 2005. *Knowing Capitalism*. Thousand Oaks, CA: Sage.

Tick, Judith, and Paul Beaudoin. 2008. *Music in the USA: A Documentary Companion*. New York: Oxford University Press.

Timberg, Scott. 2014. "David Lowery: Here's How Pandora Is Destroying Musicians." *Salon*, 31 August. http://www.salon.com/2014/08/31/david_lowery_heres_how_pandora_is _destroying_musicians/.

Tomsho, Robert. 1990. "As Sampling Revolutionizes Recording, Debate Grows over Aesthetics, Copyrights." *Wall Street Journal*, 5 November, B1.

Toop, David. 1994. "Jungle Fever Spreads in U.K.: Genre Defies Labels." *Billboard*, 29 October, 1.

Trump, Rob. 2013. "Why in the World Would You Ever Give Money through Kickstarter?" *New York Times Magazine*, 46–47.

Tsing, Anna. 2013. "Sorting out Commodities: How Capitalist Value Is Made through Gifts." *HAU: Journal of Ethnographic Theory* 3: 21–43.

Tsing, Anna Lowenhaupt. 2005. *Friction: An Ethnography of Global Connection*. Princeton: Princeton University Press.

Tupica, Rich. 2008. "Veloura Caywood! Lansing lo-fi!" *Turn It Down!*, 9 December. http://turnit -down.blogspot.com/2009/12/veloura-caywood-interview-illman.html. Last accessed 1 July 2014.

Ulin, Jeffrey C. 2009. *The Business of Media Distribution: Monetizing Film, TV, and Video Content in an Online World*. Burlington, MA: Focal Press.

UNESCO. n.d.a. "Knowledge and Practices Concerning Nature and the Universe." http://www .unesco.org/culture/ich/?pg=56. Last accessed 1 July 2014.

Vagnoni, Anthony. 1984a. "Hunter Murtaugh: Music & Sound Production at Young & Rubicam," *Back Stage*, 20 April, 28.

———. 1984b. "Music Makers Sing Out," *Back Stage*, 20 April, 55.

van Eijck, Koen. 2001. "Social Differentiation in Musical Taste Patterns." *Social Forces* 79 (March): 1163–84.

Vazsonyi, Nicholas. 2010. *Richard Wagner: Self-Promotion and the Making of a Brand*. New York: Cambridge University Press.

Veblen, Thorstein. [1899] 1994. *The Theory of the Leisure Class: An Economic Study of Institutions*. New York: Penguin.

Wakin, Daniel J. 2012a. "Ringing Finally Ended, but There's No Button to Stop Shame." *New York Times*, 12 January, A16.

——. 2012b. "Rockers Playing for Beer: Fair Play." *New York Times*, Arts Beat, 12 September. http://artsbeat.blogs.nytimes.com/2012/09/12/rockers-playing-for-beer-fair-play/?_r=0. Last accessed 1 July 2014.

——. 2012c. "Musician Changes Tune and Will Pay Volunteers." *New York Times*, 21 September, C2.

Wallerstein, Immanuel. 1974. *The Modern World-System: Capitalist Agriculture and the Origins of the European World-Economy in the Sixteenth Century*. New York: Academic Press.

Wallis, Roger, and Krister Malm. 1984. *Big Sounds from Small Peoples: The Music Industry in Small Countries*. London: Constable.

Warde, Alan. 1997. *Consumption, Food and Taste: Culinary Antinomies and Commodity*. Thousand Oaks, CA: Sage.

Watercutter, Angela. 2011. "Musicians Turn to Turntable.fm to Connect with Fans." *Underwire*, 1 November. http://www.wired.com/underwire/2011/11/turntable-fm-artist-promotion/. Last accessed 1 July 2014.

Weber, Peter. 2014. "The Baffling Revival of the Vinyl LP." 2014. *The Week*, 10 January. http://theweek.com/article/index/254901/the-baffling-revival-of-the-vinyl-lp. Last accessed 1 July 2014.

Weber, William. 1975. *Music and the Middle Class*. London: Croom Helm.

——, ed. 2004. *The Musician as Entrepreneur, 1700–1914: Managers, Charlatans, and Idealists*. Bloomington: Indiana University Press.

——. 2008. *The Great Transformation of Musical Taste: Concert Programming from Haydn to Brahms*. New York: Cambridge University Press.

Wentz, Brooke. 1993. "No Kid Stuff." *Beat* 12, no. 5, 42–45.

Werde, Bill. 2004. "We've Got Algorithm, but How about Soul?" *New York Times*, 21 March, WK12.

Wheeler, Alina. 2009. *Designing Brand Identity: An Essential Guide for the Whole Branding Team*. 3rd ed. Hoboken, NJ: John Wiley & Sons.

Wikström, Patrik. 2013. *The Music Industry: Music in the Cloud*. 2nd ed. Malden, MA: Polity.

Will.I.Am. 2011. "What Does 'Communicating' Mean???" *Advertising Age*, 17 October, 42.

Williams, Raymond. 1977. *Marxism and Literature*. New York: Oxford University Press.

——. 1981. *Culture*. N.p.: Fontana.

Williamson, Nigel. 1997. "Rolling Their Own in Havana." *Times* (London), 4 April, 33.

——. 2000. "Don't Call It World Music." *Times* (London), 7 January, 43.

Wolf, Eric R. 1982. *Europe and the People without History*. Berkeley and Los Angeles: University of California Press.

Wood, Ellen Meiksins. 2002. *The Origin of Capitalism: A Longer View*. New York: Verso.

——. 2005. *Empire of Capital*. New York: Verso.

Wortham, Jenna. 2009. "A Few Dollars at a Time, Patrons Support Artists on the Web." *New York Times*, 25 August, B1.

——. 2011. "Music Site Lets Users Play D.J. to Virtual, Yet Discerning, Crowds." *New York Times*, 10 July, B1.

Zager, Michael. 2003. *Writing Music for Television and Radio Commercials: A Manual for Composers and Students*. Lanham, MD: Scarecrow Press.

Zwerin, Mike. 1998. "Angelique Kidjo Is on a Mission." *International Herald Tribune*, 10 June, 10.

Index